Biotechnology in Comparative Perspective

The biotechnology industry is an extremely important sector in the developed world's economies. This book, with contributions from an international array of experts, explains why biotechnology companies in different countries concentrate in a small number of locations and what accounts for the success some of these companies then go on to have.

This interesting book covers such themes as:

- the role of small firms in US biotechnology clusters;
- geographic clustering in the UK;
- case studies involving the sectors in a cross-section of European companies.

With such international contributions, this book will be of interest to students and academics involved in industrial organisation, innovation studies and business organisation. In addition, professionals with an interest in international business will also find this to be a very useful read.

Gerhard Fuchs is Deputy Director of the Department of Technology, Organisation and Work at the Centre for Technology Assessment in Baden-Württemberg, Stuttgart, Germany.

Studies in Global Competition

A series of books edited by John Cantwell, The University of Reading, UK and David Mowery, University of California, Berkeley, USA

Biotechnology in Comparative Perspective

Edited by Gerhard Fuchs

Routledge
Taylor & Francis Group

LONDON AND NEW YORK

First published 2003 by Routledge
11 New Fetter Lane, London EC4P 4EE

Simultaneously published in the USA and Canada
by Routledge
29 West 35th Street, New York, NY 10001

Routledge is an imprint of the Taylor & Francis Group

Typeset in Times by Wearset Ltd., Boldon, Tyne and Wear
Printed at Chennai Micro Print Pvt. Ltd. (Export Division) 100% EOU
No. 34, Nelson Manickam Road, Aminjikarai, Chennai 600 029 (India).

First Indian Reprint 2003

British Library Cataloguing in Publication Data
A catalogue record for this book is available from the British Library

Library of Congress Cataloguing in Publication Data
A catalog record for this book has been requested

ISBN 0-415-28343-4

For sale in india, Nepal and Bangladesh only

Contents

Figures

Tables

Contributors

David B. Audretsch – Ameritech Chair of Economic Development and Director, Institute for Development Strategies, Indiana University, USA.

Tomas G. Bas – Ecole des Sciences de la Gestion, University of Quebec at Montreal, Canada.

Stefano Breschi – Libero Istituto Universitario C. Cattaneo, Castellanza and CESPRI, Bocconi University, Milan, Italy.

Philip Cooke – Centre for Advanced Studies, Cardiff University, UK.

Frederic Corolleur – Institut de Recherche Economique sur la Production et le Développement (IREP-D), Pierre Mendès University, Grenoble, France.

Christien Enzing – TNO Institute for Strategy, Technology and Policy (TNO-STB), Delft, The Netherlands.

Gerhard Fuchs – Centre for Technology Assessment in Baden-Württemburg, University of Stuttgart, Germany.

Gerhard Krauss – Centre for Technology Assessment in Baden-Württemburg, University of Stuttgart, Germany.

Stephane Lemarié – Institut National de la Recherche Agronomique (INRA)/SERD, Pierre Mendès University, Grenoble, France.

Francesco Lissoni – University of Brescia and CESPRI, Bocconi University, Milan, Italy.

Vincent Mangematin – Institut National de la Recherche Agronomique (INRA)/SERD, Pierre Mendès University, Grenoble, France.

Jorge Niosi – Department of Management and Technology, University of Quebec at Montreal, Canada, Researcher CIRANO and Chair of Management of Bio-Industries.

Luigi Orsenigo – Institute of Political Economy, and CESPRI, Bocconi University, Milan, Italy.

Martha Prevezer – Visiting Professor, Economics Department, City University, London, UK.

Gerd Schienstock – Work Research Centre, Research Institute for Social Sciences, University of Tampere, Finland.

Thomas Stahlecker – Fraunhofer Institut für Systemtechnik und Innovationsforschung, Germany.

André Torre – SADAPT, Institut National de la Recherche Agronomique (INRA), Institut National Agronomique Paris-Grignon (INA-PG).

Pasi Tulkki – Work Research Centre, Research Institute for Social Sciences, University of Tampere, Finland.

Acknowledgements

The idea for this book was developed during an international conference, held at the Centre for Technology Assessment in Baden-Württemberg, Stuttgart, bringing together scientific experts from ten different countries and thirteen different biotechnology regions. The purpose of the conference was to discuss and further develop recent scientific findings regarding the development of biotechnology clusters.

Many people have helped in various ways in producing this book. During the preparation phase of this book the authors met at a workshop held in Stuttgart. Authors and editors have profited greatly from the discussion and the contributions from the participants in the workshop. In addition, the valuable support of the reviewers Dave Casper, Edgar Grande and Maureen McKelvey has to be greatly appreciated. Sandra Wassermann and Simone Grünig helped in organising the workshop. Melanie Schneider put together a first manuscript. Bernd Luib put together the last version of the manuscript and was busy writing e-mails to the authors. Monika Baumunk provided some of the English translations and read the whole manuscript for stylistic and typographical errors. Barbara Teutsch offered organisational support all along the project. Many thanks also go to the editorial team of Routledge, who patiently supported the creation of this volume.

1 Biotechnology in comparative perspective

Gerhard Fuchs and Gerhard Krauss

Introduction

Biotechnology is one of the new rising global industries. Companies are making decisions on where to place and support research activities worldwide. Knowledge is moving beyond national boundaries. Despite its global character the industry has a very specific regional flavour; it tends to concentrate in a few specific locations. The issue of regional concentration, however, has been overlooked in much of the more recent research on biotechnology, which covers industry trends, company behaviour and national strategies to promote biotechnology, the effects of national systems of innovation on the formation of the industry, etc. (see Giesecke 2001; Senker and Zwanenberg 2001). These studies have revealed great differences in patterns of innovation. Partial explanations for these differences are provided by the conceptual framework of a national system of innovation (NSI). National case studies confirm that the R&D system, the role of the public sector including public policy, interfirm relationships, the financial system, and the national education and training system are important elements of a NSI. These country-oriented studies also show that the strength of biotechnology companies in France, Germany and in the UK seems to be related to existing national strengths in the pharmaceuticals sector. These explanations, however, leave many important questions unanswered. What accounts for the spatial disequilibrium of biotechnology firms? To what extent are successful regional clusters mirroring or transcending established structures of an NSI? Which relationship actually exists between the pharmaceutical industry and the biotechnology industry, which still mainly consists of small and medium-sized firms and many university spin-offs?

The regional orientation, in addition, has become ever more a focus of public policy discussions. A number of countries (e.g. USA, UK, Germany) have recently started to promote the idea of supporting the development of regional industrial clusters. The OECD has also published important policy statements in this regard. The questions as to what drives clustering in biotechnology, what effects of this clustering can be observed.

whether clustering is a sustainable process and whether it can be supported by public and private agencies is nevertheless still under-researched. In the context of regional and industrial development paths the question is whether new industrial sectors primarily develop in new growth regions or in mature industrial regions. So far analysis has provided a contradictory picture. In the extreme some regional planners seem to work on the assumption that clustering firms in the same neighbourhood will in itself trigger innovation. But, as various papers in this volume also suggest, clustering may simply heighten competition intensity and displace otherwise viable firms. Strong policy interventions may be required to shape a regional economy into an institutionally conducive environment for collective learning and business success. There is a growing literature on these issues which concentrates on a mantra-like reiteration of specific concepts such as networking and trust, but is short of detailed empirical analysis. This collection of chapters will try to fill this gap.

Discussing clusters

The book aims to explain why biotechnology companies in different countries concentrate in some few locations and what factors may account for the growth (or non-growth) of this industrial sector. Regional concentrations in North America (USA, Canada) and Western Europe (UK, Germany, Finland, Netherlands) will be analysed, offering truly comparative insights. The question the book then starts out with is the following: Do innovative activities in biotechnology tend to cluster in specific geographical areas? If the answer is positive, what are the determinants of these processes of agglomeration?

Definitions of clusters are abundant and various, yet have several elements in common: specialization, proximity as well as spill-over and synergies. There exists a widespread consensus about these elements as constitutive parts of clusters. Yet there is also a widespread consensus that these elements are open to interpretation, that other elements are also important, and that they imply further so far unresolved questions.

The discussion about clustering leads inevitably back to the seminal work of Alfred Marshall from the turn of the last century. He noted that most industry was concentrated in specific districts: cutlery in Sheffield, cotton in the Manchester area, lace in Nottingham, coal in Newcastle. Marshall also tried to provide an explanation for his observations. These insights were forgotten for a long time, but have received renewed interest over the last two decades. Marshall mentioned three characteristics for clusters which have been amended by a fourth in the more recent discussion:

- Economies of intra-industry specialization: a localized industry can support a greater number of specialized local suppliers of industry-specific intermediate inputs and services, thus obtaining a greater variety at a lower cost.

- Labour market economies: a localized industry attracts and creates a pool of workers with similar skills, which benefits both the workers and their employers.
- Ease of communication among firms: information about new technologies, goods and processes seem to flow more easily among agents located within the same area, thanks to social bonds that foster reciprocal trust and frequent face-to-face contacts. Therefore adoption, diffusion and innovation seem faster and more intense in geographical clusters than in scattered locations. That is, some 'knowledge spillovers' exist which are geographically bounded.
- Public intermediate inputs: local authorities may place a stronger than usual effort in providing support as soon as they recognize the importance of a specific industry for the welfare of the local communities.

The notion of so-called Marshallian districts has recently been challenged from two sides. There are those who claim that new Information and Communication Technologies and especially the Internet have undermined traditional notions of why and where individual companies settle. The Internet (theoretically) provides the possibility for every company to settle anywhere on the globe without losing contact with suppliers and customers and be excluded from a stream of valuable information.

A second line of argument says that it is true that we see agglomeration, but we still know little of what drives these agglomerations and under what conditions agglomeration acts as a beneficial or an inhibiting factor in further economic development in a globalizing world.

With respect to the third of the Marshallian advantages, Krugman insists that knowledge flows are invisible: 'They leave no paper trail by which they may be measured and tracked, and there is nothing to prevent the theorist from assuming anything about them that she likes' (Krugman 1991: 53). The co-operation of companies as an advantage, or at least a characterizing element, of clusters has also been put into serious doubt by some scholars, who could detect little actual horizontal co-operation in many of the highly acclaimed clusters. Some scholars like Zeller even state that 'spatial concentration does not necessarily imply the existence of a close network of input–output relations within a cluster' (Zeller 2001: 123). By selecting samples according to the dependent variable (i.e. district success and proximity), investigators have not been able to test the possibility that spatial proximity (1) may be important only under certain conditions, and (2) has variable consequences for firms and networks. The strengthening of global relationships and networking and the demise of some of the old clusters raise the question of whether this has not been the result of too much inbreeding within a crowded area. Parallel to the concentration of firms in a few regions, the creation and maintenance of global innovation networks has to be studied and reckoned with.

Tacit knowledge

The role of geographically bounded knowledge spill-overs is linked to tacitness. Tacitness implies that personal contacts, imitation and frequent interactions are tools which are necessary for knowledge transmission and which are clearly available at a lower cost for firms located within the same city or region. Regional economists have built upon such observation, and added many socio-economic features to the need for agglomeration. In particular, they have pointed out that the transmission of tacit knowledge requires mutual trust, a sharing of language and culture, as well as intense non-business relations. Thus social networks, such as those one can find in areas with a homogeneous social background, appear to be key carriers of tacit knowledge. However, very little is known about the precise ways by which knowledge is actually transferred among people located in the same geographic area.

These questions are particularly important for the case of biotechnology, which is usually considered as a strongly science-based technology and as such is – at least in principle – in large part dominated by the use of abstract and codified knowledge. Under these circumstances, knowledge should be theoretically available to everybody. So, what forces might lead to the agglomeration of biotechnology activities in specific clusters?

Part of the answer may lie in the observation that the mastery of biotechnology required (and still requires) a lot of complementary tacit knowledge. To the extent that the transmission of tacit knowledge is facilitated by geographic proximity, clustering may be a likely outcome. However, the diffusion of innovative activities in biotechnology does not seem to depend only on geographical proximity. So what other factors might be responsible? And is clustering a necessary condition for the development of biotechnology?

Some authors have argued that discoveries in biotechnology are characterized by high degrees of *natural excludability*, i.e. the *techniques* for their replication are not widely known and anyone wishing to build on new knowledge must gain access to the research team or laboratory setting having that know-how. In these circumstances, the discovering scientists ('superstars') tend to enter into contractual arrangements with existing firms (contract or ownership) or start their own firm in order to extract the returns from the fruits of their intellectual human capital.

Thus, it is still an open question as to what relationships actually exist between local and global knowledge links. The contributions in this book help to provide a more nuanced answer; the question of the interdependence of global and regional links is treated especially in the contribution of Gerhard Krauss and Thomas Stahlecker. The relationship between global and local connections also plays a role with regard to firms' market position. In fact, there are some indications that the firms in spatially concentrated and institutionally embedded networks (clusters) are exposed to international and global competition, which tends to be stronger the more the firms are 'high tech'. For that reason they particularly need the support from networks.[1] The question therefore is what form this support should take.

The entrepreneurial regime

Another aspect should be taken into account: unlike the more traditional and already developed or older industries, young high-tech industries are generally characterized by strong elements of what evolutionary economists call an 'entrepreneurial regime' (cf. Nelson and Winter 1982; Winter 1984). In other words, while young firms and start-ups play a minor role in the mature branches of industry, in the young developing and much more turbulent high-tech industries the innovatory contributions of young start-up firms are crucial (cf. Audretsch 1995). Thus these industries can be characterized by a high proportion of young start-up companies. On the other hand, the success of these young high-tech companies largely depends on their embeddedness in an environment of supporting institutions and organizations; the regional and local context is therefore of great interest. Here the study of biotechnology clusters offers the possibility of analysing in more detail the role of 'young' vs. 'old' companies, of global vs. regional/local networks, of competition vs. co-operation and, finally, of regional institutions. In contrast to most of the research on biotechnology, which essentially focuses on the level of the firm, we will study specifically the spatial aspects of this new industry and examine 'biotechnology clusters', each of which features a specific profile, characterized by a strong tension between competition and co-operation, as well as globalization and rationalization, and each of which occupies a specific position in the global economic space.

Particularities of the biotechnology sector

What are the further particularities of biotechnology? One could, first of all, refer to the fluidity of the innovation networks, to the great pace of innovation, as well as to the distinct technological and economic risks and chances. The technological knowledge in this field is radically new and it is therefore possible to open up completely new technological paths: 'Biotechnology represents a competence-destroying innovation because it builds on a scientific basis (immunology and molecular biology) that differs significantly from the knowledge base (organic chemistry) of the more established pharmaceutical industry' (Powell *et al.* 1996: 117). These new technological paths remain rather obscure, and the extremely broad spectrum of possible applications increases further the uncertainty under which biotechnology companies have to make their investment decisions. Due to the high technological risks it is likely that further development is influenced to no small degree by non-technical factors (cf. Tushman and Rosenkopf 1992). The complexity of the new biotechnologies seems to require, even more than in other domains, the systematic bringing together of disparate technological competencies and disciplines. That means that the generation of knowledge and its economic exploitation require intense science-based interactions between the actors, in order to bring together many, sometimes very different competencies. This presupposes a high degree of willingness to learn on the part of the actors. In some of the contributions the outstanding importance of star scientists in the context of the regional clusters and networks is stressed: the interaction between the young biotech firms and the academic scientific community turns out in practice to be crucial and the close coupling of technological progress and academic basic research following from it seems to be a very typical attribute of the young biotechnology industry.

In this context attention should be paid to the work of Audretsch and Stephan (1999) who showed that more than half of the start-up companies they studied were started by scientists having an exclusively academic trajectory and that another quarter founded their firm subsequent to a professional activity in the pharmaceutical industry. Of particular importance for the young biotech firms seems to be the direct, personal relationships to highly qualified and mature academic scientific personalities, who engage themselves for the young start-ups as advisers and/or associates. While it can generally be assumed that basic research is extremely important in the early stages in the development of any technological field, and will diminish in importance during later stages (Faulkner 1994), it can be stated that at present probably no other technological field shows an equally intensive relationship between purpose-free basic research and the research and development activities of young high-technology companies. Several of the contributions in this book consider this close interrelationship with science. The work of Lynne Zucker and Michael Darby is also of major importance in this respect; they conclude that the presence of star scientists is the decisive factor for success, while the role played by local venture capital industry is less important. Similarly, David Audretsch argues that the local presence of such star scientists is an important condition for the development of biotechnology clusters.[2]

In sum, this points out that the continuing access to fresh basic knowledge is vital for young technology firms, especially in biotechnology. In fact, many of the young biotech firms have the option to open up scientific know-how through social networks of academic scientists, because in general they have been founded by university researchers and recruit them as employees (cf. Liebeskind *et al.* 1996). These network relationships offer a number of advantages to the young firms: through direct and above all personalized relationships to academic scientists, information and new knowledge can be exchanged and acquired in the most efficient way. Such networks enable the firms to react more quickly and flexibly to new developments. Finally, networks also operate over substantial distances (Audretsch and Stephan 1996). A network of external experts enables firms to evaluate their own knowledge base critically and to adapt their strategies accordingly. Following Liebeskind *et al.* (1996: 432), it can be said that networking with a broad spectrum of external scientists, first, increases the probability of the company being the first with access to new knowledge and findings. Second, a young biotech company may be able to reduce its own costs, because it has immediate access to publicly financed top-class research, whereas mere market relationships would imply much higher costs. Third, social networks often offer better protection of intellectual property, since not all knowledge is always easily patentable (the appropriability problem). Finally, social networks may represent the only way for a young biotech start-up to access top scientific knowledge, since academic scientists would otherwise be unlikely to transfer their knowledge to the private economy.

The particularities of the biotechnology domain described so far have effects on the relationships between the main actors in the field. The generation of new knowledge that may result in the conception and production of new innovative biotechnological products and services, takes place in biotechnology according to a very specific pattern. The technology is extremely complex, its knowledge base expands continuously and knowledge and competence sources are often broadly dispersed, sometimes over wide distances (Powell 1998). As a consequence, interorganizational learning and cooperation networks develop on a large scale, in order to ensure access to new knowledge and specific competencies (Powell *et al.* 1996). Under conditions of fast technological change and fundamental scientific progress, a single company cannot possibly cover alone all the competencies necessary for technological and economic success. Thus there exists a strong incentive for the actors to co-operate. Inter-organizational cooperation is of existential importance for the actors, in order to gain rapid access to knowledge. This means that co-operation arises, to a great extent, from mere practical motives, since other options are barred for most of the time. Strong international competition, on the one hand, is paired with manifold types of cooperation on the other.

The simultaneous systematic constraint towards cooperation results [...] from the extraordinary dynamic of the generation of knowledge, the close coupling of basic and applied knowledge, the fast technological change and the multidisciplinarity of biotechnological research and development projects, which for a long time it has been impossible to handle even in big enterprises purely through the building-up of strong in-house capacities, but only through the simultaneous recourse to company-external knowledge and know-how.

(Dolata 1999: 136)[3]

On the other hand, relations are at the same time highly competitive – first, in the temporal dimension and, second, in the economic dimension: the extremely high level of investment generally necessary in the case of top-level technology projects creates a relatively strong time pressure, since the investment could be rendered valueless by a competitor being faster. Strong competition exists in the technological dimension, because the great techno-logical uncertainty means that only a few top projects will finally be brought to a successful conclusion. In addition, biotech firms are under great eco-nomic pressure to exploit their technological knowledge in the market-place, in order to be able to compensate for the necessary high initial investment, first phases of significant losses and continuing investment in R&D. In this respect it is notable that, in contrast with other areas, biotech-nology companies are still very strongly dependent on external financial sources, such as venture capital. Martha Prevezer stresses, for example, that for the United States the development of a strong venture capital industry in California during the growth of the electronics sector had created very favourable conditions for biotechnology, since the know-how available on the local level for the foundation and financing of high-technology com-panies could immediately be used for biotech start-ups. David Audretsch offers a similar argument in his contribution to this volume.

The above-mentioned importance of young and newly founded busi-ness in this technological field with regard to innovation is noteworthy. Biotechnology as a young (cross-sectional) technological domain and as a developing industry shows a big share of newly founded and young firms. Because non-routinely generated knowledge is so important for innova-tion, the new biotechnology firms may have innovation advantages *vis à vis* established enterprises. For that reason, in many cases the economic exploitation of new knowledge is initiated by start-ups which, to a great extent, are created by scientists. Only later do globally operating large incumbents take a central place in the further development of the techno-logy. This does not mean at all that the big established companies play a minor role – on the contrary, many adapt the attitude and strategies of the young biotechnology firms. In fact, they have to take an interest in the new technologies and be prepared to assimilate them. Conversely, the young firms have a marked interest in establishing relations with incumbent com-panies (cf. for instance Walker *et al.* 1997). Some of the contributors to this book, therefore, discuss more exhaustively the role of the pharmaceutical industry, i.e. of the established groups, for the development of the techno-logical field. For example, Gerhard Krauss and Thomas Stahlecker argue that in Germany the wait-and-see attitude, the lack of interest and the low preparedness for support on the part of the big pharmaceutical companies, which were dominated by chemical engineers, in the specific prevailing institutional context, *de facto* hampered the development of a domestic biotechnology industry. Similarly, Stefano Breschi, Francesco Lissoni and Luigi Orsenigo see the strategies of the pharmaceutical companies in Italy as an important impeding factor with little or no beneficial effect on the development of biotechnology. Finally, when considering the difficulties faced in opening up this new technological field in different regions and countries, one should not overlook the role politics can play and plays in practice – in not only a positive, but also a negative way. This aspect is specifically addressed in some of the contributions, for instance in the chapters by Schienstock and Tulkki, by Enzing and by Audretsch. For example, the most recent dynamic in the German bioregions cannot be understood unless the carefully directed promotion of regional biotechnology districts by the federal government in the context of the BioRegio contest is taken into account. On the other hand, as David Audretsch points out, the development of biotechnology may be determined not only by promotional measures and programmes, but also by regulatory barriers.

Thus the most essential aspects have been addressed which, in the following, will guide the study of biotechnology clusters in this book. All of the contributions in the first instance deal with specific patterns of the development of biotechnology in a given geographical space. Some of the contributions, in particular, offer a broader analysis of the problems of development of the biotechnology industry. This is the case, for example, with the contributions of Christien Enzing and Luigi Orsenigo

The papers collected in this book basically use two different approaches in addressing the issue of cluster formation. One approach is to look at the problem from a mainly statistical point of view using available or newly collected data sets (e.g. Prevezer, Breschi, Lissoni and Orsenigo). The other is to carry out in-depth case studies of various regions (e.g. Krauss and Stahlecker). In this respect the contributions conveniently supplement each other.

Contributions to the present volume

Audretsch (Chapter 2) provides an overview of the US biotech scene, focusing in particular on the strong interdependence between basic research in the biomedical sciences and the formation of biotechnology firms, and clusters of firms. The work has three broad levels of analysis: general industry structure and patterns of firm organization and networking, the emergence of biotechnology clusters and the involvement of scientific personnel within biotech firms, and the role of public policy in the United States – in particular the role of the NIH but also regional support programs.

Prevezer (Chapter 3) summarizes the structure of the US biotechnology industry, focusing in particular on cluster activity, from the formation of the industry up until the mid 1990s. The paper has two main currents. First is a description of results from a modelling exercise based on several core US biotech clusters. Key results are that:

a   the science base was a key 'attractor' for firm entry,
b   the science base tended to create therapeutic firms, which then tended to promote the entry of complementary firms in related fields, and
c   there is a negative effect of the presence of like firms in the same sector on entry.

These statistical findings are complemented by a brief history and descriptive overview of the financing, organization and policy environment in which US biotechnology clusters have emerged.

Niosi and Bas (Chapter 4) review the literature on regional agglomerations and knowledge spill-over, then suggest that a useful way to examine clusters is through extending the competency theory of the firm to the cluster level. Doing so should allow analysis to compare the 'institutional architectures' across different clusters and thus to examine more carefully performance differences across clusters. The paper applies such an analysis to Canadian biotech clusters by building up a patent database on all biotechnology patents in Canada. The analysis shows that patents tend to conglomerate within a few firms and universities that are regionally agglomerated, particularly around the Toronto area. Additionally, the chapter finds that while universities are important 'entry attractors', government laboratories play almost no role. Finally, correlation analysis shows that urban agglomeration is the most important factor associated with the existence of biotechnology clusters.

Cooke's Chapter 5 has three parts. The first part presents some very interesting new data combined with charts on the relative performance of the UK industry compared to Europe. This review shows that a) the UK has been commonly thought to be well ahead of continental Europe in the development of therapeutic and diagnostic-based biotechnology products, seen in terms of common statistics such as number of firms, employment or investment. However, b) a systematic survey of some fifty-three biotechnology-derived drugs presently available on the UK market shows that none have UK origin, while the vast majority were created in the United States; in terms of bringing biotech drugs to the market, the UK is no better off than Germany or other major European economies. But, c) looking towards the future, the UK once again appears as Europe's leader when one looks at biotech drug development pipelines or (once more), number of UK-based companies in the top ten in Europe based on market capitalization, employment and so forth.

The second part of the chapter starts with an examination of industry dynamics within the pharmaceutical industry, which suggests that networks of small biotech firms will continue to dominate discovery and related new technology areas of biotechnology. Because small firms will dominate, the paper suggests that an analysis of the regional technology clusters is the appropriate lens with which to examine on-going developments within the UK. The chapter then surveys four dominant biotech clusters in the UK, paying special attention to a new technology promotion framework in Scotland in addition to descriptions of established English clusters in Oxford, Cambridgeshire and Surrey. The chapter concludes with a prospective look at industry dynamics, which reiterates the core point that despite a continued globalization of the pharmaceutical industry (which should favour the continued development of UK and European biotech), clusters will remain the core locations within which most discovery and related high-risk or technologically volatile activities will take place.

Krauss and Stahlecker (Chapter 6) provide a detailed analysis of the Rhine–Neckar-Triangle BioRegion within the broader context of an analysis of the organization of various networks within the community, including linkages with state-actors, other firms, public research facilities and financial actors. In part the analysis concentrates on the localization of networks within the Rhine–Neckar cluster, with the interesting result that a) many start-ups did not have local origins and b) intra-firm links with the surrounding and prominent large pharmaceutical firms are forming very slowly, and that the legacy of established linkages between German pharmaceutical firms and US biotech firms have remained stable despite the recent build-up of local biotech. The chapter also provides an historical overview of the Rhine–Neckar cluster, a description of its current industrial structure in terms of firm specialization and the local science base, and its general position within the broader German biotech scene.

Corolleur, Mangematin, Torre and Lemarié (Chapter 7) examine localization effects within biotechnology, concentrating in particular on the French case. The chapter has two strands of analysis. The first consists of a detailed statistical survey of the French biotechnology sector. Among other things, the survey shows that a) localization effects within France are strong, b) in terms of dependence on local cluster infrastructures (especially universities and related public research institutes), most firms progress from an entry stage in which they are very dependent on local cluster infrastructures, to a mature phase in which their networks become more national/international in focus, and c) French firms can be grouped into four general types of firms, ranging from 'type 2' growth-oriented product firms, niche market players, subsidiaries of larger firms, and firms that have been acquired. Localization effects differ across these firms, especially across type 1 (international) and type 2 (very localized) firms. The second strand of analysis consists of a review of the localization and related cluster literature, with implications drawn out for localization and knowledge spill-over within biotech clusters.

Breschi, Lissoni and Orsenigo explain why the Lombardy region of Italy has not excelled in developing commercial biotechnology, and through doing so identify numerous institutional obstacles to sustaining biotechnology innovation networks and surrounding cluster infrastructures that are commonly found in Europe. The chapter is broken into three core sections: a) a brief description of the mostly failed history of biotechnology in Italy and Lombardy, b) an analysis of numerous institutional problems that tend to systematically undermine the orchestration of innovative competencies in Italian and broader European innovation clusters, and c) an analysis of institutional economic findings on the development of knowledge flows and related organizational devices within clusters; this summary has the somewhat unexpected conclusion that though potentially useful, there is no firm connection between the development of cluster infrastructures and the parallel development of successful organizational structures to facilitate the type of knowledge flows needed to successfully innovate in biotechnology

Enzing (Chapter 9) contributes a detailed overview of Dutch cluster policy towards biotechnology. The chapter mixes historical data on Dutch cluster policy, descriptions of Dutch biotechnology clusters, theoretical analysis about cluster formation in biotechnology, and an analysis of current Dutch cluster policy applied towards solving several problems within Dutch commercial biotechnology.

Schienstock and Tulkki (Chapter 10) present a case study of the development of the Finnish biotechnology industry. While still small, policymakers in Finland have targeted biotech as a 'fourth pillar' of industrial development, alongside IT, forestry and the metal industry. The chapter discusses the Finnish conception of biotechnology, its industry structure, and developments in three important areas in Finland: pharmaceuticals, agra/food and wood/forestry segments. While the pharma sector is off to a good start, the chapter argues that progress in the agra/food and forestry segments have been blocked due to industrial structure and regulatory lock-in of both segments, both of which have until recently delayed the introduction of new technologies such as biotechnology. The chapter concludes with a discussion of recent public policy initiatives to improve the Finnish research base in biotech.

Notes

1 Though, in contrast with the historically grown networks of older branches (such as mechanical engineering), networks in biotechnology are more likely to manifest themselves as an accumulation of project-based, temporary and mutually independent bilateral figurations and less likely as stable, long-term oriented and interaction intensive multilateral relation networks (Dolata 1999: 137).
2 Powell *et al.* (2002), however, argue that the importance of venture capital is paramount for the development of biotechnology clusters.
3 See Zeller (2002) on the importance of project-oriented work in order to cross organizational and knowledge barriers.

References

Audretsch, D.B. (1995) *Innovation and Industry Evolution*, Cambridge, MA: MIT Press.

Audretsch, D.B. and Stephan, P.E. (1996) 'Company–Scientist Locational Links: The Case of Biotechnology', *American Economic Review*, 86(3): 641–52.

—— (1999) 'Knowledge Spillovers in Biotechnology: Sources and Incentives', *Journal of Evolutionary Economics*, 9: 97–107.

Dolata, U. (1999) 'Innovationsnetzwerke in der Biotechnologie?' *WSI-Mitteilungen*, 1999(2): 132–41.

Faulkner, W. (1994) 'Conceptualising Knowledge Used in Innovation: A Second Look at the Science–Technology Distinction and Industrial Innovation', *Science, Technology and Human Values*, 19(4): 425–58.

Giesecke, S. (2001) *Von der Forschung zum Markt. Innovationsstrategien und Forschungspolitik in der Biotechnologie*, Berlin: Edition Sigma.

Krugman, P. (1991) *Geography and Trade*, Cambridge: MIT Press.

Liebeskind, J., Oliver, A.L., Zucker, L. and Brewer, M. (1996) 'Social Networks, Learning, and Flexibility: Sourcing Scientific Knowledge in New Biotechnology Firms', *Organization Science*, 7(4): 428–43.

Nelson, R.R. and Winter, S.G. (1982) *An Evolutionary Theory of Economic Change*, Cambridge, MA: Harvard University Press.

Porter, M. (1998) *On Competition*, Boston, MA: Harvard Business School Press.

Powell, W.W. (1998) 'Learning From Collaboration: Knowledge and Networks in the Biotechnology and Pharmaceutical Industries', *California Management Review*, 40(3): 228–40.

Powell, W.W., Koput, K.W., Bowie, J.I. and Smith-Doerr, L. (2002) 'The Spatial Clustering of Science and Capital: Accounting for Biotech Firm–Venture Capital Relationships', *Regional Studies*, 36: 291–306.

Powell, W.W., Koput, K.W. and Smith-Doerr, L. (1996) 'Interorganizational Collaboration and the Locus of Innovation: Networks of Learning in Biotechnology', *Administrative Science Quarterly*, 41: 116–45.

Senker, J. and Zwanenberg, P. van (2001) *European Biotechnology Innovation Systems*. TSER Project No. SOE1-CT98-1117. Final Report. SPRU, University of Sussex.

Tushman, M.L. and Rosenkopf, L. (1992) 'Organizational Determinants of Technological Change: Toward a Sociology of Technological Evolution', *Research in Organizational Behavior*, 14: 311–47.

Walker, G., Kogut, B. and Shan, W. (1997) 'Social Capital, Structural Holes and the Formation of an Industry Network', *Organization Science*, 8(2): 109–25.

Winter, S.G. (1984) 'Schumpeterian Competition in Alternative Technological Regimes', *Journal of Economic Behavior and Organization*, 5: 287–320.

Zeller, C. (2001) 'Clustering Biotech: A Recipe for Success? Spatial Patterns of Growth of Biotechnology in Munich, Rhineland and Hamburg', *Small Business Economics*, 17(1–2): 123–41.

—— (2002) 'Project Teams as Means of Restructuring Research and Development in the Pharmaceutical Industry', *Regional Studies*, 36: 275–90.

2 The role of small firms in US biotechnology clusters[1]

David B. Audretsch

Abstract

The biotechnology industry poses a particular challenge to analysis because its origins were poorly understood or even noticed at the time. The purpose of this chapter is to examine and make sense of recent developments in the US biotechnology industry. The pioneers and subsequent followers in biotechnology came from other fields. They altered their career trajectories in sciences like genetics and medical research to enter an unknown and undefined field, which only subsequently became labelled as biotechnology. Those regions exhibiting the greatest success in developing biotechnology clusters also possessed the greatest ability to unleash the potential commercialisation latent in those scientists. To generate a successful regional cluster, the existence of world-class scientific talent is a necessary condition. However, it is not a sufficient condition. The ancillary or complementary factors must also be available to translate this knowledge into a commercialised product. The complementary factors include the presence of venture capital and other forms of finance, the existence of an entrepreneurial culture, and transparent and minimal regulations fostering the start-up and growth processes.

Introduction

The purpose of this chapter is to examine and make sense of recent developments in the US biotechnology industry. This chapter tries to understand how the American biotechnology industry has evolved, with a particular emphasis on the role of public policy. The biotechnology industry poses a particular challenge to analysis because its origins were poorly understood or even noticed at the time. The pioneers and subsequent followers in biotechnology came from other fields. They altered their career trajectories in sciences like genetics and medical research to enter an unknown and undefined field, which only subsequently became labelled as biotechnology. Those regions exhibiting the greatest success in developing biotechnology clusters also possessed the greatest ability to unleash the potential commercialisation latent in those scientists.

Definitions

The terms biotechnology and biotech industry are typically used in a casual and imprecise manner. To provide more precision and a common understanding it is important that the following concepts have a more exact definition.[2]

- **Biotechnology** – a group of techniques and technologies that apply the principles of genetics, immunology and molecular, cellular and structural biology to the discovery and development of novel products.
- **Biotechnology industry** – the industry is composed of around 5,000 private companies that apply various biotechnologies to develop commercially viable products. The biotech industry is typically an input in the health care, food and agriculture, industrial processes, and environmental cleanup industries.
- **Pharmaceutical industry** – this industry is composed of around one hundred private companies whose products involve the design, discovery, development and marketing of new agents for the prevention, treatment and cure of disease. Pharmaceutical firms have a heavy reliance on scientific research. The industry may be evolving towards a new name – the biopharmaceutical industry – which reflects the heavy reliance of pharmaceutical companies on biotechnology.
- **Medical research** – this refers to science-based inquiry, both basic and applied, where the goal is the improvement in health and the eradication or mitigation of disease and disability.

Formation and development of regionally based biotech industry

The United States biotechnology industry has grown considerably over the past 15 years. In 1992 there were 1,358 patent applications by US companies in the United States. By 1997, patent applications were up to 3,014. Between 1990 and 1999, private investment in the biopharmaceutical industry grew from $10 billion to $24 billion. While the biotechnology industry in the United States has exploded over the past 15 years, this growth has not been neutral with respect to geographic location, but has been regionally concentrated in just a handful of geographic locations. The strongest presence of biotechnology companies has been in California, which accounts for around one-quarter of the biotechnology companies. Massachusetts accounts for the second highest share of biotechnology companies; nearly one-tenth of American biotech firms are located in Massachusetts. A third tier of states accounts for a significant amount, including New Jersey, Maryland, North Carolina and Texas, each having a share of around 5 per cent of US biotechnology companies. In fact, even within these states, the location of the biotechnology industry is geographically concentrated within a very small region. In California, one-fifth of the biotechnology firms is located in the East Bay area, 15 per cent in San Francisco, 18 per cent in Santa Clara, 22 per cent in Los Angeles, 18 per cent in San Diego, and 4 per cent in Sacramento (Blakely *et al.* 1993).

There are strong reasons both why the biotechnology industry remains geographically concentrated in just a few regions, and why these specific regions have emerged as the main location for the US biotechnology industry. The most important input in the biotechnology industry is specialised knowledge. In most cases, only a few scientists have the potential to acquire this knowledge. In addition, the scientists possessing that knowledge must have the information about a potential commercial market for viable products resulting from that knowledge. They must also be willing to act on that knowledge by commercialising it through a biotechnology enterprise. To commercialise requires start-up capital as well as managerial capabilities. For all of these factors to come together has been impossible, with the exception of just a few select regions.

Biotechnology is a new industry that is knowledge-based and predominantly produced by new start-ups and small firms. The relatively small scale of most biotechnology firms may be attributable to the diseconomies of scale inherent in the 'bureaucratic process which inhibits both innovative activity and the speed with which new inventions move through the corporate system towards the market' (Link and Rees 1990: 25). Zucker *et al.* (1994: 1) provide considerable evidence suggesting that the timing and location of new biotechnology firms is 'primarily explained by the presence at a particular time and place of scientists who are actively contributing to the basic science'. More specifically, they find that firms are likely to locate in geographic areas where scientists who have published articles on gene sequencing are located.

The early evolution of the biotechnology industry took place in California, and in particular in the San Francisco Bay area. This is because the key ingredients identified above were the most prevalent in this region. As Prevezer (1997) explains, there was already a strong presence of venture capital in Silicon Valley, as a result of the boom in high-technology industries such as semiconductors and computers. This also meant the existence of a very entrepreneurial culture. There was expertise in starting and growing high-technology companies, high job mobility and strong networks. This was also the location of a number of the country's most important universities and government research laboratories.

The two most significant discoveries fuelling the biotechnology industry occurred in the early 1970s, when Cohen and Boyer at Stanford University developed the recombinant DNA technique, and Kohler and Milstein produced monoclonal antibodies in Cambridge, UK. The pioneering biotechnology companies, such as Cetus, Genetech and Hybritech, were located in California near the top scientific centres, and Biogen was located in the Boston area to take advantage of the top scientists at Harvard and MIT.

According to Prevezer (1997), the San Francisco Bay area became the focal point for the incipient biotechnology industry, relying heavily upon scientific knowledge at the University of California at San Francisco (UCSF), Stanford, and CalTech. While the subsequent explosion of the biotechnology industry has remained concentrated in these regions, other regions combining the demanding requirements of scientific knowledge and a strong and vigorous entrepreneurial culture have emerged in Dallas (Texas), Research Triangle (North Carolina) and Maryland (between Baltimore and Washington, DC).

Linkages and co-operation

Linkages and co-operation are particularly important in the biotechnology industry. Linkages occur between entrepreneurial firms, between the scientists involved with the firms, between the firms and universities, and between corporations and biotech firms.

Strategic alliances between large corporations and biotechnology companies have been particularly important for biotech companies specialising in therapeutics. This is because the costs of developing a new drug – complying with the various layers of regulation, manufacturing the product, and then marketing the product – have required a level of finance that far exceeds the budgets of most small firms. Cullen and Dibner (1993) estimate that the cost of bringing a therapeutic drug from basic research to the market is around $250 million. At the same time, the average budget for research and development of a biotech firm is $12.5 million. To close this gap, biotech firms have engaged in a broad range of marketing and licensing agreements. Under these agreements, the biotech firm provides access to cutting-edge technology in exchange for an infusion of capital from their corporate partners.

In documenting the evolution of strategic alliances in biotechnology, Cullen and Dibner (1993: 18) conclude that: 'The primary strategic goal of small and medium-sized biotechnological companies was to develop products to be marketed by their partners and their primary concern was finding and developing alliances.' The obvious advantage of such a strategic alliance is that it enables a small, new company to concentrate on its core mission – moving from basic research to commercialisation through technological innovation. The strategic alliance also enables the biotech company to reduce financial risks as well as operating costs. In addition, the biotech firm is able to better offset the major liabilities associated with biotech start-ups – acquiring manufacturing capabilities, marketing and sales.

The role of established firms towards biotech enterprises

Established firms are generally quite positive and supportive towards biotechnology firms. This is because of the strong complementary nature of biotechnology firms and established firms, particularly in the pharmaceutical industry. There are a number of reasons why such a complementary relationship has evolved between established and biotechnology firms. The first is that the former have recognised that it may be a more efficient structure to engage in an arm's-length market relationship to obtain new biotechnology products than to produce them internally. The market exchange is apparently more efficient than the internal transaction. The reason for this involves agency problems in doing research that is highly uncertain and asymmetric. In addition, the exposure to legal liabilities resulting from biotechnology research is reduced when that research is done by a small firm with limited assets rather than in a large corporation with massive assets.

Sharp (1999) identifies three main phases in the relationship of established firm and biotechnology companies. The first phase involved the formation and incipiency of the biotechnology industry. Sharp (1999: 137) reports that 'most of the established pharmaceutical companies were uncertain what to make of the new technology and especially of the hype surrounding its development that grew with the small-firm sector in the US'. This uncertainty, combined with a considerable degree of scepticism, resulted in most established pharmaceutical companies distancing themselves from the fledgling biotechnology industry in this initial phase. At the same time, Sharp points out that most established companies invested in sufficient scientific expertise to enable them to keep abreast of developments in biotechnology and monitor the industry.

The second phase began in the mid-1980s, when the period of watching and waiting ended. The established pharmaceutical firms recognised that, in fact, biotechnology had a valuable market potential. While strategies pursued by the established enterprises varied, most devised and implemented a strategic biotechnology policy. One common strategy that all companies pursued was to invest heavily to develop an in-house competence in biotechnology. How this was done varied considerably from one company to another. Some companies assembled scientific teams. Other pharmaceutical companies acquired such competence through the acquisition of biotechnology firms or, in some cases, through mergers. Another strategy was to engage in external linkages with biotechnology companies. As Cullen and Dibner (1993) document, strategic alliance between biotechnology firms and established enterprises exploded in the mid-1980s.

The third phase, which started around a decade ago, involves the commercialisation of biotechnology products. The first successful biotechnology products reached the market in the early 1990s.

In this third phase, the large established companies take the new biotechnology products developed by biotechnology companies and convert them into large-scale marketed products. For example, Intron A was developed by Biogen but marketed by Schering-Plough, resulting in $572 million of sales in 1993. Humulin was developed by Genetech but marketed by Eli Lilly, for $560 million of sales in 1993. Engerix-B was developed by Genetech but marketed by SmithKline Beecham for $480 million. RecombiNAK HB was developed by Chiron but marketed by Merck for $245 million.

In addition, this third phase has undergone a shift by the established companies from the broad learning strategies of phase two and increasingly towards a more focused approach, targeting specific technologies. For example, Ciba Geigy reduced its portfolio of interests in biopharmaceuticals in 1989 in order to focus on the development of just several targeted products. Ciba Geigy subsequently increased its investment in those targeted areas and engaged in a number of research and licensing agreements with biotechnology companies. Similarly, Bayer reduced its biotechnology research in agro-chemicals while concentrating its focus on pharmaceuticals. Hoffman LaRoche similarly pulled out of agro-biotechnology to concentrate its focus on pharmaceuticals.

Investor attitudes

Investors come from established companies, venture capital and initial public offerings. A unique feature of biotechnology is that biotechnology firms have no commercial product on which to draw revenues for a substantial period. This makes evaluating their success, or whether to invest in them or not, especially complicated. In addition, the science and research upon which they are based is typically so complicated and advanced that only a limited number of experts can hope to evaluate them. The high degree of uncertainty combined with asymmetric knowledge that is prohibitively costly to transact means that investing in biotechnology is different from investing in most other industries.

Since biotechnology companies typically have no commercial products or production upon which they can be evaluated, potential investors focus instead on the major input of the biotechnology process, which involves the scientific team. In terms of bait to the investment community, biotechnology firms, in the early stages of development, miss no opportunity to signal the abilities of their scientists as well as the science they are doing. It is not uncommon for prospectuses to read like proposals to the National Institutes of Health (NIH). Stephan and Everhart (1998) have shown the importance of scientific reputation at the time a biotechnology company goes public. Based on a sample of forty-five firms, they find that the more substantial the reputation of the university-based scientific affiliates, the greater are the proceeds raised from the initial public offering (IPO).

Positioning profile of bioregion in global economy

The focus of a region's biotechnology industry generally reflects the scientific strengths at the knowledge source as well as the focus of complementary industries. For example, California's biotechnology industry is largely focused on human–diagnostic and therapeutic products (Blakely *et al.* 1993). By contrast, considerably less activity in biotechnology is devoted towards agriculture, or plant and animal, and biotechnology suppliers. This reflects the fact that the emphasis on research as a product of biotechnology is more pronounced in California than elsewhere in the United States. It also reflects the relatively weak influence of pharmaceutical companies in California. Most of the pharmaceutical companies located in New Jersey and New York. The pharmaceutical companies tend to rely on biotechnology companies also located in their own regions for new products and innovations. In addition, the presence of the United States Food and Drug Administration (USFDA) on the East Coast has resulted in the location of testing facilities in New York and New Jersey.

The Biotech Industry Research Group reports the results of a massive survey of biotechnology firms located in California as showing that the most important factors determining location, in decreasing importance, are:

1 availability of qualified workers in the geographic area. The relative importance of this factor varies somewhat across fields. It is relatively more important in therapeutics and agritech, and relatively less so in diagnostics and for suppliers;
2 proximity of research universities and other research organisations;
3 cost of industrial space;
4 county and city regulations;
5 taxes;
6 wage rates;
7 proximity of major suppliers, proximity to venture capital and financial institutions.

(Board on Science, Technology and Economic Policy, National Research Council of the National Academy of Sciences 1999)

Institutional barriers impeding regional development of biotech clusters

A number of regions have tried to develop a biotechnology industry. Many of these attempts have not proven successful; only a handful of regions in the United States have successfully developed a biotechnology industry. For example, the region around Hanover, New Hampshire tried to develop a biotechnology cluster and failed. Atlanta, Georgia has'been unable to develop a biotechnology industry. Only recently (1999) have there been signs of an emerging biotechnology industry there.

One of the greatest impediments to developing biotechnology is the existence of institutional barriers. Perhaps the most imposing constraint has been an absence of scientific talent in a region. If no cluster of scientific talent is present, either at universities, government research laboratories or private firms, then it is unlikely that a biotechnology industry can be developed. The major reason why the biotechnology industry is so geographically concentrated is that the best scientific talent is also geographically clustered in just a few regions (Audretsch and Stephan 1996).

However, the presence of a critical mass of excellence in science is a necessary but not sufficient condition for the development of biotechnology. There are numerous examples of clusters of scientific talent in the relevant fields where there is still an absence of biotechnology activity. This is attributable to the presence of other formidable institutional constraints.

For example, Hanover, New Hampshire's Dartmouth College, including its medical centre, is the home of a large number of scientists involved in biomedical research. A project to develop a biotechnology cluster failed. One of the reasons given why this attempt failed is that while the scientific talent was present, there is no base of large companies in the relevant areas, and no existence of an entrepreneurial culture.

In contrast, Atlanta not only has a very strong presence of biomedical researchers in the city, which is the home of Emory University, with one of the top medical schools in the country, and the Centre for Disease Control (CDC), but it is also rich in private industry. The inability of Atlanta to translate the scientific knowledge into a biotechnology industry may reflect the absence of venture capital and perhaps the fact that the industry has had a tradition of large corporations such as Coca Cola, but a relative absence of high-tech entrepreneurship. This would suggest two other important institutional barriers to developing a biotechnology industry: the availability of finance and venture capital, which tend to be regional and not national, and the presence of an entrepreneurial culture, which is also a regional phenomenon. Venture capital and other forms of informal finance are local because the venture capitalist needs to monitor and interact with the company. The success of the company is highly dependent upon this interaction. Thus, geographic proximity between the venture capitalist and the biotechnology firm is essential for commercial success.

The presence of an entrepreneurial culture is important because this creates the opportunities for a scientist to change his career trajectory and shift it away from research to commercialisation. In studying Silicon Valley, Saxenian (1990: 96–7) emphasises that it is the existence of such an entrepreneurial culture that provides individuals with the information and support needed to become entrepreneurs themselves:

> It is not simply the concentration of skilled labour, suppliers and information that distinguish the region. A variety of regional institutions – including Stanford University, several trade associations and

local business organisations, and a myriad of specialised consulting, market research, public relations and venture capital firms – provide technical, financial, and networking services which the region's enterprises often cannot afford individually. These networks defy sectoral barriers. Individuals move from established firms to start-ups. And they continue to meet at trade shows, industry conferences, and the scores of seminars, talks and social activities organised by local business organisations and trade associations. In these forums, relationships are easily formed and maintained, technical and market information is exchanged, business contacts are established, and new enterprises are conceived.... This decentralised and fluid environment also promotes the diffusion of intangible technological capabilities and understandings.

A fourth type of institutional constraint to the development of a regional biotechnology cluster is the high cost of regulation. Blakely *et al.* (1993: 23) document the high concern that biotechnology firms have for regulation: 'Predictable application of regulations concerning environmental and public health and the use of land are crucial to the location of biotechnology firms. Companies must be assured that their development activities will not be hindered by inconsistent applications of regulations.'

Regional and global networks

Audretsch and Stephan (1996, 1999) document the strong linkages that exist among biotechnology scientists and between universities and biotech firms. These linkages are crucial because biotechnology companies are strongly defined by their scientists. Many of these scientists, particularly senior scientists with strong reputations, do not work for the biotechnology company full-time, but instead are members of university faculties. For example, Audretsch and Stephan (1999) show that, of 101 founders of new biotechnology firms in the early 1990s, nearly half (fifty) are from universities. Of these fifty, thirty-five remain associated with their universities on a part-time basis, while the remaining fifteen founders left the university to work full-time for their biotech firm.

These university-based scientists fulfil a variety of roles within biotechnology companies. Some are founders, others serve as members of scientific advisory boards (SABs), while still others serve as directors. The degree of knowledge provided by university-based scientists varies according to the role played by the scientist. Scientific founders seek out venture capitalists in order to transform technical knowledge into economic knowledge. Scientific advisors provide links between scientific founders and other researchers doing work in the area. They, along with founders, also provide the possibility of outsourcing research into university laboratories staffed by graduate students and post-docs. The concept of scientific advisory boards also provides the firm with the option of having, at minimal cost, a full roster of the key players doing research in the firm's area of expertise.

In addition to providing knowledge to newly formed biotechnology companies, university-based scientists also provide a signal of firm quality to the scientific and financial communities. An effective way to recruit young scientists is to have a scientific advisory board composed of the leading scientists in the field. George B. Rathman, President and Chief Executive Officer of Amgen, attributes much of the company's success to an SAB of 'great credibility' whose 'members were willing to share the task of interviewing the candidates for scientific positions'.

Certain roles, such as being a founder of a biotechnology firm, are more likely to dictate geographic proximity between the firm and the scientist than are other roles that scientists play. This is because the transmission of the knowledge specific to the scientist and firm dictates geographic proximity. Presumably scientists start new biotechnology companies because their knowledge is not transferable to other firms for the expected economic value of that knowledge. If this were not the case there would be no incentive to start a new and independent company. Because the firm is knowledge-based, the cost of transferring that knowledge will tend to be the lowest when the firm is located close to the university where the new knowledge is being produced. In addition, the cost of monitoring the firm will tend to be minimised if the new biotechnology start-up is located close to the founder.

By contrast, the role of scientific advisor to a biotechnology company does not require constant monitoring or even necessarily specialised knowledge. Thus, the inputs of scientific advisors are less likely to be geographically constrained. Furthermore, geographic proximity of all major researchers in a particular scientific field is unlikely given the opportunity cost that universities face in buying into a single research agenda. Thus, if firms are to have access to the technical knowledge embodied in the top scientists in a field, they will be forced to establish links with researchers outside of their geographic area. Scientists whose primary function is to signal quality are also less likely to be local than are scientists who provide essential knowledge to the firm. Their quality signal is produced by lending prestige to a venture they have presumably reviewed – a task that can be accomplished with credibility from a distance.

To identify the links between knowledge sources, the incentives confronting individual scientists, and where the knowledge is commercialised, Audretsch and Stephan (1996) rely upon a data base collected from the prospectuses of biotechnology companies that prepared an initial public offering (IPO) in the United States between March 1990 and November 1992. A total of fifty-four firms affiliated with 445 university-based scientists were identified during this period. By carefully reading the prospectuses, it was possible to identify the names of university-based scientists affiliated with each firm, the role that each scientist plays in the firm, and the name and location of their home institutions. Universities and firms were then grouped into regions, which are generally larger than a single city but considerably smaller than a state. Certain areas, for example metropolitan New York, cross several state lines.

Only 138 of the 445 links observed between scientists and biotechnology companies are local in that the scientist and firm are located in the same region. This suggests that geographic proximity does not play an important role for links between biotechnology companies and scientists in general. However, the geographic link between the scientist and the founder is influenced by the particular role played by the scientist in working with the firm. Most strikingly, 57.8 per cent of the scientist–firm links were local when the scientist was a founder of the firm; 42.1 per cent were non-local. By contrast, when the scientist served as a member on the SAB, only 31.8 per cent of the links were local, while 68.2 per cent were non-local. This disparity suggests that the nature of the knowledge transmitted between the university and the biotechnology firm may be different between scientists serving as founders and those serving on a SAB. Presumably it is the difference in the nature and quality of the knowledge being transferred from the university to the company that dictates a higher propensity for local proximity in the case of the founders, but not for SAB members.

Innovation strategies of biotech firms

Biotechnology firms have pursued a broad spectrum of innovation strategies. The diversity of innovation strategies reflects heterogeneity of fields, backgrounds and goals. Still, several key innovation strategies have emerged in the biotechnology industry. One successful strategy has been to develop and exploit close links with university researchers. Such close links provide access to state-of-the-art research and knowledge, as well as a source of potential employees. Another important strategy involves marketing. A successful marketing agreement with a large pharmaceutical company can result in the ability for a small biotechnology company to extend its product to a mass market. Biotechnology companies are generally successful when they devote their resources and competence to their core product – research – and rely on third-party firms for clinical testing and marketing.

Characteristics of newly founded regional biotech enterprises

The biotechnology industry is composed of nearly 1,300 companies that use various biotechnologies to develop products for use in health care, food and agriculture, industrial processes, and environmental clean-up. Most of these companies are very small. Two-thirds of them have fewer than fifty employees. All but twenty of these companies are 'unencumbered by revenues' (Rosenberg 1999). As Rosenberg (1999: 69) observes: 'The biotechnology industry is a very entrepreneurial industry, but one with relatively few commercial successes.'

In order to understand biotechnology enterprises, it is essential to understand the scientists that start these enterprises. This is because the biotechnology firms are an extension of the scientific knowledge and competence embodied in those firms.

Audretsch and Stephan (1999) use a data base drawn from the prospectuses of sixty firms that made an initial public offering (IPO) in biotechnology during the period March 1990 to November 1992 to examine the sources and incentives for commercialising new knowledge. Prospectuses for the offerings were carefully read in order to identify the scientific founders of the new firms. In cases where it proved difficult to identify founders from the prospectuses, telephone calls were made to the firm. In addition, firm histories were checked and confirmed in BioScan. Founders having a PhD or a MD were coded as scientific founders for the purposes of this research. In addition, several individuals who did not have a doctorate but were engaged in research were included as scientific founders. All told, we were able to identify 101 scientific founders for fifty-two firms making an initial public offering during this period.

Biographical information was also collected from the prospectuses and was supplemented by entries from standard reference works such as *American Men and Women of Science*. Four types of job experience were identified: academic experience (which includes positions at hospitals, research foundations and the government); experience with pharmaceutical companies; training experiences (as a student, post-doc, or resident); and 'other' experience. This information was used to distinguish among five distinct career trajectories followed prior to the founding of the company:

1   The academic trajectory describes scientists who had spent all of their time since completing their training employed in the academic research sector;
2   The pharmaceutical trajectory describes those scientists whose careers subsequent to receiving training had been entirely spent working in the drug industry;
3   The mixed trajectory describes scientists who had worked in both the pharmaceutical industry and the academic research sector;
4   The student trajectory describes individuals who went directly from a training position to founding a biotechnology firm; and
5   The other trajectory, which includes scientists who have been employed by non-pharmaceutical firms.

Additional biographical information coded was ascertained concerning date of birth and educational background. Citation counts to first-authored published scientific articles were measured using the 1991 Science Citation Index produced by ISI and are used here as an indicator of scientific reputation.

Summary data, presented in Table 2.1, show that 50 per cent of the scientific founders' careers followed an academic trajectory, slightly more than 25 per cent a pharmaceutical trajectory. Half of this latter group had established their careers exclusively with large pharmaceutical companies such as SmithKline and Beecham; half had come from smaller pharmaceutical firms, some of which, like Amgen, were a first generation biotech firm. Table 2.1 also indicates that approximately an eighth of the founders had a mixed career, in the sense that prior to founding the firm they had held positions in both a pharmaceutical company as well as a university or non-profit research organisation. A handful of founders moved directly from a training position such as a residency or post-doctorate appointment to the start-up firm, thereby short-circuiting the traditional trajectories from pharmaceutical firms and/or academe. The career trajectory of the remaining scientists was either indeterminate or followed another type of path.

The employment status of the founders with the biotechnology company was also determined. Note that fifty-nine of the 101 scientific founders were working full time with the new firm at the time of the public offering; forty-one were working part time, and almost all (thirty-five) of these had followed an academic trajectory. This means that 70 per cent of the academic founders maintain full-time employment with their academic institutions, serving as consultants or members of the Scientific Advisory Boards to the start-up firms. Only fifty of the academic founders had moved to full-time employment with the firm by the time the IPO was made. By contrast, all twenty-eight scientists whose careers had been

Table 2.1 Age and citation record of biotechnology founders

	Birth date				Citations		
	N	M	SD	N_{known}	M	SD	N_{known}
All scientific founders	101	1943.18	10.20	96	92.13	171.05	99
All academic founders	50	1940.55	10.06	49	149.32	226.51	49
Part time	35	1938.79	10.29	34	172.71	259.03	35
Full time	15	1945.06	8.54	15	72.21	78.70	15
All drug founders	28	1945.61	9.20	28	29.71	46.28	28
Small	14	1945.93	9.84	14	30.30	57.40	14
Big	12	1947.00	7.67	12	34.00	34.41	14
Mixed career	13	1943.80	8.76	13	62.69	57.56	13
Student career	6	1957.00	3.54	5	58.17	83.72	6
All full time	57	1945.64	9.61	57	46.59	60.69	57
All part time	40	1939.42	10.03	37	159.30	245.52	37

Source: Audretsch and Stephan (1999).

exclusively in the pharmaceutical sector held full-time positions with the firm at the time of the IPO; nine of the thirteen careers following a mixed trajectory were full time.

The evidence from Table 2.1 supports the hypothesis that the incentive structure varies considerably between the pharmaceutical founders and the academic founders. Those founders coming from universities and non-profit research organisations have the option of having their cake and eating it too, by maintaining formal contacts with their previous employer, often in a full-time position. Even those from the academic sector who are full time with the new firm are often able to maintain some connection with the non-profit sector as adjunct or clinical faculty. By contrast, those scientists who have a career path in pharmaceuticals take full-time positions with the company, at least by the time the company goes public.

There are other differences between those scientists coming from an academic trajectory and those scientists coming from a pharmaceutical trajectory. The most notable is the difference in age at the time the public offering was made. On average, those coming from universities were born approximately 5 years earlier than those coming from the pharmaceutical sector, a difference which is statistically significant at the 95 per cent level of confidence. As would be expected, we also find that those following the academic trajectory have significantly more citations than those coming from a pharmaceutical trajectory.

Of perhaps even greater interest are the differences between the part-time academics and the full-time academics. Academic founders who remain full time with their institution, working but only part time for the new firm, were, for example, born more than 6 years earlier than academic founders who leave their institution to go full time with the firm. The part-timers are not only older; they are also more eminent, having significantly more citations than academics that go full time with the firm. This suggests that eminence gives these scientists the luxury of hedging their bets; both the firm and their research institution welcome a chance to claim them as affiliates. And, although we have not yet measured the incidence, such individuals often serve as directors and members of Scientific Advisory Boards of additional start-up firms. The full-timers, by contrast, have developed sufficient human capital to be recognised as experts but lack the lustre to hold 'dual' citizenship. In terms of both citation counts and date of birth they are remarkably similar to their fellow founders who followed a pharmaceutical trajectory.

These preliminary observations suggest that the incentive structure depends upon the career trajectory that the scientist has followed as well as upon whether the scientist has established sufficient eminence to be able to sustain multiple roles. Scientists working in incumbent pharmaceutical firms face the well-known problem of deciding whether to remain with the incumbent firm or start a new firm. Furthermore, the goal of an incumbent firm to capture their economic knowledge seldom permits a scientist to establish a reputation based solely on publication. Instead, their scientific reputations are typically established in terms of the products they helped to develop and are known primarily to 'insiders' in the industry. Scientists in academe, however, face a different incentive structure. They live in a world where publications are essential for the establishment of reputation. Early in their careers they invest heavily in human capital in order to build a reputation. In the later stages of their career, scientists may trade or cash in on this reputation for economic returns. A variety of avenues are available to do this, including the establishment of a new firm.

The data suggest that this cashing out pattern is determined in part by eminence. As noted, a number of academic founders have established sufficiently strong reputations as to be able to have their cake and eat it too. They maintain their full-time jobs in academe, while seeking part-time opportunities to gain economically from their knowledge and scientific reputation. The economic returns are tied to the shares they own in the start-up companies. A subset of academic scientists, however, go full time with the firm. They, too, hold stock in the firm; but their rewards are more immediate in terms of the salaries paid to executives in the companies. And, while they have established solid reputations, they are considerably less cited than those academic founders who maintain full-time positions in academe. Although this may be a result of age (they are, after all, about 5 years younger), it is more likely a characteristic that age cannot alter. Science, as numerous researchers have established, is noteworthy for persistent inequality which age merely amplifies.

National biotech promotion programs

There is, in fact, no official program for promoting biotechnology at the federal or national level. This, however, does not imply an absence of programs that *de facto* promote biotechnology. Because scientific research and knowledge plays such an important role in biotechnology, policies promoting the underlying scientific research also promote biotechnology. Much of this scientific research has been funded by a national agency, the National Institutes of Health (NIH). As Penhoet (1999: 41), founder and former CEO of Chron observes:

> The history of biotechnology to date has involved the commercialisation of technologies that were funded almost entirely by the National Institutes of Health (NIH). Partnership, therefore, has been a major theme of the biotechnology story – partnership between government, industry, and universities. Much of the technology commercialised by industry was developed in the university setting using NIH grants.

Rosenberg (1999) concludes that the role of advocacy of research organisations has fueled the rapid growth of the NIH: 'Effective lobbying from the Association of American Medical Colleges, Research America, Funded-First, disease groups, and others, has been responsible for the growth in support for federally-funded medical R&D over the past 30 years, and the past 10 years especially.' In 1990, the NIH budget was $8 billion; in 1999 it was $14.6 billion, with projected strong growth. This is essentially a doubling of NIH funding within a decade, and Congress doubled again the budget of NIH for the following 5-year period.

The NIH has steadily expanded its support of biotechnology start-ups. For example, in 1998, NIH and private companies entered into 166 cooperative research and development agreements (Cards), which allow for the sharing of compounds and other research materials and results, as well as for the exchange of funds. This is the largest number ever of Cards between NIH and the private sector.

The Small Business Innovation Research (SBIR) program is another federal policy that provides NIH funding of biotechnology firms (Audretsch *et al.* 2000). The United States Congress enacted the SBIR program in the early 1980s as a response to the loss of American competitiveness in global markets. Congress mandated each federal agency with allocating around 4 per cent of its annual budget to funding innovative small firms as a mechanism for restoring American international competitiveness. A Phase I award provides an opportunity for a small business to establish the feasibility and technical merit of a proposed innovation. The duration of the award is 6 months and may not exceed $70,000. A Phase II award is granted to only the most promising of the Phase I projects based on scientific/technical merit, the expected value to the funding agency, company capability and commercial potential. The duration of the award is a maximum of 24 months and generally does not exceed $600,000. Approximately 40 per cent of the Phase I awards continue on to Phase II. A Phase III award is for the infusion and use of a product in the commercial market. Private sector investment, in various forms, is typically present in Phase III.

Through the Small Business Innovation Research (SBIR) program, NIH awarded $411 million in grants to small firms for medical and biopharmaceutical research in 2001. It is expected that the SBIR program at NIH will exceed $500 million in 2003.

In addition to the NIH, the United States Department of Defense also uses the SBIR program to fund biotechnology firms. Between 1983 and 1997 more than $240 million was allocated in SBIR awards to biotechnology companies from the Department of Defense. Phase I accounted for $47 million and Phase II accounted for $194 million.

In addition, the Advanced Technology Program (ATP) funded by the US Commerce Department awarded $29 million to small biotechnology companies in 1999. The ATP, like the SBIR, is expected to grow in the future.

There is compelling evidence that the SBIR program has had a positive impact on developing the US biotechnology industry. The benefits have been documented (Audretsch *et al.* 2000) as follows:

- The survival and growth rates of SBIR recipients have exceeded those of firms not receiving SBIR funding.
- The SBIR induces scientists involved in biomedical research to change their career path. By applying the scientific knowledge to commercial-isation, these scientists shift their career trajectories away from basic research towards entrepreneurship.
- The SBIR awards provide a source of funding for scientists to launch start-up firms that otherwise would not have had access to alternative sources of funding.
- SBIR awards have a powerful demonstration effect. Scientists com-mercialising research results by starting companies induce colleagues to consider applications and the commercial potential of their own research.

Regional biotech support programs

While the SBIR is a federally funded program, it also has a regional element. Many or most states have formed programs to assist firms in applying for SBIR grants. States sponsor seminars and hire agents who contact potential recipients of SBIR grants.

In addition, a number of states and cities have developed programs to try to develop a biotechnology cluster. Most of these efforts revolve around transferring the knowledge out of universities via new-firm start-ups, most typically involving technology transfer programs and technology parks. As Blakely *et al.* (1993: 12) point out:

> State and regional policy makers are taking advantage of the lessons learned from the micro-electronics experience and applying them in recent attempts to revitalise the declining industrial areas with new technologies. Unlike traditional approaches to economic development that are aimed at luring high-technology firms from their established bases, states are becoming increasingly sophisticated in their approach to economic development through biotechnology.

In particular, the traditional incentives and instruments used to promote economic development, such as low taxes, cheap land, low-cost labour and subsidies, are not effective in developing biotechnology. In an assessment of the state's approach to economic development through biotechnology, the California State Senate Office of Research concluded:

> The strategies that states are employing in the pursuit of biotechnol-

ogy are a good deal more sophisticated and better funded than the past economic development strategies, which have been, more often than not, marketing efforts designed to encourage firms to locate new production facilities in their states.

(Blakely *et al.* 1993: 12)

For example, the University–Industry Relations (UIR) program at the University of Wisconsin has resulted in the formation of a dynamic cluster of biotechnology companies in Madison, Wisconsin. The size of the grants is generally modest. In 1995, they ranged from $2,500 to $33,000. To date, the program has funded thirty-nine biotechnology start-ups that have received subsequent private investment of $10,723,200.

Similarly, South Carolina recently established the South Carolina Research Grant Program, with one goal being to develop a biotechnology industry. Faculty at the universities was encouraged to submit proposals for funding. Not only were the proposals meant to advance science, but also contribute to the economic development of South Carolina by inducing scientists to commercialise their knowledge via a biotechnology start-up.

Conclusions

Because the biotechnology industry in the United States is rapidly evolving it is difficult to make inferences about appropriate policy in the new century. What may have been effective when the industry was incipient may be less effective or even counterproductive today. Still, several major policy lessons emerge from the experience in the United States. First, the biotechnology industry is and remains a local phenomenon. The biotechnology industry not only clusters regionally, but there are only a handful of regions that have successfully generated a viable biotechnology industry. To generate a successful regional cluster, the existence of world-class scientific talent is a necessary condition. However, it is not a sufficient condition. The ancillary or complementary factors must also be available to translate this knowledge into a commercialised product. The complementary factors include the presence of venture capital and other forms of finance, the existence of an entrepreneurial culture, and transparent and minimal regulations not hindering the start-up and growth processes.

Notes

1 I am grateful to the conference organizers and two anonymous referees for their comments and suggestions.
2 These definitions follow those provided by Rosenberg (1999) for the United States National Academy of Sciences.

References

Audretsch, D.B. (1995) *'Innovation and Industry Evolution'*, Cambridge: MIT Press.

—— (1996) 'R&D Spillovers and the Geography of Innovation and Production', *American Economic Review*, 86(3): 630–40.

Audretsch, D.B. and Stephan, P. (1996) 'Company–Scientist Locational Links: The Case of Biotechnology', *American Economic Review*, 86(3): 641–52.

—— (1999) 'How and Why Does Knowledge Spill Over in Biotechnology?', in D.B. Audretsch and R. Thurik (eds) *Innovation, Industry Evolution, and Employment*, Cambridge: Cambridge University Press: 216–29.

Audretsch, D.B., Weigand, C. and Weigand, J. (2000) 'Does the Small Business Innovation Research (SBIR) Program Foster Entrepreneurial Behaviour? Evidence from Indiana', in C. Wessner (ed.) *Evaluating the Impact of the U.S. Small Business Innovation Research (SBIR) Program*, Washington, DC: National Academy of Sciences.

Blakely, E.J., Nishikawa, N. and Willoughby, K.W. (1993) 'The Economic Development Potential of California's Biotechnology Industry', *Biotechnology Review*, 1: 11–27.

Board on Science, Technology and Economic Policy, National Research Council of the National Academy of Sciences (1999) *Government–Industry Partnerships in Biotechnology and Computing*, unpublished manuscript.

Cullen, W.C. and Dibner, M.D. (1993) 'Strategic Alliances in Biotechnology: Imperatives for the 1990s', *Biotechnology Review*, 1: 110–19.

Link, A.N. and Rees, J. (1990) 'Firm Size, University Based Research, and the Returns to R&D', *Small Business Economics*, 3(1): 1–38.

Penhoet, E. (1999) 'Biotechnology: Needs and Opportunities', in *Board on Science, Technology and Economic Policy, National Research Council of the National Academy of Sciences*, unpublished manuscript.

Prevezer, M. (1997) 'The Dynamics of Industrial Clustering in Biotechnology', *Small Business Economics*, 9(3), June: 255–71.

Rosenberg, L. (1999) 'Partnerships in the Biotechnology Industry', in *Board on Science, Technology and Economic Policy, National Research Council of the National Academy of Sciences*, unpublished manuscript.

Saxenian, A.L. (1990) 'Regional Networks and the Resurgence of Silicon Valley', *California Management Review*, 33(1): 89–112.

Sharp, M. (1999) 'The Science of Nations: European Multinationals and American Biotechnology', *Biotechnology*, 1(1): 132–62.

Stephan P. and Everhart, S.S. (1998) 'The Changing Rewards to Science: The Case of Biotechnology', *Small Business Economics*, 10(2), March: 141–51.

Zucker, L.G., Darby, M.R. and Brewer, M.B. (1994) *Intellectual Capital and the Birth of U.S. Biotechnology Enterprises*, National Bureau of Economic Research (Cambridge, MA), Working Paper No. 4653.

3 The development of biotechnology clusters in the USA from the late 1970s to the early 1990s

Martha Prevezer

Introduction

This chapter explores what caused the clusters in US biotechnology to develop. The USA was the first country where the biotechnology industry has flourished and the industry there maintains a substantial lead on any other country's fledgling industry. It is the only country where a new industry has developed on the basis of these technologies, as opposed to the technologies being taken up and used by established companies in the various user sectors. This form of new industry, with substantial numbers of new companies, operating in alliance with established companies has been a feature that other countries, especially in Europe, have wished to emulate. The development of this industry, as with many other industries, has been markedly regional in character, with striking clusters or agglomerations of activity developing in particular locations. We look at the early development of the industry from a clustering perspective, with emphasis on why the industry took root on the west coast of the USA, analysing numbers of companies in different states and the degree to which they were clustered by 1991.

This has led to questions regarding the mechanisms or dynamics which cause new firms to spring up, to understand what they are attracted by and how the process of clustering gets going, encouraging further new firms or subsidiaries of established firms to set up at particular locations. This chapter examines these causes, using models of entry of firms into clusters identifying attractors, and growth of firms in clusters, looking at what the benefits to firms are of being located in a cluster.

The relationship between the start-ups and the larger incumbent companies has also been critical in the development of the industry. The relationship has largely been one of combining complementary upstream research specialisms with downstream development expertise and resources and has been crucial to the survival of the start-ups and to the commercialisation of innovative research-based products. The focus here is on what these linkages looked like spatially between small and large companies. We consider the relationship between alliances and clusters:

How geographically local have alliances been? Have alliances been formed outside clusters? Are large incumbent companies more independent of the cluster than smaller new entrants? How far have large companies needed to locate subsidiaries within key cluster areas?

The perception is that this industry has developed in the USA without substantial state or federal guidance. This suggests a number of further questions that this chapter explores. First, we would like to know how true this perception is; we examine how spontaneous the clustering dynamic was and what kind of state intervention and policies assisted it. The fourth section examines the role of regional policy in various US states to encourage and support biotechnology clusters. The importance of building on existing resources and specialisms and of working with market forces is emphasised. We look at the successful policies building on sources of regional strength, such as research at Research Triangle Park in North Carolina or in health regulation from the expertise at the National Institutes of Health. We go on to consider the migration of clusters from the first generation clusters in California and Massachusetts to second generation clusters in Maryland and North Carolina, as well as older industrial states of New Jersey, New York and Illinois, through to the development in the early 1990s of activity in other states including Washington, Tennessee and Texas. We outline a few of the policies relating to these different generations of clusters, giving a flavour of the range and number of policies and programmes at state level and what has characterised their success.

The structure of the chapter is therefore as follows. After a brief early history of the biotechnology industry in the USA in the first section, the second section is an outline of the modelling exercise that was carried out to analyse the dynamics behind clustering in the biotechnology industry. The third section looks at the role of networks of alliances in the clustering process. The fourth section looks at the regional policy initiatives that were put in place to encourage clusters to develop. The final section concludes with policy lessons on clustering and regional growth.

Preliminary view of clustering in the US biotechnology industry

One clear way to get a notion of the importance of clustering in biotechnology in the USA is to look at the distribution of companies in the industry in 1993, based on Ernst and Young's data. The clusters in the San Francisco Bay area, the group in the New York Tri-State area and the cluster around Boston made up 45 per cent of companies in the Ernst and Young sample in 1993. Other clusters were in San Diego and Los Angeles, Washington, DC and Maryland, and Philadelphia/New Jersey and Washington State. The clusters on the east coast were not neatly confined within one state but spilled over between states, whereas California as a state was

Table 3.1 Proportion of biotechnology companies in different states, 1991

State	Number of companies	Proportion of companies (per cent)
California	197	23.2
Massachusetts	68	8.0
New Jersey	58	6.8
Maryland	57	6.7
Texas	41	4.8
New York	39	4.6
North Carolina	39	4.6
Pennsylvania	37	4.4
Total	**536**	**63.1**
Out of	**849**	**100**

Source: Dibner, M.D. (1991) *Biotechnology Guide in the USA: Companies Data and Analysis*, New York: Macmillan Press.

the home to at least two distinct clusters of companies. This is relevant when we look at the data on the distribution of clusters between states. Table 3.1 shows the proportion of biotechnology companies in different states, taken from our database from Dibner's data of biotechnology companies in 1991. Almost a quarter of companies in 1991 were based in California, with far smaller proportions in other states. The next three states in importance were Massachusetts, New Jersey and Maryland, with around 7–8 per cent of companies in each state.

The sample includes both large and small firms, with differences in composition of small and large companies between sectors (see Table 3.2).

Table 3.2 Classification of firms in sample by sector and size

	Total number of firms	Employment in firms	
		Small	Small and large
All companies	**849**	**742**	**1850.7**
Therapeutics	293	265	624.5
Diagnostics	158	151	84.5
Equipment	186	156	189.5
Agriculture	107	87	444.3
Chemicals	52	41	369.4
Food	10	7	37.0
Waste	30	28	42.1
Energy	11	7	65.3

Source: Dibner, M.D. (1991) *Biotechnology Guide in the USA: Companies Data and Analysis*, New York: Macmillan Press.

Diagnostics and waste companies were mainly small; therapeutics, agricultural and equipment companies were a mix of small start-ups and large pharmaceutical, agro-chemical and equipment manufacturers. The food, energy and chemical sectors were dominated by large multinational companies, with very few start-ups by the early 1990s. In terms of the ranking by US states by industrial sector, Table 3.3 shows that California ranked first in almost all sectors, with Massachusetts, New Jersey, Maryland and North Carolina consistently among the leading states for most sectors with start-ups in therapeutics, diagnostics and equipment. For sectors which developed slightly later, such as agriculture, chemicals and waste, states such as Iowa, Texas and Illinois were beginning to feature more prominently. The fact that California and Massachusetts developed leading clusters in several sectors of the industry suggests that clusters have tended to be multi-sectoral rather than specialising in a single sector and that there has been some cross-fertilisation of techniques between sectors, especially in the early stages of the industry.

Modelling the dynamics of clustering in biotechnology[1]

The aim of the modelling exercise was to set up two main sets of models: one set to look at entry of new companies into clusters and the other to look at the growth of companies in clusters. The entry models tried to establish whether there were common factors attracting new companies into clusters in the industry, what those common factors might be and whether firms in one sector of the industry attracted firms into other

Table 3.3 Ranking of top four states: numbers of firms per state (including large companies)

	Ranked			
	1	*2*	*3*	*4*
All sectors	CA	MA	NJ	MD
Therapeutics	CA	MA	NJ	PA
Diagnostics	CA	NJ	MD	MA
Equipment	CA	MD	MA	NC
Agriculture	CA	IA	NC = NJ	TX
Chemicals	CA	NJ	NY = IL	MD, PA, TX, WI
Food	PA	–	–	–
Waste	CA	TX	–	–
Energy	–	–	–	–

Source: Swann *et al.* 1998: 132.

Notes
– Denotes only one company per state.
CA = California; MA = Massachusetts; NJ = New Jersey; MD = Maryland; TX = Texas;
PA = Pennsylvania; NC = North Carolina; IA = Iowa; IL = Illinois; WI = Wisconsin.

complementary sectors and what that pattern of intersectoral attraction might be. The growth models were at the company level, and the question being asked was whether firms in clusters grow faster than those not in clusters, and what do firms benefit from, through being in a cluster. The literature on entry and growth and the modelling associated with them is huge and I will not summarise it here.[2] However, I relate below the results of these models here to this more general literature on entry and growth.

Entry into the biotechnology industry, as into most markets (Geroski 1995), has been common, with substantial numbers entering the industry in waves. Geroski (1995) makes the point that entry rates are far higher than market penetration rates; the survival rates of most entrants is low. Our database was a survival database: it is a register of all companies which had survived until 1991. There is no record here of companies that were founded but had failed or been swallowed up before 1991. In other words, the data represent a snapshot of the industry in 1991. However, as survival is a feature we want to capture, and as we want the cluster pattern to reflect stable firms that have grown and survived rather than the more ephemeral population of those that entered and exited, we have not been too worried by this feature.

Entry of new firms over the period and geographic concentration

Table 3.4 shows entry of new firms into the industry in our sample between 1979 and 1990. It gives four-state concentration ratios for each year and ranks the states for entry in each year. There were just over 600 surviving entrants into our dataset. Entry occurred in waves, with peaks in 1981, 1984 and 1986–1987. This concurs with the pattern of entry in many industries (Geroski 1995). There was more entry into therapeutics than other sectors, but a sizeable number went into diagnostics and equipment sectors. Entry was predominantly into those states which ranked high in Table 3.3, with California, Massachusetts, Maryland, New Jersey, North Carolina and Texas capturing over 50 per cent of new entrants. In the early 1980s the geographical concentration fell slightly, but increased again in the late 1980s. So entry patterns did not become less concentrated over the decade, despite the diffusion and diversification of companies into states such as Texas and Pennsylvania.

Data and classification of the industry for the models

The unit of location taken to define a cluster was the individual state in the USA. There were a few problems with this, as stated above. There was more than one cluster in California and clusters developed across state boundaries on the east coast. For example, the location of the National Institutes of Health encouraged entry into Maryland, North Carolina and Washington, DC. However, there is some justification for using the state

Table 3.4 Number of new firms in our sample and the four-state concentration ratio of entry by new biotechnology firms across the USA

	Number of new firms in sample (four-state concentration ratio)	Ranking of top four states by entry of new firms (% of new firms entering into the state)			
1979	19 (64%)	NC (21%)	CA (16%)	MD (16%)	MA (11%)
1980	33 (51%)	CA (33%)	NC (6%)	TX = NJ = MA (6%)	
1981	81 (55%)	CA (31%)	MA (12%)	NJ (7%)	MD = WA (5%)
1982	40 (48%)	CA (24%)	MD (10%)	NJ = NY (7%)	
1983	57 (46%)	CA (18%)	MD (14%)	NJ (9%)	NY = NC = MO (5%)
1984	69 (46%)	CA (24%)	WA (9%)	TX (7%)	MD = NJ (6%)
1985	54 (52%)	MD (17%)	CA = MA (15%)		MN = NC (6%)
1986	64 (50%)	CA (25%)	MA (13%)	NC (8%)	PA = TX (5%)
1987	88 (47%)	CA (24%)	MA (9%)	MD (8%)	TX = NC (7%)
1988	56 (55%)	CA (30%)	MD (9%)	NC (9%)	NJ = NY = PA (7%)
1989	35 (60%)	CA (26%)	TX (17%)	MA (11%)	NC = WA = PA (6%)
1990	13 (69%)	CA (38%)	MA (15%)	CO = NY = MD = NJ = PA = WA (8%)	

Source: Swann *et al.* 1998: 138.

Notes
CA = California; MA = Massachusetts; NJ = New Jersey; MD = Maryland; TX = Texas;
PA = Pennsylvania; NC = North Carolina; IA = Iowa; IL = Illinois; WI = Wisconsin;
WA = Washington; NY = New York; MO = Montana; CO = Connecticut; MN = Minnesota.

as the unit of the cluster, in that policies were developed in general at the state level, with each employing its own tax regime and pricing policies.[3]

Entry and growth models

As we lacked a time series of data on employment by sector, by state and by year, we built up to a 'full' entry model which used estimated employment data, via two simpler preliminary models of entry. The first used an analysis of entry with a single estimate of employment per sector per state, taking the time series of surviving entry into each sector and performing a latent variable analysis of it.[4] This established that the factors attracting entry into the industry were not uncorrelated, that there were some underlying common factors, although we were not able to identify them from the latent variable analysis. The next step was to estimate an average entry model, per sector, per cluster, per year and see how these correlated for each sector with employment in the industry and science base in 1991. Results are summarised in Table 3.5. These regressions told us that entry at a cluster into therapeutics, diagnostics and equipment sectors was significantly related to strength of employment in the science base as well as employment within the biotechnology industry. We could not at this stage say anything about specific sector-to-sector effects.

To do this we constructed a full entry model. For the employment data for this model, we made a rough estimate of employment in each cluster, by estimating the size of each relevant firm in each year, assuming steady long-run growth from date of foundation to 1991. This made no allowance for cycles in growth, due to business cycles for example. These estimates were then aggregated across firms, to give a rough indication of cluster strength.

The entry of firms into a particular sector (i) at a particular cluster (c) was assumed to be a function of industry strength in terms of employment in each sector at that cluster at the start of that year, and of strength in the science base in terms of employment at that cluster at the start of that year. Total entry into the sector picked up any macro cyclical effects, and the state-fixed effects summarised the extent to which a broad range of other factors which were specific to particular states led to above or below average entry or growth within sector i at cluster c, such as the California effect, Massachusetts effect, etc. This full model allowed us to identify separate sector-to-sector effects and the pull from the science base to firms in particular sectors.[5]

The results were found to be consistent with the two simpler models and are shown in Table 3.6. This shows the attractor coefficients – how much employment in one sector and in the science base affected entry in each other sector. The coefficients summarise the effect of a 1 per cent increase in relevant employment on mean entry. It should be noted that a 1 per cent increase in science base employment represented far fewer people than a 1 per cent increase in industrial employment. The results are summarised in two flow diagrams (Figures 3.1 and 3.2) indicating direction of attraction (attractor → attracted) with the thickness of the arrows indicating the size of coefficients and hence strength of attraction. Parts of the science base were the main attractors for new firms to enter the industry. There was also a group of intersectoral linkages which exerted a pull to entry. The sectors divided into two groups – therapeutics, diagnostics,

Table 3.5 Regression of mean entry in each sector and each state on industry employment and science base employment

	Biotechnology sector							
	Therapeutics	Diagnostics	Equipment	Agriculture	Chemicals	Food	Waste	Energy
In science base employment	0.0710 (0.0382)	0.0408 (0.0178)	0.0439 (0.0168)	0.0180 (0.0074)	0.0110 (0.0057)	-0.0011 (0.0022)	0.0066 (0.0037)	0.0031 (0.0013)
In industry employment	0.0866 (0.0385)	0.0486 (0.0184)	-0.4428 (0.1888)	0.0215 (0.0080)	0.0172 (0.0065)	0.0005 (0.0008)	0.0117 (0.0039)	-0.0018 (0.0011)

Source: Swann et al. 1998: 143.

Table 3.6 Entry attractors in biotechnology (mean change in number of entrants for given percentage increase in employment in each sector)

	Entry into							
	Therapeutics	Diagnostics	Equipment	Agriculture	Chemicals	Food	Waste	Energy
R^2	0.103	0.102	0.101	0.129	0.058	0.111	0.084	0.108
Std error	0.696	0.52	0.56	0.395	0.234	0.083	0.223	0.102
Attracted by:								
Total entry into sector (all states)	0.022 (0.004)	0.021 (0.005)	0.02 (0.004)	0.022 (0.004)	0.023 (0.006)	0.021 (0.007)	0.021 (0.006)	0.022 (0.007)
Therapeutics	−0.01 (0.048)	0.091 (0.036)	0.043 (0.039)	0.048 (0.02)	0.017 (0.016)	0.005 (0.006)	0.000 (0.015)	−0.000 (0.007)
Diagnostics	0.006 (0.057)	−0.089 (0.042)	−0.026 (0.046)	0.006 (0.024)	−0.002 (0.019)	0.003 (0.007)	−0.003 (0.018)	−0.008 (0.008)
Equipment	0.037 (0.061)	−0.022 (0.045)	−0.064 (0.049)	0.019 (0.026)	0.01 (0.02)	−0.005 (0.007)	0.021 (0.019)	0.017 (0.009)
Agriculture	0.054 (0.068)	0.026 (0.05)	−0.007 (0.055)	−0.084 (0.029)	0.017 (0.023)	−0.012 (0.008)	−0.017 (0.022)	0.011 (0.01)
Chemicals	−0.019 (0.065)	−0.075 (0.048)	−0.022 (0.052)	0.025 (0.028)	−0.048 (0.022)	0.011 (0.008)	0.056 (0.021)	0.012 (0.01)
Food	−0.052 (0.084)	−0.057 (0.062)	0.014 (0.068)	−0.045 (0.036)	0.017 (0.028)	−0.061 (0.01)	0.042 (0.027)	−0.002 (0.012)
Waste	−0.157 (0.089)	−0.06 (0.066)	−0.098 (0.072)	−0.13 (0.038)	−0.026 (0.03)	−0.009 (0.011)	−0.141 (0.029)	0.022 (0.013)
Energy	−0.14 (0.124)	−0.136 (0.092)	−0.317 (0.099)	−0.066 (0.052)	−0.019 (0.042)	−0.012 (0.015)	0.019 (0.04)	−0.11 (0.018)
Science base Agriculture	−0.023 (0.157)	0.025 (0.117)	−0.006 (0.127)	−0.003 (0.067)	−0.019 (0.053)	0.003 (0.019)	−0.032 (0.05)	−0.015 (0.023)
Biology	0.021 (0.09)	0.052 (0.067)	0.057 (0.073)	0.034 (0.038)	0.02 (0.03)	0.004 (0.011)	0.002 (0.029)	−0.018 (0.013)
Medical	0.029 (0.104)	0.03 (0.077)	0.119 (0.084)	0.029 (0.044)	−0.011 (0.035)	0.017 (0.012)	0.029 (0.033)	0.008 (0.015)

Source: Swann et al. 1998: 146–7.

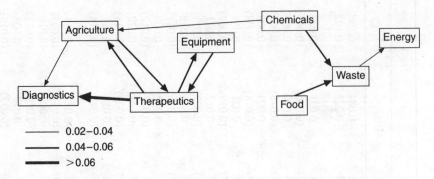

Figure 3.1 Principal new entry attractors in US biotechnology: sectors

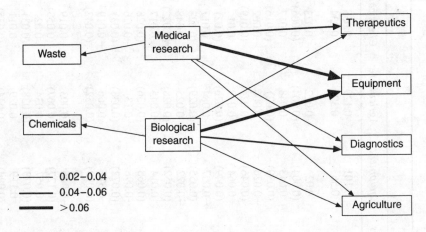

Figure 3.2 Principal new entry attractors in US biotechnology: science base

equipment and agriculture – where there was feedback between sectors, and another group – chemicals, food, waste and energy – where there was no feedback. A firm's own sector acted as a mild repellent to new entry with negative coefficients.

The growth model was a company-level model and examined how the growth of employment in each company depended on the age of the company, own sector employment at that cluster, employment in other sectors than the one to which the company belonged at that cluster, and employment in the science base at that cluster. Thus the model estimated the trend rate of growth, but made allowances for growth to be influenced by the presence of like firms (in the same sector) or unlike firms (in other sectors) or the science base.

It fits into the profusion of growth models looking at the patterns of growth rates in many different types of population: manufacturing or non-financial companies, using national censuses and proprietary databases; some sampling small units, others cutting off at a threshold (Caves 1997). The literature has been concerned with testing Gibrat's Law (Sutton 1997) to see whether growth rates of firms in a population have been independent of their initial sizes, whether there is standard variance in growth rates with size and whether serial correlation of growth rates exists. The more recent models have established exceptions and extensions to Gibrat's model. This work has established that the variance of growth rates is not independent of size but that the variability of a firm's growth decreases with size, that mean growth rates decline with size and age, and that firms' growth rates may be serially correlated (Caves 1997). It also establishes that average growth rates are large, in terms of both expansion and contraction and that there is a long-run regression to the mean as the large contract and the small grow, although there is a stickiness in leaders' positions which is perhaps explained by first mover advantages and structural rigidities. A relatively small percentage of growth is accounted for by inter-industry shifts; most is accounted for by intra-industry mobility (Caves 1997). There is some evidence that countries with smaller size establishments display higher growth rates, consistent with the Gibrat's Law literature. Some work has been done to try to pin down determinants of growth, such as the learning models where firms invest in innovations and grow if successful or exit if they are not.

The growth model here is concerned not so much to examine growth rates *per se* but the relation between growth and clusters. The benefits and costs of being in a cluster are examined in Swann *et al.* (1998). It is more concerned with whether the spillovers which are beneficial to growth come from firms in the same sector (with similar specialisations) or from firms in other related sectors (with complementary specialisations). The questions being asked are whether, as with new entrants, the benefits of clustering are stronger between complementary firms, exploiting inter-sectoral factors such as demand by other sectors which are users of innovations in that sector. Alternatively, incumbent firms may benefit more from being close to similar types of firms, for example due to knowledge spillovers within that sector which cannot be absorbed from other sectors.

Table 3.7 gives us the growth parameters. There were not enough companies in the energy sector to compute the growth promoters. It was employment within the company's own sector and cluster which were found to have promoted growth of any company, whereas strength of employment in other sectors at that cluster detracted from company growth (with mainly negative coefficients). The strength of the science

Table 3.7 Growth promoters in biotechnology (company employment and other sector employment) as function of age of company, own sector employment and other sector employment)

	Growth in							
	All biotechnology	Therapeutics	Diagnostics	Equipment	Agriculture	Chemicals	Food	Waste
R^2	0.483	0.477	0.275	0.435	0.473	0.673	0.850	0.698
Std error	1.707	1.794	1.678	1.539	2.031	1.657	1.534	1.273
Promoted by:								
Age of company	0.058	0.058	0.064	0.052	0.053	0.073	0.055	0.065
	(0.003)	(0.005)	(0.009)	(0.007)	(0.006)	(0.008)	(0.012)	(0.021)
Own sector employment	0.203	0.252	0.200	0.316	0.107	0.114	0.262	0.324
	(0.028)	(0.069)	(0.081)	(0.082)	(0.078)	(0.101)	(0.218)	(0.198)
Other sector employment	−0.006	−0.038	−0.033	−0.076	0.057	0.095	−0.173	−0.06
	(0.027)	(0.076)	(0.057)	(0.054)	(0.082)	(0.068)	(0.093)	(0.088)
Science base employment	−0.023	−0.081	0.006	−0.131	0.066	0.043	0.335	−0.097
	(0.053)	(0.102)	(0.127)	(0.118)	(0.133)	(0.146)	(0.263)	(0.15)

Source: Swann et al. 1998: 148.

base at a cluster was found not to assist company growth; again, more often coefficients were negative. Coefficients of 'age' simply represent the trend growth rate of a company in the relevant sector.

Interpretation

The science base was found to have been a significant attractor of new entrants into the industry, which concurs with our observations in the initial section and is explored further in the third section. This strong relation in a science-based industry, where medical research in particular forms the basis for innovation in industry, has been well documented (Zucker *et al.* 1994, Audretsch and Stephan 1996, Audretsch, Chapter 1 of this volume). The attraction by the science base was in part due to early company founders being based there, and was also due to a continuing need for links to scientific expertise in the specialist disciplines that could not be developed in-house within companies. Research centres also formed an important market for the development of research equipment, and interaction between science base and equipment sector was strong.

The links between science base and companies were supplemented by links between a number of industrial sectors. The therapeutics sector exerted a strong pull for new diagnostics, agricultural and equipment firms, with some positive feedback effects of equipment and agricultural companies attracting therapeutics companies. Activity in one's own sector served as a mild deterrent to entry. So the process of attraction was self-reinforcing between one group of sectors, but the feedback mechanism was limited to the healthcare companies, equipment and agricultural companies. This implies that firms with complementary rather than similar specialisations are attracted to each other and tend to enter a cluster together. This result is supported by Audretsch and Feldman (1999) who stress that diversity of the science base at a location supports innovative activities to a greater extent than specialisation. They find that the presence of diverse industries within the same science base in a city leads to increased innovation.

In contrasting the entry and growth results, several features emerge. The advantage to a firm of locating in a cluster of like firms (in the same sector) was strong for all sectors, whereas attraction to new entrants was confined to a group of sectors. In addition there was a negative effect of the presence of like firms (in the same sector) on entry, whereas this was positive for growth of existing firms. So the presence of therapeutics firms at a cluster discouraged new therapeutics entrants, but encouraged firms from related sectors such as diagnostics and equipment firms, while benefiting those therapeutics firms that were already there.

Entry and growth processes were markedly different in relation to the effects of the science base on them, with a strong pull from the science base for new entrants, but no positive effects for established companies. This suggests that entrants and incumbents had different capabilities and competencies, which gave them different capacities to absorb spillovers from the science base and industrial sectors. Entrants appear to have been effective at absorbing spillovers from the science base and related sectors, whereas incumbents absorbed the benefits of being in a cluster which occurred within their own sector but were not good at absorbing spillovers from the science base or from interrelated sectors.

Another difference between the two processes was the spreading across all sectors of the benefits of clustering for growth, whereas the benefits of clustering for new entrants were confined to a group of sectors and did not extend to the chemicals, food, waste or energy sectors. The non-entry sectors were either dominated by large companies or were underdeveloped in the early 1990s. It is possible that the science base was less central to the chemical and food companies, which relied more on their in-house research.

Another possibility is that in those sectors dominated by large companies, local spillovers were absorbed by them, deterring new entrants by potential competitors. Moreover, large companies were not dependent on locating close to the science base in order to absorb spillovers, which they could accomplish as effectively through alliances over longer distances.

Relating these results to the growth and entry literature discussed above raises further issues in the context of biotechnology about the relationship between entry and growth. There appear from these results to be two distinct populations: entrants attracted to clusters by spillovers of various sorts from related sectors – user sectors or supplier sectors such as diagnostics and equipment sectors' attraction to therapeutics; and incumbent firms which benefit from strength within their own sectors – due to specialised labour or inputs for example – but do not absorb spillovers from related sectors. At what point do these surviving entrants become incumbents? How is that transition made? What are the barriers to market penetration in these biotechnology sectors? These questions take us to the relationships between entrants and incumbents, their synergies and complementarity which have tended to outweigh the potential displacement of incumbents by newer firms. The next section examines the role of these relations, in particular through alliances, in building up clusters.

Role of networks in building clusters

This section examines the role of networks, both of the more formal type of alliances, but also informal networks of communication between companies and universities in the local area. The fluidity and density of these networks is thought to have played a key role in the diffusion of ideas, technical expertise and commercial opportunities related to high technology areas. These networks of alliances served various purposes: to bring together complementary assets between different types of company, especially upstream research capabilities of dedicated biotechnology firms (DBFs) with downstream processing and marketing capabilities of incumbent user companies (Dodgson 1991), and to learn about and absorb new technologies outside the core competencies of the incumbent user companies (Arora and Gambardella 1994). Symbiosis has existed both between the new entrants (DBFs) and incumbents and between DBFs specialising in different technologies. Alliances have also been formed for motives of strategic choice and due to technological competition (Barley *et al.* 1992). These networks of alliances were also methods of coping with uncertain appropriability between firms (Levin *et al.* 1987) and difficulties in learning and absorbing the new technologies into organisational structures with well-established existing competencies and routines (Cohen and Levinthal 1990).

The question that concerns us here is how far alliances reinforced the clustering process, or how far they could operate over distances and could escape the need to be located close to the partner company. Evidence on whether or not alliances reinforced clusters rests partly on determining whether they have been predominantly local in character, between firms in the same state, or whether they have occurred between companies in different states with distance being no object. There is some evidence that DBFs operated differently from the larger incumbent firms in this respect. Alliances between DBFs have tended to be more local than those between entrants and incumbents, in part because established companies have not tended to be located within clusters of new companies, and clusters have not grown up around incumbent companies but rather around scientific research centres.

In a study of networks of alliances in California and Massachusetts between 1988 and 1991, it was found that DBFs based within the state were most central to their respective networks: they had the greatest number of ties with other firms (high 'degree centrality'), were more linked indirectly as well as directly in alliances (high 'betweenness centrality') and were closer to other firms in the network (higher 'closeness centrality') than were the large incumbent firms involved in those networks in California and Massachusetts. The incumbents tended to be based in other states or abroad, whereas the DBFs were located within the respective states where the networks were centred (Lomi and Prevezer 1997).[6] It seems therefore that DBFs have tended to form alliances within their own states to a greater extent than have incumbents, and this would have reinforced the clustering tendency of entrants to seek information and complementarities more locally than did incumbents.

However there has also been a trend for incumbent companies to set up subsidiaries within clusters. They have clearly not felt entirely self-sufficient located outside the mainstreams of scientific developments going on within clusters. During the 1980s some established companies located

Table 3.8 Examples of large established companies locating in clusters

Large company subsidiary	Location of cluster
Baxter Healthcare Hyland Biotechnology	California
Abbot Biotech	Massachusetts
Ciba Corning Diagnostic Corp	Massachusetts
Lubrizol Agrigenetics	California
Glaxo	North Carolina Research Triangle Park
Burroughs Wellcome	North Carolina Research Triangle Park
BASF Bioresearch Corp	Cambridge and Worcester, Massachusetts
Hitachi Chemical Research Center	California
Tanabe Seiyaku	Acquired R&D laboratories of Immunetech San Diego
Berlex Laboratories, subsidiary of Schering	On site of Codon Corp, California

Source: Swann, Prevezer and Stout 1998: 170–1.

biotechnology subsidiaries within clusters (see Table 3.8). Clearly it has been important for both large incumbents and smaller DBFs to be located close to the centres of the main clusters, and to establish formal alliances and informal linkages within those clusters.

Regional policy initiatives

This section examines the role of regional policy in various US states to encourage and support biotechnology clusters. The first main finding is that there have been a substantial number and range of policy initiatives, even in the states of California and Massachusetts where it might seem as though clusters developed through market forces and spontaneously. The role of policy was significant in bolstering those developments. A second general finding was that it mattered that policy initiatives should make use of local strengths and resources, and should work with the current of market forces, rather than try to lure companies to locations against their market inclinations. The success of policy initiatives hinged on focusing on initial conditions needed to foster particular sectors or niches that were appropriate to those sectors. In other words, focusing on boosting research conditions – the quality of infrastructure, its concentration, conditions for transferability into the industrial sector, the availability of skilled research labour – was germane to fostering clusters of therapeutics companies, which have had the greatest need for good research conditions. The strength and accessibility of the user community, in the form of users of new instruments and medical technology, were critical features for the development of clusters of diagnostics and equipment companies. The cost of labour was a greater consideration in the location decisions of those firms specialising in manufacturing or scaling-up processes. For firms specialising in commercialising research, the fact that skilled research labour was more expensive in Boston, San Francisco or San Diego, which stemmed from demand for that quality of scientist, was not a deterrent for companies reliant on the science base and with a need for access to top-class research scientists.

We turn now to examine the initiatives that were put in place across the USA in biotechnology, mainly in the form of biotechnology centres located in particular states as part of local government policy. These centres varied enormously in their aims and focuses, but had a number of common elements. They were:

1   encouraging the specialisms of that area and enhancing and making use of local expertise, such as strength in research at Research Triangle Park in North Carolina, or expertise in health regulation in the area around the National Institutes of Health in Maryland;
2   tax breaks or other fiscal and financial inducements to entry of new companies;
3   the creation of infrastructure that could be shared between small companies that would otherwise not have had access to such facilities, for example research parks, incubator buildings, pilot plant facilities, DNA libraries or gene banks.

It is hard to determine the precise results of these policies, in terms of numbers of companies brought into the state or area as a consequence of them. Here we assess their success in relation to their appropriateness to local conditions, and according to how well the biotechnology industry appears to have been developing in that state. In a survey of Biotechnology Centre Strategies, Dibner and Hamner found that in 1991 there were seventy-five centres in thirty-three states, an increase from thirty-six centres in twenty-three states in 1987. Sixty per cent of those in 1991 were based at single universities, a quarter were not aligned to a university and covered the whole state, and 15 per cent were for general technological development, including biotechnology. In terms of dispersion, in 1991 there were seven centres in California, ten in Maryland, three in Massachusetts, one in North Carolina, three in New Jersey, two in New York, three in Ohio and three in Pennsylvania (*Genetic Engineering News*, January 1992).

We look now at the policy contribution to the earliest and most successful clusters, in terms of numbers of companies in them, in California and Massachusetts, and then at the creation of the 'second generation' of clusters in newer industrial areas in Maryland and North Carolina, as well as those based in the older industrial states of New Jersey, New York and

Illinois. The more recent development of biotechnology clusters, in an 'outer' group of states, included clusters in Washington State, Idaho and Tennessee, Texas, Michigan and Delaware. This third group has focused more on agriculture, chemicals and bioprocesses, as well as healthcare where there were particular healthcare resources. This is not a comprehensive review of all biotechnology activity in all states, but gives a flavour of the type of policies and their range which seemed to provide a stimulus to the location of companies in those areas.

The earliest clusters in northern California and Massachusetts were based near leading-edge research, a process which has already been described. High-calibre scientists needed to be close to centres of research excellence and were not going to be attracted away from those academic centres. Manufacturing facilities on the other hand were located further away from the science base. Similar strengths applied to southern California. There were many research centres concentrated in this area, such as the Scripps Institute, Salk Institute, La Jolla Cancer Research Foundation, Whither Institute for Diabetes and Endocrinology. The Universities of California in the south included Irvine, Riverside, San Diego, Los Angeles as well as private universities. Some of these research institutes were well endowed; the Salk and Scripps Institutes had over 500 scientists each. So size and concentration of research activity has mattered. There have also been specific programmes, such as CONNECT in southern California, to help establish linkages between institutions and to foster commercial development. These clusters in California have been built on diverse and decentralised planning, taking advantage of local strengths. For example, Stanford's Office of Technology Licensing ran a policy of fixed royalty rates or membership fees to gain access to a pool of licences for the use of basic biotechnology patents (*Bio/Technology*, May 1983). This speeded technology transfer and gave wider access to the licences of participating universities. The universities benefited through being insulated to some extent from the corporations and through lower negotiation and administration of patenting and licensing. In Massachusetts, the centre at Worcester was important in fostering activity, aimed at imitating MIT's encouragement of Route 128. As for California, the Worcester centre was based around research centres: Worcester Polytechnic Institute, Clark University, the University of Massachusetts Medical Centre. It fostered links with the Massachusetts Biotechnology Research Institute with its incubation facility, shared instrumentation and fermentation pilot plant, nuclear magnetic resonance (NMR) facility, downstream processing equipment, biotechnology library, conference centre and training facilities. In 1991 there were fifteen biotechnology companies based at that centre, alongside five research institutes. So these early clusters benefited from various local policy initiatives and biotechnology centres, which moved with market forces to encourage and underpin the location of companies in those areas.

The newer industrial states which have grown in importance in this industry have been North Carolina and Maryland. In North Carolina the emphasis was on academic strength at Research Triangle Park, promoted as a research-oriented park with a campus-like atmosphere. Its focus has been multi-institute and multidisciplinary research and policies encouraged education and business development. It has also housed the largest incubator facility in the USA. The climate is thought to have benefited from clear regulation under the Genetic Engineering Organisms Act. The Park attracted start-ups, in addition to the biotechnology units of Glaxo and Ciba Geigy, research laboratories of Burroughs Wellcome, IBM and General Electric as well as various other subsidiaries of leading companies. In 1985 North Carolina had 110 small companies. The North Carolina Biotechnology Center was established in 1984, which is estimated to have spawned 38 biotechnology companies at that location (*Bio/Technology*, June 1992).

Maryland's expertise has been centred on the National Institutes of Health and the National Bureau of Standards as well as other research institutes, such as the Gillette Research Institute. The Center for Advanced Research in Biotechnology was established with the backing of the University of Maryland, and this has been linked to the National Bureau of Standards to encourage standardised measurement and techniques. The Shady Grove Life Science Center in Montgomery County has also been a focal area for many firms to locate, close to research institutes and other companies, and also to exploit access to NIH scientists, and information sources at the National Library of Medicine. In 1984 Montgomery County was home to 250 bioscience firms (*Genetic Engineering News*, January 1984), such as Genex, Litton Bionetics, Microbiology Associates, as well as subsidiaries of larger firms such as Boehringer Mannheim and the first Japanese research facility in the USA, Otsuka Pharmaceuticals. By 1987 it was estimated that there were over 400 high-technology companies in the area.

The older industrial states of New Jersey, New York or Illinois have focused on the presence of leading large industrial user companies in pharmaceuticals in particular, as well as prowess in research. Two out of four high-technology centres were devoted to biotechnology: one based at Cornell University specialising in agricultural applications and the other at the State University of New York at Stony Brook, specialising in diagnostics. In Illinois the focus has been on attracting inward investment based on the three large pharmaceutical companies there – Abbott, Searle and Baxter Travenol. Specific inducements have included a research park and incubator building, financing programmes and tax breaks, as well as urban renewal projects to encourage high-technology industry in older industrial areas.

The more recent spread of the biotechnology industry in the early 1990s has been towards Washington State, focusing on the Washington State

University Research and Technology Park, the Tennessee Technology Corridor and the University of Utah Park in Salt Lake City. Industrial focus has been on agriculture in Washington State and Utah, and on bio-medical research in Tennessee. The state of Michigan has also targeted agriculture, building on its agricultural expertise at Michigan State University and the presence of companies such as Upjohn, Kellogg and Dow Chemical. Again an effort has been made at the state level to diversify resources away from its reliance on automobiles and towards high-technology industries. In similar fashion Delaware has concentrated on agricultural and chemical applications, to build on the presence there of Du Pont.

The common elements in all these initiatives have been the involvement of a spectrum of companies and research institutes, the creation of linkage and transfer institutions to help with patenting and licensing activities, as well as pilot plants and incubator facilities. Competition between states to attract companies, with decentralised funding at the state level, has probably also been beneficial to the process, plus the searching for niches and specialisms that are particular strengths of that area has helped to diversify activity both geographically and across industrial sectors. The scale of these resources and their range have been important features in achieving a critical mass of support and activity for clusters of companies to be attracted to those areas.

Conclusions on clustering and regional growth

There are three main sets of conclusions that may be drawn from this chapter on the mechanics of clustering and policies to foster regional growth:

1   on the clustering mechanisms and how to understand them;
2   on the differences between entrants or start-up companies and incumbent established companies in their relationships with each other and their needs for being in a cluster; and
3   on the role of regional policies in particular in fostering these sorts of clustering dynamics.

Clustering mechanisms

Understanding the structure of an industry and its intersectoral linkages and dependencies is critical for understanding clustering dynamics. In the computing industry, the strongest attracting linkages were between hardware and software sectors, so the presence of strong hardware companies encouraged entry by software companies at that location. In the biotechnology industry there are three types of linkages that are relevant to development of the industry.

- Vertical links between start-ups and established companies, i,e. therapeutics to pharmaceuticals, agricultural to agro-chemical companies.
- Well-established in the literature and borne out by these models is the stimulus to the creation of new companies through proximity to research centres which are the sources of innovations in research. The mechanisms by which spin-offs from research are created have been described elsewhere (Audretsch, Chapter 2 in this volume, Zucker *et al.* 1994) and the importance of being near the 'star' scientists responsible for the path-breaking research has been established.
- Very important for clustering are horizontal linkages between different sub-sectors – within healthcare, for example, between therapeutics and diagnostics or between therapeutics and equipment companies. There is a further element here of linkages between 'primary' research technologies and 'secondary', platform, process technologies with companies specialising in platform technologies clustering to service those research firms with new specialised products of research. The results from the model on the attraction to clusters between new entrant equipment companies to therapeutics and agricultural companies fall into this type of relationship.
- Another result from the clustering models is the clear emphasis on the strength in complementarity of different sectors; attraction is to a diverse cluster rather than one that is specialised in only one sector or technology.
- Results from the growth model of clustering indicate benefits for established companies to being located in a cluster. However, they are not so dependent on proximity to the science base as are new entrants, and appear to absorb spillovers from within their own sector rather than from inter-related sectors. This suggests that as companies become established, they become more specialised in their particular fields of expertise and the most beneficial sources of tacit knowledge in the vicinity are those relating most closely to their particular specialisms.

Start-up and incumbent companies

There are clear differences between entrants and incumbents, both in terms of the benefits they derive from a cluster and therefore what attracts them to it, and also the relationships between them and the way clustering facilitates making alliances, especially between small companies. The larger incumbents make alliances across distances, but there is still a tendency for them to locate subsidiaries within a cluster. A question for the later development of the industry in the 1990s is the transition from start-up to established company. Orsenigo *et al.* (Chapter 8 in this volume) establishes that there appear to be first-mover advantages, giving the early entrants to the industry an enduring role; they look at the changing role of these early entrants who become established and start to play the role of an established company to later entrants, in terms of alliances, development support, etc.

Regional policies

Conclusions on the role of regional policies suggest that their influence has been substantial, despite the impression given of US industry that it is of relatively free market orientation. The combination has been one of substantial federal funding of the science base via the NIH (Orsenigo 1989), but few federally directed biotechnology policies, combined with more tailored regional initiatives geared to the strengths and circumstances of that state. We have seen some engineering of the migration of clusters from initial states to second-wave clusters and then third-wave clusters. So regional policy has been active and probably quite effective. It has worked with market mechanisms, building on existing strengths and not building from scratch.

Notes

1 The models outlined here were developed by Peter Swann (Swann 1993) and details can be found in Swann and Prevezer (1996), Prevezer (1997) and Swann *et al.* (1998).
2 This literature is surveyed and summarised in papers by Caves (1997), Geroski (1995) and Sutton (1997).
3 For details of the company data and research centres data used in these models see Prevezer (1998).
4 For details of this see Swann *et al.* 1998: 142.
5 For full details see Swann *et al.* 1998: Chapter 3.
6 For details of these measures of centrality, derived from social network analysis, see Wasserman and Faust (1994).

References

Arora, A. and Gambardella, A. (1994) 'The Changing Technology of Technical Change: General and Abstract Knowledge and the Division of Innovative Labor', *Research Policy*, 23(5): 523–32.
Audretsch, D. and Feldman, M. (1999) 'Innovation in Cities: Science-Based Diversity, Specialisation and Localised Competition', *European Economic Review*, 43(2): 409–29.
Audretsch, D. and Stephan, P. (1996) 'Company–Scientist Locational Links: The Case of Biotechnology', *American Economic Review*, 86(3): 641–52.
Barley, S., Freeman, J. and Hybels, R. (1992) 'Strategic Alliances in Commercial Biotechnology', in N. Nohria and R. Eccles (eds) *Networks and Organizations: Structure, Form and Action*, Boston, MA: Harvard Business School Press.
Caves, R. (1997) 'Industrial Organization and New Findings on the Turnover and Mobility of Firms', *Journal of Economic Literature*, 36(4), Dec. 1998: 1947–82.
Cohen, W.M. and Levinthal, D.A. (1990) 'Absorptive Capacity: A New Perspec-

tive on Learning and Innovation', *Administrative Science Quarterly*, 35(1): 128–52.

Dibner, M.D. (1991) *'Biotechnology Guide USA, Companies, Data and Analysis'*, New York: Macmillan.

Dodgson, M. (1991) 'Strategic Alignment and Organizational Options in Biotechnology Firms', *Technology Analysis and Strategic Management*, 3(2): 115–25.

Ernst and Young (1992) *'Biotech 93 Accelerating Commercialization'*, San Francisco, Ernst and Young.

Geroski, P.A. (1995) 'What do we Know about Entry?', *International Journal of Industrial Organization*, 13: 421–40.

Levin, R., Klevorick, A., Nelson, R. and Winter, S. (1987) 'Appropriating the Returns from Industrial Research and Development', *Brookings Papers on Economic Activity*, Vol. 3: 783–820.

Lomi, A. and Prevezer, M. (1997) 'Networks for Innovation in Biotechnology', in J. Butler and A. Piccaluga (eds) *Knowledge, Technology and Innovation*, Milan: Guerini e Associati: 363–77.

Orsenigo, L. (1989) *'The Emergence of Biotechnology'*, London: Pinter Publishers.

Orsenigo, L., Pammolli, F. and Riccaboni, M. (2001) 'Technological Change and Network Dynamics. Lessons from the Pharmaceutical Industry', *Research Policy*, 30: 485–508.

Prevezer, M. (1996) 'The Dynamics of Industrial Clustering in Biotechnology', *Small Business Economics*, 8: 1–17.

—— (1997) 'The Dynamics of Industrial Clustering in Biotechnology', *Small Business Economics*, 9: 255–71.

—— (1998) 'Clustering in Biotechnology in the USA', in P. Swann, M. Prevezer and D. Stout (eds) *The Dynamics of Industrial Clustering. International Comparisons in Computing and Biotechnology*, Chap. 6, Oxford: Oxford University Press: 124–93.

Sutton, J. (1997) 'Gibrat's Legacy', *Journal of Economic Literature*, Vol. 35: 40–59.

Swann, G.M.P. (1993) 'Can High Technology Services Prosper if High Technology Manufacturing Doesn't?', *Centre for Business Strategy Working Paper No. 143* London Business School.

Swann, G.M.P. and Prevezer, M. (1996) 'A Comparison of the Dynamics of Industrial Clustering in Computing and Biotechnology', *Research Policy*, 25: 1139–57.

Swann, G.M.P., Prevezer, M. and Stout, D. (1998) *'The Dynamics of Industrial Clustering. International Comparisons in Computing and Biotechnology'* Oxford: Oxford University Press.

Wasserman, S. and Faust, K. (1994) *'Social Network Analysis: Methods and Applications'*, Cambridge: Cambridge University Press.

Zucker, L., Darby, M. and Brewer, M. (1994) 'Intellectual Capital and the Birth o US Biotechnology Enterprises', *National Bureau of Economic Researc Working Paper 4653*, Cambridge: MA.

4 The competencies of regions

Canada's clusters in biotechnology

Jorge Niosi and Tomas G. Bas

Abstract

Knowledge-intensive industries tend to concentrate geographically, because of the many spillovers that they generate. Thus new biotechnology firms often set up in regions that have innovative firms, government laboratories and universities, which attract them to enter. In this chapter we unveil some of the characteristics of Canadian clusters in biotechnology: the key regions, their relative importance, and the main firms and government laboratories that attract new entrants. Moreover, we develop the concept of regions as nexus of competencies, a notion already put forward for firms, but one that may be relevant to regions within nations and, ultimately, to nations as well. Capabilities of organisations and regions vary, and a thorough study of organisational and regional capabilities should precede the analysis of knowledge spill-overs.

Toronto is the main centre of biotechnology in Canada, followed by Montreal and Vancouver. The total population of the metropolitan area (a proxy for immediate market size and venture capital) explains the size, location and characteristics of most Canadian clusters. University research is also a key factor explaining the size of the biotechnology clusters once population is held constant.

Within nations, scientific and technical competencies vary strongly among regions. Some regions within countries concentrate a disproportionate share of the capabilities of all developed and developing nations. Moreover, regions tend to concentrate competencies on a few domains of expertise. This is what the literature calls 'agglomeration effects': companies active in the same field of technology tend to cluster geographically. They do so in order to share a common labour pool, and to obtain ready access to research institutions such as government laboratories and universities, or to key markets and customers, such as large assemblers or government facilities (Feldman 1999). The specialised literature calls these institutions and key markets/customers 'entry attractors' (Swan *et al.* 1998).

In many types of science-based industries (SBIs), such as biotechnology, information technology and advanced materials, the major attractors are universities and government laboratories. In a few more mature SBIs, including aerospace and aircraft, large assemblers tend to naturally attract smaller producers of parts, components and specialised software.

In this respect Canada is similar to other nations (Niosi 2000). Its competencies cluster around a few large and medium-sized urban agglomerations, such as Toronto, Montreal, Vancouver, Ottawa, Edmonton and Calgary. Specialised clusters have also developed around smaller cities. This study builds a theory of the competencies of regions using biotechnology as a case study. Government laboratories, as well as universities and a few large firms, attract entry. The goal of the chapter is to examine – using quantitative data – the relative competencies of regions in biotechnology, and the role of National Research Council (NRC) laboratories and university research.[1]

Context

Clusters in biotechnology

Comparative analysis suggests that biotechnology tends to cluster regionally (Prevezer 1998, Shohet 1998). In both the United States and the United Kingdom, a few states or metropolitan areas concentrate the majority of firms. Factors leading to this strong clustering include access to university and public sector research, to venture capital and large markets in major cities. American biotechnology clusters developed around the US science base. Strong clusters exist in California (in Los Angeles and San Francisco), Maryland and Washington, DC, Massachusetts (Boston), New Jersey (Princeton), New York City, North Carolina (the Triangle Research Park), Pennsylvania and Texas. These agglomerations undertake almost two-thirds of US biotechnology activity. Conversely, British clusters are closer to industrial agglomerations and concentrations of graduates. Analysts also consider the hypothesis that in Britain, the size of the biotechnology cluster varies with population: the triangle region delimited by London, Oxford and Cambridge has 50 per cent of British dedicated biotechnology firms (DBFs) (Shohet 1998: 218). Greater London has the biggest agglomeration. However, no variable was highly significant in the United Kingdom to explain biotechnology clustering.

Knowledge spill-overs, or externalities, are responsible for the geographical clustering of biotechnology firms. Innovative organisations generate knowledge, some of which 'leaks' towards other organisations. As much of this knowledge is tacit – particularly in new activities such as biotechnology – geographical proximity is the key factor for all organisations absorbing such externalities. However, most of the neoclassical literature in economics assumes that all organisations (firms, government laboratories and universities) are equally innovative (Hodgson 1993). We challenge this assumption and inquire about their different capabilities in this area. We also analyse the relationship between those capabilities and the clustering success of entry attractors. For this purpose, we extend the discussion of competencies from business administration to cluster theory.

A theory of the competencies of regions

The resource-based theory of the firm explains the different performance of firms by their different endowment of factors (Hamel and Prahalad 1994, Foss 1997). Some firms develop internally or secure externally these resources to become more competitive than others in a specific field or industry. Thus some firms get superior rents and maintain these idiosyncratic advantages for some time (Williams 1994). A differential performance may arise both from divergent endowment of resources, and from their novel combination of resources. The competence theory of the firm thus goes one step beyond the resource-based theory, recognising that superior routines and organisation may yield better performance (Foss and Knudsen 1996, Durand 1998). Competitors do not immediately imitate these performances because routines can not be observed easily, and because there is always some level of ambiguity about the causes of this superior attainment.

The competence theory for regions has identical assumptions for firms concerning this point. Like firms, regions may be understood as sets of competencies and resources both tangible (physical infrastructure, corporate physical assets, research and development [R&D] laboratories) and intangible (skills and human capital, routines, institutions). Not only resources are important for regions, but also the capacity to use them to produce superior results. In the evolutionary theory of the firm (Winter 1987, Dosi and Marengo 1995, Foss and Knudsen 1996), as well as in the capabilities and competence approach (Teece *et al.* 1997), 'organisational forms do matter because information flows and behaviours differ according to the particular "institutional architecture" of each system. In particular, if each system's performance rests on specific learning dynamics by individuals or groups (such as firms), the institutional architecture affects the scope in which such learning can occur' (Dosi and Marengo 1995: 158). Universities, of course, enhance regional capabilities by producing knowledge that facilitates wealth creation and the quality of life.

Similarly, regions within nations, like firms within industries, differ persistently in resources, behaviour and performance. Thus their different outcomes and growth rates may be affected by some hidden variable, such as competencies, particularly core competencies. These variations in outcome suggest unequal resource endowments particularly in skills, information and preferences, different attitudes towards risk and contrasting institutions related to technology and innovation (such as government laboratories and universities), learning routines and financial institutions (such as venture capital firms).

Core competencies of regions include those that create economic value for markets outside the region, that are co-specialised, and difficult to imitate (Durand 1998). In traditional industrial districts, as well as in the Perroux poles (Perroux 1982), regional competencies consist of, first and foremost, those of the region's firms, including their capacity to co-operate with each other. Core competencies usually transcend those of firms: in science-based agglomerations and technological districts, where SBIs prosper, they include the propensity and capacity to co-operate with and learn from other institutions in the regional system of innovation (RSI), such as local universities, government laboratories and venture capital firms.

Competencies, like knowledge in general, increase with use and decline if they are not used. Being closely related to and made of knowledge, they increase with practice, usually procuring sustained advantage to regions as well as firms.

Much knowledge is produced in an interactive way (Lundvall 1992). Some authors have suggested that the density of the interactions between economic agents within a region also influences knowledge creation and thus performance (Héraud *et al.* 1997). According to some authors, a region such as Alsace – where there is only little interaction among firms and with local universities and public laboratories, and where most firms are branch plants operating within an international network – does not constitute a regional system of innovation. The question of course remains open how much local co-operation and how many local spill-overs constitute a local or regional system of innovation.

As is the case in business organisations, the results for a region are not always evident. There is much causal ambiguity in the factors and/or their combination, that explain the performances of regions. Thus economic actors as well as governments act under assumptions of bounded rationality. In an opaque, murky environment, they invest and operate without precise knowledge of future results. We see below that some government laboratories and university research efforts generate few economic spill-overs in certain regions.

Finally, competence theory goes beyond institutional analysis. Competencies point to skills, both personal and social or organisational. One may find the same institutions (universities and government laboratories for instance) in developed and developing countries, but endowed with totally different individual and organisational capabilities or competencies. Competence theory thus draws a link between human capital theories and institutional and evolutionary approaches (Montgomery 1995, Foss and Knudsen 1996).

Canadian biotechnology

Canadian biotechnology started some years after the American competitors, but is comparable proportionately to the US field. By 1997, Canada had 282 domestic biotechnology DBFs, and close to 350 in 2000, seventy-one of them public. The total market capitalisation of these seventy-one firms was about C$12.9 billion by the end of May 1999, two-thirds of it in the four largest. Forty-two other firms had a market value under C$50 million each, and ten of these had less than C$10 million. Moreover, the window of opportunity seemed to be closing for biotechnology initial public offerings (IPOs): in the first 6 months of 1999 only one new firm entered the market, with an offer that collected C$22 million. Table 4.1 offers a list of the largest Canadian biotechnology companies by market capitalisation in September 1999. Note that almost all of the largest firms are active in human health products.

Among the 282 DBFs existing in 1997, last year (in 1999), according to official figures, some 129 were active in human health (46 per cent), sixty-two in agricultural biotechnology, thirty-two in environment, twenty in

Table 4.1 Largest Canadian biotechnology firms by market capitalisation (at 4 September 1999, C$ million)

Company	Sector	Metropolitan area	Capital. (C$ million)
Biochem Pharma	Therapeutics	Montreal	3,839
QLT Phototherapeutics	Therapeutics	Vancouver	3,450
Biovail	Therapeutics	Toronto	2,100
Patheon	CRO	Toronto	391
Forbes Meditech	Therapeutics	Vancouver	375
Visible Genetics	Genomics	Toronto	276
Cangene	Therapeutics	Toronto	273
World Heart	Biomedical devices	Ottawa, Ontario	235
Biomira	Therapeutics	Edmonton	204
Dimethaid Research	Therapeutics	Toronto	159
Hemosol	Therapeutics	Toronto	153
Anormed	Therapeutics	Vancouver	140
Angiotech Pharmaceuticals	Therapeutics	Vancouver	133
Aeterna Laboratories	Therapeutics	Quebec, Quebec	133
Technilab	Therapeutics	Montreal	128
Axcan Pharma	Therapeutics	Montreal	126
Bioniche Life Sciences	Therapeutics	London, Ontario	109
Nymox Pharmaceuticals	Diagnostics	Montreal	100
Vasogen	Therapeutics	Toronto	97
Synsorb Biotech	Therapeutics	Calgary	87
Draxis Health	Therapeutics	Toronto	79
Inex Pharmaceuticals	Therapeutics	Vancouver	77

Sources: *Canadian Biotech News*, Vol. 8, No. 36, 11 September 1999: 6.

food products and thirty-nine in all other areas. These 282 firms employed 9,800 people. Human health had over two-thirds of the employees, with an average size of eighty-one per firm, against forty-two in agricultural biotechnology, twenty-two in environment, twenty in food production and forty-three in other areas. DBFs had total annual revenues of C$11.2 billion, including exports amounting to C$4.9 billion.

The Canadian venture capital market has developed very rapidly in the last 10 years. By the end of 1998, the total pool was estimated at C$10 billion, and the same year more than C$1.66 billion was invested in some 1,200 companies, sixty of them active in biotechnology. Seed money was the most frequent type of investment in DBFs, the average investment being around C$1 million. With some 210 firms outside the capital market, it is apparent that many demands for venture capital have not been accepted. In other words, even if the Canadian venture capital market is sizeable, it cannot accommodate all the demands from domestic DBFs.

University research in health sciences concentrates in a few major metropolitan areas, such as Toronto, Montreal and Vancouver. In 1997, according to the latest figures available, metropolitan Toronto hosted 1,149 university professors in health science (at University of Toronto and McMaster University), in comparison to only 780 in Montreal (at McGill University, the University of Montreal and University of Quebec). Vancouver was third with 506 professors, all of them at the University of British Columbia. Calgary followed with 325 (University of Calgary), Edmonton with 305 (University of Alberta) and Quebec City (Laval University) with 249.[2]

The research design

Methodology

We based this chapter on an empirical analysis of technical competencies of DBFs, as indicated on the number of biotechnology patents granted in the United States to Canadian corporations, to Canadian government laboratories and to Canadian universities.[3] Patents are uniquely revealing to study competencies, pointing not simply to resources (such as R&D personnel or laboratories), but to the ability to use resources in order to produce valuable results. Patents are thus the output of those resources, and represent a more useful indicator of competencies than simply R&D inputs. Due to a high propensity to patent in biotechnology, patents represent good indicators of competencies in this particular area.

In order to study technical competencies, we chose the US patent database instead of the Canadian one, for several reasons. First, all major inventions are patented in the United States as most Canadian companies, government laboratories and universities seek to protect intellectual property of their most valuable knowledge assets in the largest, most inventive and most affluent nation in the world. Second, the US patent database, unlike the Canadian one, indicates the geographical location (country, city and state or province) where the invention has been made, thus allowing precise identification of the region and of the competence that has produced the invention. Third, more Canadian firms patent their novelties in the United States than in Canada. For instance, between 1980 and 1999 sixty-two Canadian biotechnology enterprises sought patents in the United States, and only thirty-seven in Canada.

Biotechnology presents a major methodological problem: it has no precise classification code – be it a patent code, an industrial (or SIC) code, or a trade code – because it is a 'genetic technology' used across a variety of industries. Thus we decided to identify DBFs (by means of the 1998 BIOTECanada Biotechnology Directory). We examined the patents of these companies, and ascribed them to biotechnology, unless they were totally unrelated. The presence of a set of keywords in the patents' names and abstracts decided whether the patent was biotechnological or not. These key words included terms such as 'DANN', 'monoclonal antibodies' and 'genetic material'. We decided that DBFs produce biotechnology patents, but we checked for supplementary proof of capabilities in the specific areas by examining patent descriptions.

An additional problem for studies using patents is the propensity to patent products rather than processes (Winter 1989). Thus, we may have missed some process capabilities in biotechnology.

Government laboratories

We examined government laboratories and all Canadian universities regarding their role in attracting or nurturing private firms' competency. We found six public laboratories (five with the National Research Council of Canada (NRC), and one provincial unit) with Canadian patents. A brief description of these laboratories is presented here.

The NRC launched five institutes for biotechnology in Canada after the passing of Canada's biotechnology strategy in 1983. Some of these institutes started from scratch while others benefited from the experience and assets of pre-existing NRC laboratories. These are the Biotechnology Research Institute (BRI), the Institute for Biodiagnostics (IBD), the Institute for Biological Sciences (IBS), the Institute for Marine Biosciences (IMB) and the Plant Biotechnology Institute (PBI).

The Biotechnology Research Institute of Montreal started from scratch in 1987 and now employs almost 200 scientists, plus another 200 guest researchers in pharmaceutical, environmental and bio-processing industries. The recently founded (1992) Institute for Biodiagnostics in Winnipeg is concentrated in developing technologies for disease diagnostic. The Institute for Biological Sciences in Ottawa, one of the oldest of the NRC

(1916) focuses on immunochemistry. The Institute for Marine Biosciences, originally established in 1952, works on marine biotechnology, including plants, shellfish toxins and natural chemistry. In 1948, NRC created an institute for plant biology in Saskatoon, known as the Prairie Region Laboratory; under the new strategy, it was revamped and became the Plant Biotechnology Institute in 1985, hosting some forty-five staff and seventy guest researchers.

Each institute has been an 'entry attractor' for new DBFs in its respective technology and region. As Canada had few DBFs in 1983, the NRC laboratories have antedated the founding of most of them. All these institutes, however, were created on or near university campuses, which already had departments or faculties of medicine, biology and biochemistry.

The Alberta Research Council (ARC) set up laboratories in Edmonton in 1936 and created biotechnology facilities in the late 1970s and the early 1980s. In terms of patents, ARC is the most active public laboratory in Canadian biotechnology.

Universities

Several Canadian universities have produced patents in biotechnology. The metropolitan areas of Montreal, Toronto, Saskatoon and Vancouver are among the most important centres of university research in biotechnology. We examined the competencies of a university via the patents held under its name, whatever the department or faculty having invented the product or process. Canadian universities have requested and obtained biotechnology patents since 1976, but most of them in the 1980s and 1990s. Research universities with a proven track record in medicine, plant and/or human biology include the Universities of British Columbia, Laval, McGill, McMaster, Montreal, Saskatchewan and Toronto.

Patents: the evidence and its significance

We collected patent data, as well as foundation dates, for the largest Canadian census metropolitan areas: Toronto, Montreal, Vancouver, Ottawa, Edmonton, Calgary, Winnipeg, Halifax, Quebec City and Saskatoon. Only a few are hosts to public laboratories, but all have research universities. We present the results in Tables 4.1 to 4.8.

The number of DBFs, of patents and patenting firms indicate that Toronto is the centre of Canada's biotechnology with nearly 50 per cent of the patents that have been granted to Canadian DBFs by the United States Patent Office since 1989. Despite the creation of the BRI, Montreal remains a distant second (Tables 4.1 to 4.3).

The two most inventive DBFs in terms of US patents are Toronto's Connaught and Allelix, followed by BioChem Pharma of Montreal. Two other Toronto firms come fourth and fifth: Visible Genetics and Spectral

Table 4.2 Biotechnology: year of foundation of patenting firms existing in 1998

Year	Toronto	Montreal	Vancouver	Ottawa	Saskatoon	Quebec City	Winnipeg	Edmonton	Calgary	Other	Canada
Before 1980	4	2	0	IBS 3	1	1	1	0	0	IMB	12
1980	1	0	0	0	0	0	0	0	0	0	1
1981	0	0	0	0	0	0	0	0	0	0	0
1982	0	0	0	0	0	0	0	0	0	0	0
1983	0	0	0	0	0	0	0	1	0	0	1
1984	1	1	0	0	0	0	0	0	0	0	2
1985	1	0	0	0	PBI 0	0	0	2	0	0	3
1986	2	1	1	0	0	0	0	0	0	0	4
1987	1	BRI/0	0	0	0	0	0	0	0	0	1
1988	1	1	0	0	0	0	0	0	0	0	2
1989	0	2	1	0	0	0	0	0	0	0	3
1990	0	0	1	0	0	1	0	0	0	0	2
1991	2	0	2	0	0	0	0	0	0	0	4
1992	1	2	1	1	1	1	IBD 0	0	0	0	7
1993	1	2	1	0	1	0	0	0	0	0	5
1994	2	3	1	0	1	1	0	0	2	1	11
1995	0	0	2	0	0	0	0	0	1	0	3
1996	0	0	1	0	0	0	0	0	0	0	1
1997	0	0	0	0	0	0	0	0	0	0	0
1998	0	0	0	0	0	0	0	0	0	0	0
Total	17	14	11	4	4	4	1	3	3	1	62

Sources: Canadian Patent Office: Canadian Patent Database; US Patent Office: US Patent Database, 1999.

Note: Firms with either Canadian or US Patents.

Table 4.3 Biotechnology: year of foundation of firms existing in 1998

Year	Toronto	Montreal	Vancouver	Ottawa	Saskatoon	Quebec City	Winnipeg	Edmonton	Calgary	Halifax	Other	Canada
Before 1980	34	25	8	IBS/4	3	6	2	4	1	IMB/4	10	101
1980	5	1	1	0	1	0	0	0	0	0	2	10
1981	1	0	7	0	0	0	0	0	1	1	0	11
1982	1	1	1	0	0	0	0	0	1	0	0	4
1983	2	1	3	0	1	1	2	1	0	1	1	13
1984	4	3	2	0	0	2	0	4	1	0	1	11
1985	5	4	5	0	PBI 1	1	0	1	1	1	1	16
1986	4	4	3	0	4	2	0	1	1	0	3	23
1987	5	BRI/0	2	1	1	3	0	0	2	1	1	17
1988	3	4	3	1	2	0	0	1	1	0	3	21
1989	6	4	6	0	0	2	0	0	0	1	4	22
1990	6	5	5	0	2	2	0	1	1	2	4	21
1991	5	5	8	0	2	0	IBD 1	0	1	1	0	22
1992	5	6	6	0	2	2	0	1	0	2	2	28
1993	5	3	4	0	1	2	0	0	2	1	2	20
1994	4	1	2	2	2	5	0	2	2	1	5	27
1995	1	5	4	0	0	3	0	4	0	2	1	22
1996	1	1	3	0	0	0	0	0	0	0	2	9
1997	3	4	1	0	0	0	0	0	0	0	0	5
1998	0	3	0	0	0	0	0	0	0	0	0	0
Total	104	75	71	8	21	25	7	19	12	17	38	400

Source: BioteCanada: Canadian Biotechnology Directory 1993, 1995 and 1998.

Diagnostics. Moreover, one major DBF dominates invention capability in Montreal (BioChem Pharma), and one each in Edmonton (Biomira), Vancouver (QLT (Quadra Logic Technologies) Phototherapeutics), and Saskatoon (Biostar). Each firm has between 38 and 75 per cent of the privately held patents in the region. Toronto appears more economically decentralised in terms of technological competencies in biotechnology (Tables 4.4 and 4.5): several firms own a large portfolio of patents.

As for public laboratories, IBS in Ottawa remains the most productive of the NRC's five (in terms of patents), but the Alberta Research Council in Edmonton is the most productive public inventor of biotechnology. Some of the public laboratories are not strong in terms of patented novelty and thus probably have less spillover potential in knowledge.

Concerning firm creation, BRI (Montreal) and PBI (Saskatoon) seem to have been major entry attractors: substantially more companies were created or attracted to the region after their creation. The other large NRC institutes in Ottawa, Halifax or Winnipeg did not have as much impact. Regions with major research universities, such as Toronto, Vancouver and Quebec City (the suburb Ste-Foy) seem to bring in many DBFs even without the help of government units. Research universities seem to be as important magnets as government laboratories, which possess some of the largest concentrations of R&D resources and competencies in the region where they are present.

The largest firms, measured by market capitalisation, are located almost all in Toronto, Montreal and Vancouver, with a few in Ottawa, Edmonton, Quebec City and London, Ontario. The dominance of the three majors in the capital market (Montreal's Biochem, Vancouver's QLT and Toronto's Biovail) is phenomenal. They represent nearly three-quarters of the total capitalisation of Canadian biotechnology (Table 4.1).

University laboratories

With regard to universities, the regions are different in rank (see Tables 4.6 to 4.9). The University of British Columbia in Vancouver has most patents, followed by the University of Calgary, the University of Saskatchewan, McGill University and the University of Montreal (both in Montreal), and the University of Alberta in Edmonton.[4] By urban agglomeration, Montreal and Saskatchewan share the first place in university patents, followed by Vancouver and Toronto (including those of the University of Toronto, with the universities of McMaster and Waterloo).

Some agglomerations with university attractors did not bring in DBFs (i.e. Kingston, Ontario and Sherbrooke, Quebec). Conversely, Canada's largest city, Toronto, has only one attractor (its university), but it is probably the most important centre for biotechnology in the country.

We thus proceeded to measure the precise weight of each factor (Table 4.9). How important are public attractors (public laboratories and univer-

Table 4.4 Biotechnology: US patents of Canadian companies and major government laboratories, granted between 1989 and 1999

Company	Toronto	Montreal	Edmonton	Vancouver	Calgary	Saskatoon	Ottawa	Quebec City	Winnipeg	Other
1	51	28	39*	8	3	9	24**	2	4**	1**
2	50	15**	11	3	2	8**	3	1	3	1
3	23	4		2	2	3	3	1		1
4	13	3		2			2			
5	12	3		2						
6	8	3		1						
7	5	3		1						
8	4	2		1						
9	3	2		1						
10	3	1								
11	3	1								
12	1	1								
13	1									
14	1									
Total	178	66	50	21	7	20	31	4	7	3

Source: US Patent Office: US Patent Database, 1999.

Notes: * Alberta Research Council; ** NRC laboratories.

Table 4.5 Biotechnology: economic concentration ratios of total patents of
Canadian firms (1989–99)

Ratio	Total number of patents	Percent of patents
CR4 (4 firms with most patents)	180	43
CR8 (8 firms with most patents)	238	57
CR12 (12 firms with most patents)	279	67
CR20 (20 firms with most patents)	330	79
Total	418	100

Source: US Patent Office: US Patent Database, 1999.

Note: Only private firms.

Table 4.6 Biotechnology: regional concentration of US patents of Canadian firms
(1989–99)

Region	Number of patents	Percentage
Toronto	178	61
Montreal	51	17
Vancouver	21	7
Saskatoon	12	4
Edmonton	11	4
Calgary	7	2
Ottawa	7	2
Quebec City	4	1
Winnipeg	3	1
Other	2	1
Total	292	100

Source: US Patent Office: US Patent Database, 1999.

Note: Only private firms.

sities) to biotechnology clusters? Correlation analysis suggests that some
of the government laboratories are of little importance. In fact, government laboratory capabilities measured by patents are negatively correlated
with the three dependent variables: number of patents held by DBFs,
number of DBFs and the number of patenting DBFs.

Conversely, university research strongly correlates with two of the three
dependent variables: number of DBFs and number of patenting DBFs.
University research thus seems to attract DBFs and to contribute to
enhance their competencies. However, a university is not enough to
entirely explain the location of firms.

Table 4.7 Biotechnology: regional concentration of patents of Canadian firms, universities and main government laboratories (1989–99)

Region	Number of patents	Percentage
Toronto	191	37
Montreal	96	18
Edmonton	59	11
Saskatoon	50	10
Vancouver	44	8
Ottawa	37	7
Winnipeg	9	2
Calgary	8	2
Quebec City	7	1
Other	19	4
Total	519	100

Source: US Patent Office: US Patent Database, 1999.

Table 4.8 NRC patents by institute (1989–99)*

Year	IBS (Ottawa)	BRI (Montreal)	PBI (Saskatoon)	IBD (Winnipeg)	IMB (Halifax)
1989	0	0	0	NA	0
1990	1	0	0	NA	0
1991	$3\frac{1}{2}$	3	0	NA	0
1992	$\frac{1}{2}$	0	0	0	0
1993	0	0	1	0	1
1994	2	2	0	0	0
1995	3	2	0	1	0
1996	4	2	2	0	0
1997	2	2	$1\frac{1}{2}$	1	0
1998	5	1	1	1	0
1999	3	3	$2\frac{1}{2}$	1	0
Total	24	15	8	4	1

Source: US Patent Office: US Patent Database, NRC Web site; personal communication with the Institutes, 1999.

Note: The IBD was founded in 1992.
*Half patents are design patents where NRC is one of two co-assignees.

The major overall attractor, however, is population. When we bring in the data from the 1996 Census Metropolitan Areas (CMAs), the three dependent variables strongly correlate with their total population. In other words, activity in biotechnology clusters where most people live, and secondarily, where Canadian universities do research. Population is at first sight a proxy for the size of the immediate market. Total population may

Table 4.9 Correlation

	Privpat	Privcos	Patgcos	Univpat	Govpats	Attrapat	Popul96
Privpat	1.000						
Privcos	0.8359**	1.000					
Patgcos	0.8821**	0.9707**	1.000				
Univpat	0.2513	0.5454	0.5924	1.000			
Govpat	−0.1459	−0.1588	−0.0614	0.1055	1.000		
Attrapat	0.0522	0.2268	0.3260	0.7005	0.7836	1.000	
Popul96	0.8875**	0.9297**	0.9542**	0.4005	−0.0193	0.2364	1.000
Ungrad96	0.1908	0.0985	0.1718	−0.1564	−0.0948	−0.1658	0.1644

Source: Jorge Niosi, based on BIOTECanada Directory, 1998.

Notes: Pearson coefficients; *significant at 0.05 level (2-tailed); **significant at 0.01 level (2-tailed).

Privpat = the number of patents granted to private companies
Privcos = the number of private firms
Govpats = the number of patents held by government laboratories
Univpat = the number of patents held by universities
Patgcos = the number of patents held by private firms and government laboratories
Attrapat = the number of patents held by attractors (i.e. university and government laboratories)
Popul96 = the population in 1996
Ungrad96 = the number of undergraduates produced in the regions in 1996

also cover variables such as the size of the local pool of venture capital. (Unfortunately, we do not have figures in Canada showing the distribution of venture capital by cities.) The proportion of a CMA's population with university degrees is barely relevant. Only the size of the CMA and the scale of its university research matters.

Normalised correlation, holding population constant, confirms the significance of university research, at least for both total patents by DBFs and number of patenting DBFs (Table 4.10). We calculated three ratios, dividing the three values of the dependent variables by the population for each CMA. Government patenting still has little impact – or even a negative one – on the dependent variables.

Finally, we conducted cluster analyses combining the patent productivity of DBFs, and of universities and government laboratories. The analysis uncovered three types of regions (Table 4.11). The first type, consisting of Toronto, Montreal, Vancouver and Saskatoon, strong DBF and university patenting, combined with moderate government patenting. The second type, formed by Edmonton and Ottawa, has strong government patenting associated with weak DBF and academic patenting. The third group has weak DBF and public patenting, innovative dynamism is low. This group includes Calgary, Halifax, Kingston, Quebec City and Winnipeg.

It is to be noted that the regional pool of venture capital corroborates the previous ranking. Toronto, Montreal and Vancouver, in this order, are the centres of Canadian venture capital specialised in biotechnology (Table 4.12). All the other regional agglomerations are far behind concerning the availability of venture capital funds for biotechnology. The university base, and the venture capital pool both reinforce the sheer effect of market size in the pecking order of Canada's clusters in biotechnology.

Conclusions and policy implications

In biotechnology, economic concentration of competencies goes hand in hand with regional concentration: only twelve firms hold over two-thirds of the patents. Six of them are in Toronto, two in Montreal, and one each in Edmonton, Ottawa, Saskatoon and Vancouver.

Toronto enjoys indisputable leadership as Canada's top biotechnology cluster, measured by the number of DBFs, the number of patenting DBFs and the patents. Montreal follows, Vancouver appears in the third rank. In other words, the three main Canadian biotechnology clusters are located in the three largest cities; all of them have at least one major research university and the largest venture capital pools.

With regard to theory, this analysis brings credibility to the competency theory of the region. Knowledge spillovers do not only depend on the (variable) amount of industrially useful knowledge produced by firms, universities and government laboratories, but also on the size of the immediate

Table 4.10 Normalised correlation

	Patgcos	Univpat	Govpat	Attract	Ratio1	Ratio2	Ratio3
Patgcos	1.000						
Univpat	0.592	1.000					
Govpat	−0.061	0.106	1.000				
Attract	0.326	0.701*	0.784*	1.000			
Ratio1	0.422	0.627*	−0.220	0.255	1.000		
Ratio2	0.002	0.493	0.133	0.213	0.721*	1.000	
Ratio3	0.008	0.650*	0.030	0.427	0.822**	0.898**	1.000

Source: Jorge Niosi, based on BIOTECanada Directory, 1998.

Note: Pearson coefficients; *significant at 0.05 level (2-tailed); **significant at 0.01 level (2-tailed).

Table 4.11 Cluster analysis

	Clusters		
Variable	1	2	3
Patcos2	18.85	5.74	2.62
Unipat2	19.05	5.95	2.38
Govpat2	6.32	34.62	1.1
No. of clusters	4	2	5

Source: Jorge Niosi, based on BIOTECanada Directory, 1998.

Table 4.12 The venture capital pool in biotechnology in 1999

Metropolitan area	Venture capital pool (C$ million)	Number of DBFs financed	Average size of financing (C$ million)	Median size of financing (C$ million)
Toronto	110	11	7.9	1.3
Montreal	76	23	2.6	1.7
Vancouver	68	11	4.9	3.0
Edmonton	15	2	7	7
Saskatoon, Sk.	14	3	2.8	0.7
Quebec City	11	8	1.2	0.7
London, Ont.	7	1	7	7
Kingston, Ont.	2	1	2	2
Calgary, Alta	2	1	2	2
Sherbrooke, P.Q.	0.6	1	0.6	0.6
Halifax, N.S.	0.45	1	0.45	0.45
Ottawa, Ont.	0.25	1	0.25	0.25
Unknown location of firm	7.22	14	0.5	0.6

Source: Jorge Niosi, based on BIOTECanada Directory, 1998.

Note:
Several DBFs have been financed several times in 1999 (Macdonaiu and Associates 2000).

market and other related characteristics of the urban agglomeration. Relevant characteristics may include availability of venture capital (certainly much more readily obtainable in larger cities such as Montreal, Toronto and Vancouver than in smaller ones such as Edmonton or Saskatoon, whatever the quality of their university research and government facilities). 'Star scientists', as most researchers and university graduates in the health sciences, may also prefer larger cities.

Because of causal ambiguity, government laboratories have only marginally countered the market forces that tend to concentrate biotechnology activities in a few large cities with strong university and venture capital environments. If university creation represents a 'bottom-up' strategy and government laboratories a 'top-down' one, then the bottom-up approach to biotechnology seems adequate: universities are at the basis of most new firms and industrial dynamics. This analysis suggests that governments might reinforce Canadian biotechnology clusters if they relocated their laboratories and research universities in the largest metropolitan areas, enjoying the strongest venture capital pools. Canada's citizenry and cities may not be large enough to bear the dispersion of efforts in ten or more urban metropolitan areas. In other words, government effort must concentrate where the potential for clustering is, thus in larger cities.

The size of the metropolitan area, the other major variable related to industrial clustering, may be a surrogate for other underlying variables, the existence of large hospitals (where clinical essays can be conducted) and a wider pool of human capital.

Notes

1 The NRC laboratories are the five biotechnology units in Halifax, Montreal, Ottawa, Saskatoon and Winnipeg.
2 Association of Universities and Colleges of Canada (AUCC), special compilation.
3 We based this work on the study by Antonelli (1986) on Italian industrial districts, though Antonelli used the Italian patent database, and had other research goals.
4 One has to bear in mind the different intellectual property regimes of Canadian universities. UBC requires all professors and researchers on the campus to grant ownership of inventions to the University, while Toronto does not. Existing figures probably underestimate the importance of such universities as Toronto and Calgary where the owners of the patents may or may not be the University.

References

Antonelli, C. (1986) *L'attività innovativa in un distretto tecnologico*, Turin: Fondazione Giovanni Agnelli.
BIOTECanada Biotechnology Directory, 1998, Contact Canada.
Dosi, G. and Marengo, L. (1995) 'Some Elements of an Evolutionary Theory of Organizational Competencies', in W. England (ed.) *Evolutionary Concepts in Contemporary Economics*, Ann Arbor: University of Michigan Press: 157–78.
Durand, T. (1998) 'The Alchemy of Competence', in G. Hamel *et al.* (eds) *Strategic Flexibility*, New York: Wiley: 303–30.
Feldman, M. (1999) 'The New Economics of Innovation, Spillover and Agglomeration: Review of Empirical Studies', in *Economics of Innovation and New Technology*, 8(1–2): 5–25.
Foss, N. (1997) *Resources, Firms and Strategies*, New York: Oxford University Press.
Foss, N. and Knudsen, C. (1996) *Towards a Competence Theory of the Firm*, London: Routledge.
Hamel, G. and Prahalad, C.K. (1994) *Competing for the Future*, Boston: Harvard Business School Press.

Héraud, J.-A. *et al.* (1997) 'Réseaux d'innovation et tissu industriel régional', in B. Hauteville, J.A. Héraud and M. Humbert (1997) *Technologie et performances économiques*, Paris: Economica: 97–122.

Hodgson, G. (1993) *Economics and Evolution*, Ann Arbor, University of Michigan Press.

Lundvall, B.-A. (1992) *National Systems of Innovation*, London: Pinter.

Macdonald, M. and Associates (2000) *Venture Capital Deals Done and Disclosed 1999*, Ottawa.

Montgomery, C. (1995) *Resource-Based and Evolutionary Theories of the Firm. Towards a Synthesis*, Boston: Kluwer.

Niosi, J. (1995) *Flexible Innovation*, Montreal: McGill-Queen's University Press.

—— (2000) *Canada's National System of Innovation*, Montreal: McGill-Queen's University Press.

Perroux, F. (1982) *Dialogue des monopoles et des nations*, Grenoble: Presses de l'Université de Grenoble.

Prevezer, M. (1998) 'Clustering in Biotechnology in the USA', in P. Swan, M. Prevezer and D. Stout (eds) *The Dynamics of Industrial Clustering*, New York and Oxford: Oxford University Press: 124–93.

Shohet, S. (1998) 'Clustering and UK Biotechnology', in P. Swan, M. Prevezer and D. Stout (eds) *The Dynamics of Industrial Clustering*, New York and Oxford: Oxford University Press: 194–224.

Swan, P., Prevezer, M. and Stout, D. (1998) *The Dynamics of Industrial Clustering*, New York and Oxford: Oxford University Press.

Teece, D.J., Pisano, G. and Shuen, A. (1997) 'Dynamic Capabilities and Strategic Management', *Strategic Management Journal*, 18(7): 509–33.

Williams, J. (1994) 'Strategy and the Search for Rents: The Evolution of Diversity Among Firms', in R.P. Rumelt *et al.* (eds) *Fundamental Issues in Strategy*, Boston: Harvard Business School Press: 228–46.

Winter, S. (1987) 'Knowledge and Competence as Strategic Assets', in D.J. Teece (ed.) *The Competitive Challenge*, New York: Harper and Row: 159–84.

—— (1989) 'Patents in Complex Contexts: Incentives and Effectiveness', in V. Weil and J.W. Snapper (eds) *Owning Scientific and Technical Information*, New Brunswick, NJ: Rutgers University Press: 41–60.

5   Geographic clustering in the UK biotechnology sector

Philip Cooke

Introduction

It is widely thought that the UK is Europe's leading biotechnology economy despite lagging behind the position of the US very markedly. This tends to be argued in terms of UK ownership of large pharmaceutical companies, the strength of the science base and the possession of some 270 specialist biotechnology firms, compared to, say, Germany's 220 and France's 140 (Ernst and Young 1999). However, if we look at the position in terms of market penetration of UK-originated therapeutic products derived from biotechnology, the position is little better, and may indeed be worse than that of Germany, which in 1998 had only Boehringer Mannheim's (now Roche) Reteplase cardiac drug on the market. This is because it is hard to find a single UK-originated product derived from recombinant or genetically modified organisms or cells, despite the presence of fifty-three distinct products on the UK market. The data on which the following text is based are provided through the UK BioIndustry Association by the UK Department of Health Medicines Control Agency (MCA). A great deal of sleuthing has to be performed with the MCA data since they depend on the data of the European Agency for the Evaluation of Medical Products who, in granting market authorisations, do not always provide full details of the manufacturer of the active substance. Further, they note that details of the manufacturer of the active substance is also confidential. What is not confidential is the licence holder details, but that information is very misleading when seeking the product originator. So, an attempt has been made to penetrate the veil of confidentiality by reference to consultancy reports and databases which do note some product originators (e.g. Schitag, Ernst and Young 1998, Ernst and Young 1999, BioCentury 1999) and biosciences directories which, in giving local firm profiles, sometimes list also the drugs they have originated, described by brand-name. Of the fifty-three approved drugs, forty-eight have been traced. Further research is then presented on the likely growth in the capability of UK biotechnology firms to compete with the USA as they develop therapeutic and other products. Many of these are already in the pipeline. The development of biotechnology clusters in the UK is central to the strong future prospects for the biotechnology sector to lessen the product gap with the USA.

Market penetration in the UK

In Table 5.1, twenty-five of the twenty-eight UK-licensed biopharmaceutical products have been traced to the product originator. Of the remaining three, none are marketed by UK-owned licence holders; Roche Products, Schering-Plough and Unigene being the marketers in question. We see that market penetration by non-UK products is overwhelming and that UK giants like Glaxo, SmithKline Beecham and Zeneca are not marketing them. The industry is, therefore, highly globalised. Moving on to the twenty-five therapeutic products derived from biotechnology that are sold on the UK market by foreign or UK firms based in a licence holder country outside the UK (e.g. France, Netherlands, Belgium) we find that origination data can thus far be tracked down for twenty-three drugs.

These are presented in Table 5.2. Here, SmithKline Beecham (now Glaxo) is active as a marketer, but from its Belgium base. From the analysis the conclusion that no UK-originated, biotechnology-derived therapeutic product is currently on sale in the UK market is difficult to avoid.

The future

If the present reveals the UK market for biotechnology-derived drugs to be dominated at the end of the twentieth century by products largely originating in US entrepreneurial biotechnology firms, where does the challenge for the next century lie? If it is to come from Europe, it seems likely that the fledgling UK therapeutic products industry will have a greater impact in the next few years. Let us look, first, at some of the key milestones in the development of biotechnology, since these give a hint of the evolving basic science which is the resource for future commercialisation if exploitation opportunities can be taken.

It is clear from Table 5.3 that the UK has been a leading location for many of the main research breakthroughs in biotechnology in the second half of the twentieth century. This began with the pioneering work of the UK/US team of Watson and Crick working at Cambridge's Cavendish Laboratory, supported crucially by Rosalind Franklin's X-ray diffraction results at Wilkin's laboratory in Kings College, London. However, if we look at milestones in commercialisation of biotechnological knowledge, it is the USA that takes the early lead. Thus Genentech was set up by recombinant DNA technologist Boyer and venture capitalist Swanson in 1976. Amgen followed in 1980 and in 1982 Humulin, the first genetically produced human insulin, developed by Genentech with Eli Lilly, was given US Food and Drug Administration approval. The Massachusetts

Table 5.1 Approved biotechnology drugs in the UK (UK-licensed)

Product	Developer	Marketer	Active substance	Marketer home base
Zenapax	Protein Design Laboratories Inc. (CA)	Roche Registration Ltd (UK)	Daclizumab	Switzerland
Recormon	Genetics Inst. (MA)	Boehringer M. (UK)	Epoetin beta	Germany
Recombinate	Genetics Inst. (MA)	Baxter Healthcare Ltd (UK)	Factor VIII	USA
Neupogen	Amgen (CA)	Roche Products Ltd (UK)	Filgrastim	Switzerland
Gonal F	Ares-Serono (Italy/Switzerland)	Ares-Serono (Europe) Ltd (UK)	Hormone alpha	Switzerland*
Vaqta	Merck (US)	Pasteur-Merieux MSD Ltd (UK)	Hepatitis A	France
HIB-Vax	Connaught Laboratories (Canada)	Pasteur-Merieux MSD Ltd (UK)	Hepatitis B	France
Humulin	Genentech (CA)	Lilly Industries Ltd (UK)	Human Insulin	USA
Humaject	Genentech (CA)	Lilly Industries Ltd (UK)	Human Insulin	USA
Liprolog	Eli Lilly (US)	Lilly Industries Ltd (UK)	Insulin Lispro	USA
Insulatard	Novo Nordisk (DK)	Novo Nordisk Pharma Ltd (UK)	Human Insulin	Denmark
Penmix	Biogen (MA)	Novo Nordisk Pharma Ltd (UK)	Human Insulin	Denmark
Mixtard	Biogen (MA)	Novo Nordisk Pharma Ltd (UK)	Human Insulin	Denmark
Actrapid	Biogen (MA)	Novo Nordisk Pharma Ltd (UK)	Human Insulin	Denmark
Roferon	Genentech (CA)	Roche Products Ltd (UK)	Interferon alpha 2a	Switzerland
Intron-A	Biogen (MA)	Schering-Plough Ltd (UK)	Interferon alpha 2b	USA
Rebif	Ares-Serono (Italy/Switzerland)	Ares-Serono (Europe) Ltd (UK)	Inteferon beta 1a	Switzerland
Immukin	Genentech (CA)	Boehringer Ingelheim Ltd (UK)	Interferon gamma 1b	Germany
Granocyte	Merrell Dow/Immunex (US)	Chugai Pharma (UK) Ltd	Lenograstim	Japan
Leucomax	Genetics Institute (MA)	Schering-Plough Ltd (UK)	Molgramostin	USA
Kogenate	Miles Laboratories/Genentech(CA)	Bayer plc (UK)	Factor VIII	Germany
Genotropin	Genentech (US)	Pharmacia Laboratories Ltd (UK)	Growth Hormone	Sweden/USA
Humatrope	Genentech (CA)	Lilly Industries Ltd (UK)	Growth Hormone	USA
Norditropin	Genentech (CA)	Novo Nordisk Pharma Ltd (UK)	Growth Hormone	Denmark
Saizen	Serono (Italy/Switzerland)	Serono Laboratories (UK) Ltd	Growth Hormone	Switzerland

Source: UK Medicines Control Agency (1999).

Note: *Serono, Cambridge, MA is noted as the originator of this product in Massachusetts Biotechnology Council (1998).

Table 5.2 Approved biotechnology drugs in the UK (EU country-licensed)

Product	Developer	Marketer	Active substance	Licence holder country
Proleukin	Chiron (CA)	Chiron BV	Aldesleukin	Netherlands
Bioclate	Armour Pharma (USA)	Centeon Pharma GmbH	Antihaemophilia	Germany
Revasc	Ciba (Switzerland)	Rhône-Poulenc-Rorer SA	Desirudin	France
Neorecormon	Genetics Inst. (MA)	Boehringer Mannheim GmbH	Epoetin beta	Germany
Recormon	Genetics Inst. (MA)	Boehringer Mannheim GmbH	Epoetin beta	Germany
Puregon	N.V. Organon (NL)	N.V. Organon	Follitropin beta	Netherlands
Twinrix	Chiron (CA)	SK Beecham SA	Hepatitis B	Belgium
Infanrix	Chiron (CA)	SK Beecham SA	Hepatitis B	Belgium
Tritanrix	Chiron (CA)	SK Beecham SA	Hepatitis B	Belgium
Primavax	Pasteur Merieux (F)	Pasteur Merieux MSD	Hepatitis B	France
Benefix	Genetics Inst. (MA)	Genetics Inst. of Europe BV	Factor VIII	Germany
Cerezyme	Genzyme (MA)	Genzyme BV	Imiglucerase	Netherlands
Protophane	Novo Nordisk (DK)	Novo Nordisk A/S	Human Insulin	Denmark
Remicade	Centocor Inc (CA)	Centocor Europe BV	Infliximab	Netherlands
Humalog	Genentech (USA)	Eli Lilly Nederland BV	Insulin lispro	Netherlands
Procomvax	Pasteur Merieux (F)	Pasteur Merieux MSD	Hepatitis B	France
Avonex	Biogen (MA)	Biogen SA	Interferon beta 1a	France
Betaferon	Chiron (CA)	Schering AG	Interferon beta 1b	Germany
Refludan	Merrell Dow (USA)	Hoechst Marion Roussel	Lepirudin	Germany
Rofacto	Genetics Inst. (MA)	Genetics Inst. Of Europe BV	Factor VIII	Germany
Helixate	Miles Laboratories/Genentech (CA)	Bayer AG	Factor VIII	Germany
Triacelluvax	Chiron (CA)	Chiron s.p.a.	Pertussis toxin	Italy
Novoseven	Biogen (MA)	Novo Nordisk A/S	Factor VIIA	Denmark

Source: UK Medicines Control Agency (1999).

biotechnology lead-firms were founded as follows: Biogen (1978), Genetics Institute (1980) and Genzyme (1981). Qiagen Germany's entrepreneurial biotechnology firm was established in 1984, and the UK's first firm, Celltech, was founded with Labour government funding in 1979. Celltech recently merged with Chiroscience, one of the UK's leading biotechnology firms.

During the 1990s the commercialisation climate changed in the UK and Germany and there has been an increase in the number of biotechnology firms, especially in the health care and biopharmaceuticals sectors, with a slower rate of growth in agro-food biotechnology and bio-environmental technology businesses. Growth in the number and scale of UK biotechnology firms occurred earlier than in Germany, for example. In the latter case, a serious push to break the commercialisation logjam occurred in the late 1990s in the wake of the federal Ministry of Science, Education, Research and Technology's (BMBF) BioRegio competition. Prospects for the emergence of independent biotechnology firms are explored below, but for the moment, given the future perspective in this section, the focus is on developments in the pipeline regarding firms and therapeutic products in Europe as a whole. This inevitably draws particular attention to the UK, as Europe's leading biotechnology product development economy. There are a number of ways of engaging in such a prospective look at the sector. We can look first at firm-specific information in terms of market capitalisation, turnover, profit and loss, R&D expenditure and employees. We can then look at therapeutic products by stage in the pipeline regarding clinical trials and, as appropriate, cross-reference the two sets of indicators.

In Table 5.4 statistics are provided on Europe's top ten performing 'entrepreneurial' biotechnology (pharmaceutical) firms. Three things are

Table 5.3 Selected key biotechnology innovations

Date	Innovation	Scientists	Country
1953	DNA Structure	Watson/Crick	UK
1974	*In vitro* recombinant DNA	Cohen/Boyer	USA
1975	Monoclonal Antibodies	Milstein/Kohler	UK
1977	DNA Sequencing	Sanger *et al.*	UK
1978	Polymerase chain reaction	Mullis	USA
1979	p53 Cancer gene	Lane	UK
1982	Cascade superfusion bioassay	Vane	UK
1985	DNA Profiling	Jeffreys	UK
1988	H2 – receptor antagonist	Black	UK
1996	Transgenic sheep	Wilmut	UK
1998	Antibody protein engineering	Winter	UK
1998	Nematode worm sequence	Sulston	UK

Source: Schitag *et al.* (1998); BioIndustry Association (1999).

Table 5.4 Top ten European biotechnology pharmaceutical firms, 1998 ($ million)

Company	Market capitalisation ($m)	Turnover	Profit/ loss	R&D costs	Employees
Qiagen (G)	959	103	12	12	785
Shire Pharma (UK)	844	75	6	9	426
Innogenetics (NL)	737	46	−14	20	630
Powderject (UK)	540	48	−7	11	87
Genset (F)	522	29	−16	37	479
Celltech (UK)	480	18	−17	33	218
Chiroscience (UK)	437	40	−36	56	302
Neurosearch (DK)	387	8	−6	16	113
Oxford Asymmetry (UK)	338	23	4	2	219
British Biotech (UK)	334	1	−70	66	445

Sources: BioCentury (1999); Ernst and Young (1999).

of immediate interest. First is the predominance of UK firms (60 per cent) in the listing, with only one from each of four other European countries entering the rankings. Second, for all of them, the striking difference between their valuation, in terms of market capitalisation, and their much lower turnover is testimony to the speculative confidence of stock market investors in the industry. Third, biotechnology has high-value lead firms, the overwhelming majority of whom are making losses not profits. A further feature probably worth noting about these knowledge-intensive businesses is the often high R&D costs per employee ratio most display. Hence, what are such investor expectations based upon? Table 5.5 lists the new products in the pipeline and, while some of the firms featuring in Table 5.4 are the origin of these products-in-trial, other, smaller firms also enter the scene.

Once again, and bearing in mind these are selected therapeutic products in trial, the dominance of UK companies at the various trial stages from preclinical to phase 3, which is close to market, is most striking. Eleven of the sixteen firms and nineteen of the thirty products are UK-originated in Ernst and Young's latest list of innovative products expected from European biotechnology specialist firms. These therapeutic products are subject to exacting preclinical and clinical trials (phases 1, 2 etc.) and it is this testing process which explains the high level of R&D investment noted in Table 5.4; since this is the stage at which the cash 'burn rate' is high, venture capital has accordingly had to be accessed and firms are seeking to enter public markets to recoup the finance invested. Moreover, many such firms have already entered partnership agreements with big pharma companies for licensing of technologies which, when granted approval, are marketed and distributed by the multinationals, as we have seen. For example, Cantab Pharmaceutical's two therapeutic vaccines

Table 5.5 Pipeline products from European biotechnology companies, 1998

Company	Product	Indication	Trials status
British Biotech (UK)	BB-10153	Cardiovascular	Phase 1
	BB-3644	Cancer treatment	Preclinical
Cantab Pharma (UK)	TAGW	Genital warts	Phase 2
	DISC HSV	Genital herpes	Phase 1
Celltech (UK)	CDP 571	Crohn's disease	Phase 2b
	CDP 870	Rheumatoid arthritis	Phase 2
Chiroscience (UK)	D2163	Cancer inhibitor	Phase 1/2
	Dermal Powderject	Anaesthetic	Phase 2
Cortecs (UK)	Ulsastat	Ulcer immunity stimulator	Preclinical
	Cellcom	Cancer treatment	Preclinical
Flamel (France)	Asacard	Cardiovascular	Phase 2
	Basulin	Diabetes	Preclinical
IDM (France)	MAK	Ovarian bladder cancer	Phase 2
	MSC-DC	Cancer vaccine	Preclinical
Innogenetics (NL)	Toleri Mab	Prevent organ rejection	Preclinical
Peptide Therapeutics (UK)	Tolerizing peptide	Hay fever	Phase 2
	HSP immunotherapeutic	Rheumatoid arthritis	Preclinical
Phytopharm (UK)	P54	Colonic cancer treatment	Phase 2a
Powderject (UK)	Alprodastil	Erectile dysfunction	Phase 1
	PJ2204	Acute migraine	Preclinical
Neurosearch (NL)	NS 2710	Anxiety disorders	Phase 2
	NS 2330	Dementia	Phase 2
Scotia Holdings (UK)	Epakex	Cancer treatment	Phase 2
	Meglumine-GLA	Bladder cancer	Phase 1
Shire Pharma (UK)	TriClimactol	Hormone replacement therapy	Phase 3
	Galantamine	Chronic fatigue syndrome	Phase 2
Transgène (France)	Adenovirus-CFTR	Cystic fibrosis	Phase 1
	Adenovirus-IFN	Immune enhancement	Preclinical
Vanguard Medica (UK)	VML 530	Asthma	Phase 1
	VML 600	Hepatitis C	Preclinical

Sources: BioCentury (1999); Ernst and Young (1999).

noted in Table 5.5 have been licensed to Glaxo Wellcome and SmithKline Beecham (now merged to form Glaxo), while Transgène licensed its two gene delivery systems to Schering-Plough. Companies such as Cantab Pharmaceuticals, Transgène and the German firm MediGene are thought to be capable of head-to-head competition with US firms in the field of therapeutic vaccines because there is no dominant company globally in this field which seeks to stimulate immune responses to genetic diseases. MediGene has a development partnership with Germany's leading big pharma firm Hoechst Marion Roussel (now Aventis), to advance its tumour vaccination technologies.

If therapeutic vaccines are a relative European strength, the other future growth sector of biochips is primarily led by US diagnostics firms. Biochips aim to miniaturise biological assay processes so that the whole genetic make-up of a particular human being can be analysed simultaneously by the family doctor. Firms such as Affymetrix and Hyseq lead the field, although Amersham (UK) acquired Molecular Dynamics of the USA giving them a globally competitive market position. Biochips link to *functional genomics*, a growth field dealing with the relationships between gene functions and the diagnosis and eventual treatment of human diseases. In 1998 Affymetrix entered partnerships with twelve firms, including bioMérieux (France), Gemini Research (UK), Glaxo (UK) and Roche (Switzerland) to develop biochips. Gemini is the UK's first clinical genomics firm. Amersham's purchase of Molecular Dynamics also means that it has access to the Genetic Analysis Technology Consortium involving leading biochip firm Affymetrix. Hence, the technological lead of the USA in biochips is likely to narrow with European firms more actively involved. From the point of view of these two leading technology areas of the future, it seems likely that Europe, and most particularly the UK, shows signs of levelling-up compared to the position in the 1980s when US firms dominated biotechnology applications and products.

This is underlined by the emergence of many new spin-out firms from leading UK research centres. In Cambridge, Pharmagene and Hexagen are both involved in functional genomics, seeking therapeutic treatments from genomics information. Brax, Gemini and Chiroscience (now Celltech) are also operating in fields using genomics data, the last-named having acquired Darwin Molecular of Seattle to boost its genomics capabilities. Hexagen was also acquired in 1998 by US genomics specialist Incyte Pharmaceuticals, joining Incyte's new pharmacogenetics division Incyte Genetics. As well as these Cambridge-focused firms, there are important growth firms evolving from genomics research in Oxford, such as Oxagen, Oxford Glycosciences, Oxford Molecular and Oxford Asymmetry. Firms such as Oxford Asymmetry and Oxford Glycosciences possess bioinformatics libraries that are of major value to large pharmaceutical firms. Thus Bayer and Dow AgroSciences both signed deals with Oxford Asymmetry to access drug discovery information from its libraries, while

Oxford Glycosciences contracted similarly for access to its proteomics library.

The existence of such firms, formed to take commercial advantage of the major public and charitable investments that have been placed in genomics research both at Oxford and, especially, Cambridge, remind us of the highly localised but also simultaneously globalised relationships among firms that characterise the cutting edge of biotechnology research and commercialisation. According to Mihell *et al.* (1997) Cambridge has some seventy-six biotechnology firms and research organisations while Oxford has forty companies directly involved in biotechnology. Another agglomeration, of thirty-seven firms, is centred upon Surrey, to the south of London, with yet another concentration of over fifty in Scotland. However, research conducted by the UK Department of Trade and Industry (DTI 1999) differentiated Surrey from Cambridge and Oxford. The last two displayed the characteristics of clusters, whereas Surrey and Scotland did not and Scotland was seen as a latent cluster. The main rationale for this judgement about Surrey (but not Scotland) was the relative absence of local linkage to the science base and systematic start-up and spin-out activity centred on established, university-based technology licensing, transfer and enterprise support within science park and incubator settings. Both Cambridge and Oxford display these specialist characteristics in close proximity to the science base, something Prevezer (1995) highlights as the key characteristic also defining successful US biotechnology clusters.

Globalisation and clustering: the new balance of power

We have seen how smaller new firms from the USA, expert in applications of basic science findings often discovered elsewhere, notably the UK, became dominant sources of commercialisation of biotechnology. They remain dependent upon big pharma companies for the finance to produce, market and distribute the drug treatments eventually emanating from the lengthy gestation process typical of many biotechnology products. The 'absorptive capacity' of big pharma regarding this new industry was insufficient to enable it to displace the Genentechs and Amgens from their position of primary innovator, though many have retained sufficient of this capability to understand the meaning of cutting-edge research if not to replicate it (Cohen and Levinthal 1990). The reason for this is that the production of core knowledge was and has remained in university and other public research laboratories more than in the R&D laboratories of big pharma itself. Such was the relative strength of public laboratories over private in this respect that the initial strategies of firms such as those noted as early-movers in California and Massachusetts were to become fully integrated pharmaceutical companies (FIPCOs) and thus to challenge the predominant pharmaceutical firms, as has occurred in the IT industry with

Intel and Microsoft in relation to IBM and others. However, today this is not the case for a number of reasons. First, firms attempting the FIPCO strategy failed to achieve it because barriers to entry were relatively low for competitors focusing more on a stage or stages in the development of a particular drug. Second, the cost of drug development in biotechnology is extremely high. Third, the time taken through research and trialling until final approval stages of a new drug is enormously long. Fourth, the risk that a trialled drug will not in fact prove itself workable or effective is very high, perhaps only one in ten proving successful. Finally, the industry is turbulent, with many emerging technologies and a reasonably supportive environment for new, niche strategies by emergent small firms.

Thus, current and past industry dynamics point strongly to a continuation of the importance of a cluster model of business co-ordination. Opportunities associated with commercialisation of genomics information have strengthened rather than weakened the salience of this model by adding new phases to the drug discovery process, into which specific niche-oriented firms can fit. Hence, firms focus on developing 'platform technologies', which accelerate the prospects of drug discovery. In biopharmaceuticals, these link core genomics technologies such as genome analysis, bioinformatics, protein analysis and functional genomics to diagnostics and therapeutic products via such technologies as biosensors, DNA arrays, biochips, monoclonal antibodies and polymerase chain reaction, amongst others. The largest of these companies are of US origin, such as Millennium, Myriad Genetics, Axys, Incyte, Genome Therapeutics and Human Genome Sciences. Millennium and Monsanto have formed a partnership, as did Hexagen (UK) acquired by Incyte (USA). German firms like MorphoSys (Pharmacia-Upjohn, Swedish/US) and Evotec Biosystems (Novartis of Switzerland and Glaxo SmithKline of the UK) have also become involved in partnerships with foreign big pharma. Thus we see that entrepreneurial biotechnology firms are, if anything, strengthening their control over the product development process while courting big pharma for licensing and downstream marketing and distribution. Proximity to the science base and capability rapidly to transform potential knowledge into products remain defining characteristics of biotechnology. The clustering model which predominated early in the USA has developed more recently in the UK, notably at Cambridge and Oxford.

Cambridge, Oxford and Surrey

UK commercial biotechnology effectively started with the establishment of Celltech in 1979. High-level concern at the failure of the Medical Research Council's (MRC) Molecular Biology Laboratory to patent their discovery of monoclonal antibodies, and efforts by the Callaghan government to try to remedy the UK's lagging position in new, high technology markets led to the National Enterprise Board and MRC supporting the formation of a state-funded firm. Intended to be set up in Cambridge in proximity to the science base, property availability resulted in Celltech setting up in Slough, west London, where it remains. In 1999 it merged with Chiroscience, one unit of the merger to be known as Celsis.

Oxford

The UK's most notorious indigenous biotechnology firm, British Biotechnology, was a spin-out from the American firm Searle (part of Monsanto) of High Wycombe (near Oxford), when the latter closed UK operations in 1985. Two research directors established British Biotech and by 1992 it had become the UK's first publicly floated biotechnology company. Its site at Cowley is close to other Oxford-based biotechnology ventures such as Oxford Glycosciences, Oxford Molecular and Xenova. In 1997 British Biotech was Europe's largest biotechnology company in terms of market capitalisation and R&D costs, and second to Qiagen of Germany in employment, with 454 employees. Then the company suffered a $2 million stock-market decline because of delays in gaining approval for its two leading products. Confidence was badly hit everywhere in Europe by this setback to its leading company. Subsequent disclosures of potentially fraudulent practices in stoking-up the stock-market price did not help. Celltech also received a big setback with Bayer's announcement of withdrawal of support for its septic shock treatment, leading to a 48 per cent price drop. Investor confidence was further damaged by poor drug trial results from Scotia Holdings and Stanford Rook. The British Biotech clinical trials head, who was fired for questioning the effectiveness of the firm's cancer treatment in public, moved to Oxford Gene Technology (OGT) Operations, a commercial offshoot of Oxford University biochemist Ed Southern's pioneering research in DNA biochip technology. In 1999 OGT was in legal dispute with Affymetrix over the invention of the DNA biochip, which the American firm has patented. Oxford University retains a 10 per cent stake in OGT, set up in 1995 to manage income from Southern's DNA microarray patents.

Other Oxford firms of significance in biotechnology include Oxford University spin-out Oxford GlycoSciences, the world's leading proteomics firm, now partnered with Incyte Pharmaceuticals of California, Oxagen (functional genomics) based in nearby Abingdon, and therapeutics company Oxford Molecular. Other firms in the extended Oxford cluster, which is aligned down the A34 highway corridor, are near Abingdon and Didcot on the Milton Science Park and include Prolifix, a cell cycle control therapeutics firm, Oxford Asymmetry (bioinformatics) and Cozart BioSciences (immunodiagnostics). A number of newer firms are located at Oxford Science Park, including Progenica (diagnostics), Oxford Therapeutics (drug development), Oxford BioResearch, Kymed (biopharmaceuticals) and Evolutec (drug discovery). Other centres, such as the Medawar Centre and Abingdon Science Park, also house biotechnology firms.

The Institute of Molecular Medicine at the John Radcliffe Hospital, Oxford (part of Oxford University's Clinical School) is a leading research institute which spins out new firms, notably specialising in oncology and AIDS/hepatitis vaccines, in partnership with Isis, the Oxford University technology licensing and spin-out support organisation, private investors and venture capitalists. Oxagen, in Abingdon, is a recent spin-out from the Wellcome Trust Centre for Human Genetics in Oxford, and Prolifix was spun out from the Medical Research Council's National Institute for Medical Research in London. Yamanouchi Research Institute is the first privately funded biotechnology research institute to be established in the area (1990). In 1999, Oxfordshire BioScience, a network association for the industry, was established. Oxford has some fifty biotechnology firms and 200 supply, service or intermediary firms and organisations. Although still relatively small, it has most of the features of a cluster, including rising costs of industrial and domestic property, congestion and shortages of venture or other kinds of investment capital (partly caused by the negative British Biotech effect upon investor confidence). A study by Mihell *et al.* (1997) has shown that of forty biotechnology firms identified in 1995 (fifty in 1999), nine out of twelve interviewed were spun out from the university or other public research base, and all firms interviewed had grown swiftly in employment and revenues in the previous 5 years. Collaboration among local firms and with both the local science base and more distant big pharma are central to firm strategy, though local networking between firms was not as developed as the other links, signifying the comparative immaturity of the cluster. At the time of the survey, in 1996, 2,200 people were employed in the forty firms identified, and new firms were forming at a rate of three to four per year.

Cambridge

Cambridge's core biotechnology industry consists of no less than fifty firms and the broader cluster (venture capitalists, patent lawyers, etc.) probably consists of not much more than 200 firms, including the core biotechnology firms. The growth in number of biopharmaceutical firms was from one to twenty-three over the 1984–97 period, an average of just under two per year, but the rate was four per year in the last 2 years of that period. Equipment firms grew from four to twelve between 1984–97, and diagnostics firms from two to eight. Table 5.6(a) shows the breakdown of technology-based companies in Cambridgeshire, while Table 5.6(b) shows that for support services. Key firms include Cambridge Antibody Technologies, one of twelve spin-outs from the Molecular Biology Laboratory, Chiroscience (now Celltech), a start-up originally based at the Babraham incubator (see below), Cantab Pharmaceutical, Brax Genomics, Churchill

88   *Philip Cooke*

Table 5.6 Shares of biotechnology and services functions

5.6a Biotechnology firm distribution		5.6b Biotechnology services distribution	
Biopharmaceuticals	41%	Sales & Marketing	29%
Instrumentation	20%	Management Consulting	23%
Ag-food Bio	17%	Corporate Accounting	15%
Diagnostics	11%	Venture Capital	15%
Reagents/Chemicals	7%	Legal & Patents	8%
Energy	4%	Business Incubation	10%

Source: ERBI (1999).

Applied Biotechnology and American offshoots Chiron and Amgen. Many of the UK firms originated in Cambridge research laboratories and retain close links with them.

The infrastructure support for biotechnology in and around Cambridge is impressive, much of it deriving from the university and hospital research facilities. The Laboratory of Molecular Biology at Addenbrookes Hospital, funded by the Medical Research Council; Cambridge University's Institute of Biotechnology, Department of Genetics and Centre for Protein Engineering; the Babraham Institute and Sanger Institute with their emphasis on functional genomics research and the Babraham and St John's incubators for biotechnology start-ups and commercialisation, are all globally recognised facilities, particularly in biopharmaceuticals. However, in the eastern region are also located important research institutes in the 'green bio' field of agricultural and food biotechnology, such as the Institute for Food Research, John Innes Centre, Institute of Arable Crop Research and National Institute of Arable Botany. Thus in research and commercialisation terms, Cambridge is well placed in biopharmaceuticals; and, with respect to basic and applied research, but perhaps less so commercialisation, agro-food biotechnology also.

Within a 25-mile radius of Cambridgeshire are found many of the specialist biopharmaceutical firms with which commercialisation development by smaller start-ups and R&D by research institutes must be co-financed. Firms like Glaxo Wellcome, SmithKline Beecham, Merck, Rhône-Poulenc Rorer, Hoechst Pharmaceuticals in the 'big pharma' category are represented, and in the specialist biopharmaceutical sector: Amgen, Napp, Genzyme and Bioglan among others. Thus on another of the criteria for successful cluster development, namely access within reasonable proximity to large customer and funding partner firms, Cambridge is, again, fortuitously positioned.

Finally, with respect to 'agro-food bio', Rhône-Poulenc (now Aventis), Agrevo, Dupont, Unilever and Ciba are situated in reasonably close proximity to Cambridge. Hence the prospects for linkage, though more occluded by public concerns about genetically modified organisms than in the case of health-related biotechnology, are nevertheless propitious in locational terms.

Cambridge is relatively well-blessed with science and technology parks, though the demand for further space is significant. At least eight of the aforementioned 'biopharmaceuticals including vaccines' firms are located on Cambridge Science Park itself. St John's Innovation Centre, Babraham Bioincubator, Granta Park, the Bioscience Innovation Centre and Hinxton Science Park are all recently completed, under construction, or under planning review. Most of the newer developments are taking place within short commuting distance of Cambridge itself, on or near main road axes like the M11, A11, A10 and A14. This is evidence of the importance of access for research-applications firms to centres of basic research, reinforcing also the point that not everything concerning biotechnology must occur 'on the head of a pin' in Cambridge city itself.

The final, important, feature of the biotechnology landscape in Cambridge and the surrounding eastern region is the presence of both informal and formal networking between firms and research or service organisations and amongst firms themselves. Cambridge Network Ltd was set up in March 1998 to formalise linkages between business and the research community, connecting both from local to global networks in a systematic way. It is mostly IT-focused, though some of this spills over into biotechnology, given its demand for IT equipment and opportunities for IT-delivered patient and clinician services through, for example, telemedicine. Of more direct relevance to the biotechnology community are the activities of the Eastern Region Biotechnology Initiative (ERBI). This biotechnology association is the main regional network with formal responsibilities for newsletter, organising network meetings, running an international conference, website, sourcebook and database on the bioscience industry, providing aftercare services for bio-businesses, making intra- and international links (e.g. Oxford, Cambridge, MA, San Diego), organising common purchasing, business planning seminars, and government and grant-related interactions for firms.

Surrey

Moving to Surrey, this county contains an agglomeration of some thirty-seven biotechnology firms, according to Mihell *et al.* (1997), but differs from Cambridge and Oxford in having a great variety of types of firm and relatively few biotechnology research centres. Moreover, there is little interaction between firms in the locale, despite the existence of Southern BioScience, a regional industry association. In 1995 there were thirty-seven 'entrepreneurial' biotechnology firms and related organisations in Surrey. Unpublished figures from the UK Department of Trade and Industry note some 120 of all sizes between Surrey and Kent in 1998.

Pharmaceutical firms of multinational status such as Pfizer, Rhône Poulenc Rorer (now Aventis) and Eli Lilly are found across the two counties, but most firms are SMEs. Despite this, start-up activity has been less noticeable than at Cambridge or Oxford, partly because, despite there being a large number of universities in the wider regional setting, few if any have cutting-edge biotechnological research or pronounced commercialisation strategies. Southern Bioscience, the regional industry association, had assisted eleven new enterprises in biotechnology by 1999. Only one bioincubator exists in the region, at Sittingbourne in Kent where there is a Research Centre on a former Shell plc property. Surrey Research Park has no dedicated 'wet lab' space available. Poor availability of suitable premises was cited as a growth barrier in a Southern Bioscience study of the local industry. Other barriers noted were funding gaps, skills weaknesses and poor communication between industry and academia. Moreover, strong networking has been directed outside rather than inside the region, and the regional industry association itself recognises the absence of cluster-like characteristics such as those enjoyed in Oxford and Cambridge.

An exemplar of that firm type is Vanguard Medica, a leading drug development firm originating in Surrey, accessing early stage compounds and commercialising them. Frovatriptan is one of Vanguard's successful products for treating acute migraine. Partnerships with academia are directed towards London, Scotland, Europe and the USA, and collaborating companies include Abbott, Roche and 3M Pharmaceutical. Biocompatibles is a user of biotechnology in its core products, ranging from contact lenses to 'stents' (biomedical devices) using polymer synthesis to prevent protein build-up. The company, in interview, said that the Surrey biotechnology industry did not constitute a cluster because of poor linkage with local universities, absence of firms for local outsourcing and testing and the fact that firms have little in common around which to build partnerships. Microgen is a diagnostics firm which conducts environmental and food health monitoring, but has scarcely any local inter-firm links; its sources technology from the USA, where it was once acquired by Centocor, the US biopharmaceuticals firm, before being spun back out into private ownership in 1994. The view in the firm was that it was not part of a cluster, and in this respect there was remarkable unanimity with the other two firms profiled here. Hence, without further labouring the point, the key absence of strong local linkages to knowledge centres, supply chains or horizontally to other biotechnology firms, despite the presence of a regional industry association, points to the absence of clustering despite the presence of considerable industry agglomeration. Nevertheless, biotechnology firms in this area have prospered, demonstrating the importance of global networking even in the absence of the proximate hard and soft infrastructures of the localised, systemic innovation capabilities offered by clusters (Porter 1998).

Scotland

As in Wales, the approach to encouraging cluster growth in biotechnology involves the public funding bodies more centrally than in the market-driven clusters of Cambridge and Oxford or even the agglomeration of biotechnology firms in Surrey. However, while Wales has some fifteen biotechnology firms in mini-agglomerations in Cardiff and Swansea, Scotland has over fifty biotechnology firms. The biggest geographical concentration is in Glasgow, but there is strong science and spin-out firms in Dundee and Edinburgh, as well as near Aberdeen. The sector is thus seen as occupying a 'biotechnology triangle' between Dundee, Edinburgh and Glasgow at its heart.

The role of the public sector has been important in Scottish biotechnology in three ways. First, as elsewhere, the finance for basic scientific research in the universities is mainly provided by UK Research Councils and, to a lesser extent and influenced by the measures of scientific legitimacy conferred by the high public ranking of biosciences schools, university hospitals and the like; this also attracts private sector funding from big pharma or charitable trusts. Second, the sector has benefited from the adoption of a cluster strategy by Scottish Enterprise, the development agency for Scotland. Scottish Enterprise commissioned Michael Porters' consultancy, Monitor, to conduct a scoping exercise and provide intensive, back-up training for developing four pilot clusters, one of which was biotechnology. This has now begun in earnest and the methodology by means of which cluster-building is taking place is established (see Figure 5.1). It is noteworthy that this methodology, the whole cost to Scottish Enterprise for which was $2 million, is unlike what might be termed a

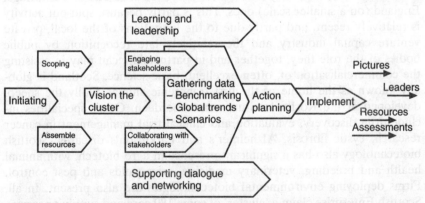

Stakeholders: industry, academia, education, research, government and other institutions

Figure 5.1 The Scottish enterprise cluster approach in biotechnology

Stakeholders: industry, academia, education, research, government and other institutions.
Source: Scottish Enterprise.

more normal planning and programming approach. Instead, it places great emphasis on the processes of scoping, picturing and resourcing a 'vision' of the cluster. Then, armed with the cluster-vision, stakeholders and leaders willing to show strong commitment bring together key actors and engage in interactive learning. Only then, at the third stage, does data-gathering, benchmarking and scenario-building begin. This leads to action planning based on consensus and concrete agreements, followed by implementation guided by cluster pictures, leaders, expenditures and evaluation. This is a market-influenced model of public enterprise based on the ideas of 'picture, manage and monitor', rather than 'survey, analysis and plan'.

The third way in which public intervention has a generic impact on biotechnology in Scotland flows from the consensus agreement on the cluster strategy at Scotland-wide level, and the collaboration by governance bodies to pool funding to assist in the process of supporting, in this case, the biotechnology sector (see Scottish Office 1999). Thus, Scottish Enterprise, the Scottish Office and the Scottish Higher Education Funding Council created a fund of some £11 million to enable all clusters to develop by innovative means. As an example, funding is being made available to 'buy-out' or 'free-up' the time of bioscientists and biotechnologists to concentrate on research and commercialisation activities instead of teaching and administration. This is administered with local knowledge and sensitivity through the decentralised Scottish Local Enterprise Companies with whom candidate academics discuss their prospects for receiving funding.

Despite this excellent public support, the existence of biotechnology as one of the cluster-building projects is testimony to the fact that, although having considerable potential, the biotechnology sector does not yet constitute a cluster in the way that Cambridge, Massachusetts or Cambridge, England (on a smaller scale) does. This is partly because spin-out activity is relatively recent, and partly due to the limitations of the local, private venture capital industry and the relatively late recognition by public bodies of the role they, together and in partnership, can play in assisting the commercialisation of, often excellent, basic science. Scotland is globally known as the home of the first transgenic animal, Dolly the sheep, developed at the Roslin Institute near Aberdeen. Other specialities include drug discovery, evaluation and clinical trial management in cancer research, cystic fibrosis, Alzheimer's and Parkinson's diseases. Scottish biotechnology also has a significant presence in agro-biotech, with animal health and breeding, veterinary medicine, crop yields and pest control. Firms deploying environmental biotechnologies are also present. In all, Scottish Enterprise claim a 'cluster' of some 180 core and supply or service firms engaged to some degree in the 'cluster'. In truth, the core is some forty to fifty firms which are quite geographically dispersed and focused mainly on their scientific home bases.

The industry in Scotland is made up broadly as shown in Table 5.7. It is

Table 5.7 Composition of biotechnology sector in Scotland

Activity	Number of firms (core activity)
Biopharmaceutical therapeutics	24
Biopharmaceutical diagnostics	18
Biopharmaceutical clinical trials	10
Biopharmaceutical contract R&D	14
Bioprocessing	17
Environmental bioremediation	3
Environmental diagnostics	7
Environmental waste treatment	5
Agro-food therapeutics	1
Agro-Food plant breeding	2
Agro-Food diagnostics	4
Agro-Food contract R&D	2
Supplies	23
Support services	26

Source: Scottish Enterprise (1999).

clear that biopharmaceuticals is the strong core part of the industry in Scotland, with a substantial number of firms in therapeutic product development, fewer in diagnostics, research and clinical trials (many of the contract R&D entries are universities, some with firms attached, others not). There is also a reasonably well-endowed supplies (reagents, chemicals, etc.) and support services (legal, consultancy, etc.) infrastructure. Hence, as a whole, Scotland has a robust basis for future growth in biotechnology, but it may lack, at present, the interactive capacities and sophisticated support arrangements found more extensively in Cambridge and Oxford. Having said that, it is undoubtedly closer in type to those university-based clusters and quite unlike the rather amorphous agglomeration found in Surrey. In Dundee, there are a number of highly rated bioscience departments in the university, and a new Wellcome Trust-funded biotechnology institute. Cyclacel, which will be described below, and Shield Diagnostics, a manufacturer of immunoassays in cardiovascular diseases, are spin outs, the first located on the nearby innovation park of Dundee University, the second having graduated beyond it as it has grown in size. The Ninewells Hospital Medical School has some 250 bioscience researchers to contribute to the total of 1,000 life scientists in Dundee. Of these 170 are in the Wellcome Trust Institute (which opened in 1997), rising eventually to 240.

Dundee thus has the science base for possible future cluster development but as yet lacks a critical mass of firms. Cyclacel is a contract R&D spin-out specialising in drug discovery for cancer genomics; the key connection is with the Ninewells Medical School, headed by David Lane (co-owner of Cyclacel) who discovered the p53 anti-cancer gene. Venture capital of £2.5 million was accessed from London-based Merlin Ventures, headed by biotechnologist Chris Evans, who founded Chiroscience, one of the UK's leading biotechnology firms. Chiroscience recently merged with the UK's first biotechnology firm (based in west London) Celltech, and recently they made news by being the UK's first biotechnology acquirers of a pharmaceutical firm, Medeva, since spinning off its vaccines division to PowderJect.

Cyclacel contracts in research from American headquartered Quintiles, one of the world's leading biotechnology contract research firms from Boston – the subsidiary is based in Edinburgh. Quintiles entered Scotland by acquiring Innovex, an upstream biosciences spin-out from academia. Another firm, now located in Perth, called Quantase is present near Dundee because of Shield Diagnostics based on the Technology Park at Dundee. Quantase conducts neonatal screening and was acquired by Shield in 1994. Shield specialises in cardiovascular neonatal diagnostics. In September 1997, however, Quantase was subject to a management buy-out; the firm employs eight people, of whom three are research scientists, and has won government innovation awards to support development of its leading product. Expansion has been funded by venture capital from UK firm 3i and bank loans. Quantase, like Cyclacel and Quintiles, find the environment in Perth highly suitable for their business activities. Linkages between firms are regular and established even though geographical co-location is not considered a prerequisite. Communication links between Dundee and Edinburgh, particularly, are extremely easy and swift. More-over, Glasgow is well linked to both by high-grade transportation links.

This small snapshot of biotechnology in Scotland shows that the sector has the characteristics of close inter-firm interaction often found in clusters, and taking the form of network linkages. In Scotland as a whole, there are largely adequate business infrastructures to sustain a successful biotechnology sector. Private capital for biotechnology investment is not abundant in Scotland, but this is partly compensated by the presence of public sector support in this well-networked, latent cluster.

Concluding remarks

This chapter began with a commentary on how dependent big pharma has become upon significantly smaller technology-driven start-up and spin-off firms. This was demonstrated in detailed analyses of biotechnologically derived therapeutic treatments manufactured, marketed or distributed by the multinational pharmaceutical companies. Whichever way diverse data sources are analysed, big pharma is overwhelmingly dependent for drug origination upon independent, lesser-scale, biotechnology firms. Of course, the latter are dependent on the former to at least as great an extent for the large cash investments required to test and trial potential products over lengthy time periods and at a high risk. Big pharma is cash-rich enough to continue this asymmetrical power game for as long as biotechnology firms fail to make the scale breakthrough to become fully integrated pharmaceutical companies or FIPCOs This kind of relationship of double, but asymmetrical, dependence is probably unique in the business world, though it has a resonance with the way the IT industry operated in its earlier days, when electronics multinationals quarried Silicon Valley for technologically sophisticated start-ups. By the end of the millennium, of course, some of the bright start-ups of the 1970s and 1980s had themselves outgrown or displaced the larger predators, as the histories of Microsoft and Intel exemplify. It is not possible to predict that a comparable process of independent, technology-focused firm growth from start-up to market leader will happen in biotechnology as it has, to a growing extent, in IT. This is not ruled out, but what can be stated with confidence is that the model of venture capital-driven, start-up and spin-out growth, usually in business clusters, has now spread from the USA to Europe, particularly in the UK, and that, if anything, big pharma shows less signs of being at the research cutting-edge of biotechnology in the era of the human genome than it did in the days of monoclonal antibodies and recombinant DNA. Moreover, a first case of biotechnology acquiring pharmaceuticals occurred with the Chiroscience-Celltech purchase of Medeva in November 1999 in the UK. There has also been some equalisation of the technological lead in product commercialisation between the USA and Europe as the climate for academic entrepreneurship has improved in the latter.

There are even some signs in the USA that the biotechnology firm formation rate has declined, with merger and acquisition practices among biotechnology specialist firms. This may signify a new stage in the industry's slower evolution towards a less bifurcated structure than hitherto. Peak years for new firms in Massachusetts, for example, were 1991–3, with annual start-up rates of fifteen, twenty-one and fifteen. Between 1996 and 1998 seven Massachusetts firms merged or were acquired by others (Massachusetts Biotechnology Council 1998). Alternatively, it may be a lull before the storm of potential new firm formation associated with functional genomics as gene-sequencing, bioinformatics and a host of other commercial applications of human genome science are explored. More of this kind of activity is likely to occur in the UK, as well as elsewhere in Europe, than happened in the first wave of biotechnology applications growth in the 1980s when key discoveries remained unpatented in UK laboratories, leaving US technologists a clear field for early adoption and application. Despite its European lead in the biotechnology product potential the UK is, in 1999, as dependent on the USA for biotechnological therapeutic products, marketed and distributed by big pharma in the UK, as Germany. However, independent UK biotechnology firms dominate the European pipeline for future biopharmaceutical products, and many of these involve alliances, as with UK pharmaceutical firms. Cantab Pharmaceutical's past vaccine partnerships with Glaxo and SKB, Powderject's with Glaxo, and Peptide Therapeutics with SKB are illustrative of this tendency. But UK alliances with non-UK pharma, like Cambridge Antibody Technology with Eli Lilly, Chiroscience with Schering-Plough, Bristol Myers Squibb and AstraZeneca, and Scotia Holdings with Boehringer Ingelheim are noteworthy and show that the levelling-up between US and European entrepreneurial firms is now a reality in prospect rather than mere hype.

The final inference to be drawn from this analysis of global–local power dependencies and asymmetries is two-pronged. First, 'strength-in-numbers' characterises the practices of the small-firm ecosystem defining the originators of potential biopharmaceutical products and platform technologies. The cluster is the definitive organisational mode of the creative community of firms that risk oblivion to pursue discovery and commercialisation. Investment is tight, so situations that can lower transaction costs or remove them via trustful exchange, reputational trading and collective learning in localised knowledge networks is of key importance. Further, the prospects of long-term profit continue to attract the complementary business, legal and financial services companies into the cluster alongside the research laboratories, incubators and start-up firms. This is an 'extended campus' milieu rather than the 'extended workbench' metaphor applied to clusters in more traditional industries such as those of northern and central Italy. This also highlights, however, the second feature of the 'triple-helix' relationship between industry, university and government (Etkowitz and Leydesdorff 1997), which is that big pharma and the entrepreneurial biotechnology firms are also inordinately dependent upon the public purse. For example, some $770 ($1.3 billion in 2001) million of public research funding flows through the Boston biotechnology community per year, and it is at least $1 billion each in San Francisco and San Diego. The US biotechnology funding agencies had at their disposal $20 billion of public money in 1999 ($21.3 billion in 2003), more than twice as much as the business R&D budget of $9 billion. This is by no means only an innovation process involving venture capital, management support and start-ups to transfer research results from laboratory to market. It is fundamentally fuelled by public research budgets. Estimates of the value of the market at $70 billion in 2000 give an indication of the public market value ratio. Keep in mind also that UK government annual expenditure on bioscience research is some £1 billion and Germany's a further $1 billion, if the large public element in biotechnology venture capital is included, and we see something of the scale of modern public investment in this industry of the future (Cooke 1999; DTI 1999). In conclusion, the globalisation of bioscience and its commercialisation in biotechnology is a study in variable geometry between multinationals and entrepreneurial start-ups, competition and collaboration, public subsidy and private profitability, or as some might also say, the devil and the deep blue sea.

References

BioCentury (1999) *Biopharmaceutical Database*, Oxford: BioCentury International.

BioIndustry Association (1999) *BioScience UK: Fundamental, Influential, Exponential*, London: BioIndustry Association.

Cohen, W. and Levinthal, D. (1990) 'Absorptive Capacity: a New Perspective on Learning and Innovation', *Administrative Science Quarterly*, 35: 128–52.

Cooke, P. (1999) *The German Biotechnology Sector, the Public Policy Impact and Regional Clustering: an Assessment*, Report to the UK Department of Trade and Industry, Cardiff: Centre for Advanced Studies.

DTI (Department of Trade and Industry) (1998a) *Our Competitive Future: Building the Knowledge-Driven Economy*, London: DTI.

—— (1999b) *Biotechnology in Germany: Report of an ITS Mission*, London: DTI and Foreign and Commonwealth Office.

—— (1999) *Biotechnology Clusters*, London: DTI.

ERBI (Eastern Region Biotechnology Initiative) (1998) *Sourcebook '98*, Cambridge: ERBI.

—— (1999) 'Background Information for Cambridge and E. Region Biotechnology Cluster' (mimeo), Cambridge: ERBI.

Ernst and Young (1999) *European Life Sciences 99: Sixth Annual Report*, Ernst and Young.

Etkowitz, H. and Leydesdorff, L. (1997) *Universities and the Global Knowledge Economy*, London: Pinter.

Massachusetts Biotechnology Council (1998) *Massachusetts Biotechnology Directory*, Cambridge: MBC.

Mihell, D., Kingham, D. and Stott, M. (1997) *The Development of the Biotechnology Sector in Oxfordshire: Implications for Public Policy*, Oxford: Oxford Innovation Ltd.

Porter, M. (1998) *On Competition*, Harvard: Harvard Business School Press.

Prevezer, M. (1995) 'The Dynamics of Industrial Clustering in Biotechnology', *Small Business Economics*, 9: 255–71.

Schitag, Ernst and Young (1998) *Germany's Biotechnology Takes Off in 1998*, Stuttgart: Schitag, Ernst and Young.

Scottish Enterprise (1999) *Biotechnology Scotland Source Book*, Glasgow: Scottish Enterprise.

Scottish Office (1999) *Biotechnology Clusters*, Edinburgh: Scottish Office.

6 The Rhine–Neckar-Triangle BioRegion

Scientific excellence and catching up in development

Gerhard Krauss and Thomas Stahlecker

Introduction

In biotechnology, flexible innovation networks play a significant role in generating and exploiting knowledge for commercial purposes. Although such know-how/knowledge networks may in certain ways function over large geographical distances (Audretsch and Stephan 1996), there are also indications that intensive social exchange relations exist on a regional level. The question, therefore, is the nature of the relationship between global and regional networks. There is obviously a strong incentive in biotechnology, on the one hand, to participate in new international findings and, on the other, in view of commercial exploitation, to engage in certain kinds of exchanges favoured – or indeed facilitated – by face-to-face relationships and intense informal contacts. The more one is dealing with tacit knowledge, the more advantageous is geographical proximity to the people with the know-how.

The significance of geographical proximity in relation to the global transfer of know-how in this field of technology is a question which has not yet been answered. To what degree does the commercialisation of biotechnology know-how bind certain spheres of competence to the region, leading to the formation of integrated, regional biotechnology clusters? What kind of competence profile can a region develop in such a young field of technology as biotechnology, the distinguishing features of which are the tremendous importance of basic research, high technological risks, strong global competition paired with the extreme necessity for co-operation and highly fluid co-operative networks?

The present chapter is intended to demonstrate and analyse the status and significance of the process of cluster formation in the Rhine–Neckar-Triangle BioRegion, seen against the background of global networking. To this end, we have based our work, on the one hand, on the evaluation of secondary analyses of existing material on this region and, on the other hand, on numerous interviews with specialists and with members of new biotechnology companies which were carried out as part of an accompanying study on the development of biotechnology industries in the

Rhine–Neckar-Triangle BioRegion and as part of a project financed by the Deutsche Forschungsgemeinschaft (German Research Association) on 'The formation of high-risk companies'.

The chapter is structured in six sections. The first describes the region under scrutiny; the next deals with the unsuccessful cluster formations in the field of biotechnology in the 1980s. The fourth section examines the subsequent development of clusters in the 1990s, particularly in the context of a purposeful cluster-promoting policy by the former German federal government as part of the Bio-Regio Programme. The fifth section goes on to introduce the institutional infrastructure for supporting the development of biotechnology. The development of the institutional environment creates important conditions for the formation of a biotechnology cluster rooted in the region. The final section presents the main results in a concluding summary.

The area under survey: the Rhine–Neckar Triangle

The polycentric system of the Rhine–Neckar Triangle is marked today by a high density of main and medium-sized centres, with the nucleus towns of Ludwigshafen, Mannheim and Heidelberg contrasting quite clearly with the surrounding, less dense (in part rural) counties. The Rhine–Neckar-Triangle BioRegion also includes the towns of Kaiserslautern (university city as technology centre) and Darmstadt (due to the Merck KgaA company which is involved in the regional BioRegio initiative). The main agglomeration advantages of the area stem from a highly efficient transport infrastructure, a large sales and purchase market and the proximity to research and education centres (Egeln *et al.* 1996: 24–8). What makes the region special is its position at the intersection of three *Länder* (federal states) – and thus at the intersection of three administrative areas. This administrative structure determined the development of the region and still has a significant impact on it today (Strambach 1995: 63).

From the point of view of their economic structures the three nucleus towns are very different from one another: while Mannheim has traditional industrial characteristics, Ludwigshafen is distinguished by the predominance of just a few large-scale enterprises in the chemical and pharmaceutical industries (BASF, Knoll, Rasch, Guilini) (Strambach 1995). Heidelberg's main strength lies in education, science and research, the clearly identifiable emphasis of which are the fields of molecular biology, genetics and cancer research. Seen as a sector, industry has an above-average standing, both in terms of the proportion of employees (44.3 per cent) and gross product (42.7 per cent), by comparison with the rest of the country (Arbeitskreis Rhine–Neckar-Dreieck e.V. 1998). The main reason for these high values is evidently the chemical and pharmaceutical industries which, in spite of gradually reduced numbers of employees, still constitute the economic backbone of the region (10.9 per cent of the national insurance contributors; see Grammel and Iwer 1998: 6).

Involving 6.3 per cent of national insurance contributors, the intensity of research by the companies in the Rhine–Neckar Triangle is almost twice as high as the average for the rest of Germany (Egeln *et al.* 1996: 28, 119). This is in part due to the traditionally research-intensive chemical and pharmaceutical industries. However, this is by no means a mono-structured region, since it has an extremely strong service industries sector with almost 55 per cent of the national insurance contributors (1996) (in Heidelberg it is as high as 72 per cent) and there are many innovative companies responsible for setting modern trends in the area.

Lack of cluster formation in the 1980s

Conditions for the development of biotechnology in the region

The Rhine–Neckar Triangle is traditionally one of the most important chemical and pharmaceutical industrial areas in Germany. Ludwigshafen, with BASF located there, constitutes a special concentration as the largest employer in the region. In the past, the chemical and pharmaceutical industries developed almost completely independent of regional research potential in biotechnology. Up to the 1980s biotechnology procedures and processes were mainly only applied in state-financed basic research and for experimental purposes. This involved the University of Heidelberg and such research institutions as the Deutsches Krebsforschungszentrum (DKFZ) (German Cancer Research Centre), the European Molecular Biology Laboratory (EMBL) and the Max-Planck-Institut für medizinische Forschung (Max Planck Institute of Medical Research) specialising in molecular genetics, oncology, chemistry and bioinformatics.

Processes for exploiting the research for commercial purposes were, however, first initiated in locations in other parts of the world. In the mid-1970s, the most important impulses for the commercial development of biotechnology came from the newly founded life sciences companies in the United States. They were the first to back the commercial exploitation of research results. A broader spectrum of use of biotechnology began in the 1980s (Dolata 1994, 1999). By contrast, the large, established companies in North America, Japan and Western Europe were relatively late and hesitant in becoming involved in this new field of technology. However, due to the strength of their position in terms of research, production and the market, they were soon able to close this gap (Dolata 1994).

The large chemical and pharmaceutical companies in the Rhine–Neckar Triangle – BASF, Boehringer Mannheim (now Roche) and Merck – acted in the same way. It was not until the second half of the 1980s that BASF extended its genetic engineering activities, which were indeed concentrated on relatively few projects in the comparatively small pharmaceuti-

cals sector. The clearest sign of an intention to catch up was the establishment of a new pharmaceutical research centre, the BASF Bioresearch
Corp. in Worcester, near Boston, one of the world's leading life sciences
regions. In 1990 the Bayer subsidiary in Berkeley followed; it started production of coagulation factor VIII (Theisen 1991, Dolata 1994).

By contrast, Boehringer Mannheim entered into genetic engineering
research relatively early (in the mid-1970s). However, it concentrated
most of its research and production on the locations in Penzberg arrd
Tutzing (Dolata 1994). The Boehringer Mannheim Group's competence in
the molecular biology processes in the diagnostics industry was instrumental in the take-over decision by Roche AG, leading to the formation of the
world's largest producer of diagnostics (Roche Boehringer Mannheim
Diagnostics). In the context of Roche AG's innovative network, the industrial location of Mannheim situated in the Rhine–Neckar Triangle,
however, will play a less important part in the future. The biotechnological
activities will be much more concentrated in Penzberg.[1]

Against the background of the development in the USA, the German
federal government initiated the modernisation of the biotechnology
research infrastructure in Germany and promoted know-how transfers
between science and industry. 'Genetic engineering centres' were established and publicly funded with the intention of bringing about the interdisciplinary concentration of (academic) research capacity and direct
co-operation between university institutes, scientific organisations and
business all under one institutional roof (Dolata 1991, BMFT 1993).
Nevertheless, the genetic engineering centres were not able to fulfil their
mission to mediate between academic and industrial research. The focus
of these centres was clearly on academic basic research (Dolata 1996: 153).

Next to Cologne, Berlin and Munich, the genetic engineering centre in
Heidelberg received public funding from 1982 to 1993. The effort was concentrated around the Heidelberg Centre for Molecular Biology (ZMBH)
at Heidelberg University and the German Cancer Research Centre
(DKFZ) in Heidelberg. Apart from the temporary start-up funding by the
BMFT and institutional aid from participating federal state governments,
local big chemical and pharmaceutical industry branches also became
involved. BASF AG and Merck AG both owned participating interests in
industry in the Rhine–Neckar Triangle. These private funds, however,
represented only a relatively insignificant part of the total budget of these
centres.

On the commercial side of biotechnology a – relatively modest –
number of businesses had already been established in the Rhine–Neckar
Triangle (mainly in Heidelberg) in the first half of the 1980s. This trend
still continued after the law governing genetic engineering was amended in
1993 so that, together with Munich, Heidelberg became a centre of competence in biotechnology, not only in the scientific and academic fields, but
also in economic terms.[2]

Institutional barriers

The main strength of the innovation system in Germany – and in particular in Baden-Württemberg – lies in process innovation and incremental improvement innovations in experience-based technology paths. The institutional environment is to a large degree geared towards supporting incremental, continuous and routine innovations (Krauss 1999a, Casper 1999). This system is internationally acknowledged for its special competence in product and process innovations in the field of complex and highly advanced, i.e. mature, technologies. The technological basis in Baden-Württemberg lies in the strong industrial clusters which have evolved over the decades with a high concentration of the material and nonmaterial resources available in the *Land* (Heidenreich and Krauss 1998).

The large-scale chemicals industries located in the Rhine–Neckar Triangle constituted a similar point of attraction. In view of the fact that the large-scale chemicals industry provides a well-developed associated sector of business which could well have served as a launching pad for developing structures for the commercial exploitation of biotechnology, it is surprising how slowly and hesitantly this economic sector has been developed in the region. For a long time there was little progress in integrating life sciences from an economic and social point of view in the Rhine–Neckar Triangle. Significant factors were the wait-and-see attitude of the regional and national state, the poor orientation of academics towards possible economic and industrial applications, as well as a lack of support for the young life sciences companies formed in the region from established companies in associated economic sectors such as the chemical and pharmaceutical industries; the latter showed little inclination to co-operate and start business relations with new biotechnology companies in the region.

> The often hesitant, sometimes even forced looking entry of German companies into the new biotechnology is ... primarily due neither to the (pretended) weaknesses of the research location Germany nor to an expression of a consciously calculated restraint of early, risky investments in this new and still uncertain field of technology, but above all the product of a narrowing of company strategies over decades: for a long time the new biotechnology simply remained out of the perception of the big groups mostly dominated and directed by chemists.
>
> (Dolata 1996: 115)

In addition, the institutional environment was hardly geared towards the requirements of the biotechnology industry, involving various aspects such as finances (too little resources and risk capital, investors and banks with an aversion to risks), problems in gaining public acceptance and, in the past, additional, complicated and long-winded licensing procedures (which de facto constitute a hindrance to development).

By tradition, the *Land* government of Baden-Württemberg also sets other points of emphasis in its industrial and innovation policies. The low interest of the *Land* government in the pharmaceutical and chemical industries (compared to the powerful core branches of industry) and in the innovation potentials of biotechnology relevant to these branches presented a certain handicap. In addition, the polycentric structure of Baden-Württemberg is inclined to make any concentrated promotion of biotechnology in individual sub-regions, such as Heidelberg or in the Baden-Württemberg part of the Rhine–Neckar Triangle, more difficult.[3] Furthermore, any development assistance policy requires co-ordination and co-operation across *Land* borders: the Rhine–Neckar Triangle of which Heidelberg is a part, is also the intersection between no less than three different Federal *Länder* (Hesse, Rhineland Palatinate and Baden-Württemberg).

For a long time it was typical of the situation in Germany and in the Rhine–Neckar Triangle that established companies were extremely hesitant to invest in biotechnology located in the area. To begin with, there was little interest in more recent developments in life sciences in Germany; instead there was a trend towards co-operation with American biotechnology firms. During a conference in 1995, the Director of the German Cancer Research Centre (DKFZ), Professor Harald zur Hausen emphasised that co-operation with German industry required improvement:

> Without question co-operation could well be achieved, in particular with industry in Germany which in the past rarely anticipated anything significant from the institutes in their own region and was sometimes so sceptical about some pioneering discoveries that they ended up being produced by foreign companies.
> (Industrie- und Handelskammer Rhein–Neckar/Deutsches
> Krebsforschungszentrum 1995: 40)

Only in a few individual cases, such as the model company ORPEGEN in Heidelberg, was any support to be seen from the business establishment; in the aforementioned case this was crucial to the development of the company (Industrie- und Handelskammer Rhein–Neckar/Deutsches Krebsforschungszentrum 1995: 43–56).

The company Orpegen was set up as one of the very first new high-tech companies to be directly initiated by science in Germany. It is a pioneering biotechnology company in Heidelberg and the Rhine–Neckar Triangle. In 1985, Deutsche Shell AG took out a 49 per cent participating interest in Orpegen; when Shell AG withdrew in 1987, Heidelberger Zement AG (Heidelberg Cement) purchased the 49 per cent. Both companies invested in the hope of gaining access to innovative technology developments which might be of relevance to them.[4]

This interest by established companies in technology developments being implemented by the new biotechnology companies was the exception to what was a generally indifferent attitude towards young life sciences companies in Germany.

Picking up on cluster formation in the 1990s

The BioRegio campaign by the Federal Ministry for Education and Research (BMBF) has since brought about some changes and stimulated a boom in the formation of new biotechnology companies. From the financial point of view, young life sciences companies now have an enormously extended range of potential ways of financing available to them.[5] In the course of this campaign new networks have emerged and existing ones have been extended and intensified in the respective regions. What was special about the BioRegio Programme was an approach which offered to assist the development of regional biotechnology clusters, making regions compete with one another and then, in the final phase, concentrating on just a few selected, promising regions. The Rhine–Neckar-Triangle Bio-Region won distinction as one of a total of three model regions in Germany. This involved state funds to the tune of DEM 50 million for a period of 5 years (starting in 1997).

The development of the biotechnology industry in the Rhine–Neckar-Triangle BioRegion

The first biotechnology companies were founded in Heidelberg in the early 1980s. Since then, the number of young companies has continually increased; in particular a boom set in in the second half of the 1990s. The first German Biotechnology Report by Schitag, Ernst and Young in 1998 showed that half of all German biotechnology companies were located in just three Federal *Länder*, the largest proportion of which was in Baden-Württemberg, followed by North Rhine-Westfalia and Bavaria. Berlin and Hesse ranked fourth and fifth (Köhler 1998, Schitag *et al.* 1998: 14). In the meantime these relative positions have changed considerably: whereas Bavaria ranked third in 1997, it has succeeded in becoming number one of all German bioregions, not least thanks to the modern and aggressive industrial policy of the Bavarian government which concentrates resources on the bioregion of Munich. This region comprises a good infrastructure, a wide range of financing possibilities (venture capital among others) and a well-developed research structure of high international reputation. By contrast, Baden-Württemberg lags behind and now ranks only second, the polycentric structure of the *Land* making an industrial policy focused too much on a particular region or sub-region difficult.[6] A comparison of sixteen bioregions in Germany in 1998 (Barnett *et al.* 1998) showed that the Rhine–Neckar-Triangle BioRegion ranked only eighth among newly founded biotech firms (in 1998 about twenty biotech firms were located in this region, of which nine started up after 1996). However, in terms of the number of jobs created, the outcome is much better. But it seems that the dynamics in terms of newly founded biotech firms is lower than in the rival bioregions,[7] especially Munich and, recently, the regions of Berlin and Brandenburg (Ernst and Young 2000). In Baden-Württemberg, the Freiburg region recorded the greatest number of newly founded companies.

Among the biotechnology companies located in the Heidelberg area, however, are also examples of fast-growing firms. Some of the biotechnology companies especially formed in the late 1990s were positioned in a growing market segment and usually started up with a relatively high number of employees. Since, by comparison with other fields of technology, a fairly high volume of investment is required to form biotechnology companies (for the basic equipment requirements), it may be assumed that it also has an above-average impact on secondary and tertiary suppliers. Whether these frequently highly specialised suppliers (optoelectronic components, medico-technical equipment, laboratory equipment, etc.) are also located or are formed in the Rhine–Neckar Triangle, thus establishing a high-performance background of suppliers, cannot be conclusively stated at present. The supply structures are more likely to be supra-regional and international.

The majority of life sciences companies located in the Rhine–Neckar Triangle are situated in the Heidelberg Technology Park, in direct proximity to scientific institutions such as the German Cancer Research Centre and the University clinics, as well as the central co-ordinating, counselling and financing institutions of the BioRegio Rhine–Neckar Triangle e.V. (registered association), Heidelberg Innovation GmbH and the Seed Capital Fund administered by the latter. In spite of the predominant position of Heidelberg in the Rhine–Neckar-Triangle BioRegion, it became clear in various talks with those involved locally that besides Heidelberg, the Mannheim and Rhineland-Palatinate parts of the Rhine–Neckar Triangle are close enough to the most important bearers of tacit knowledge of the technology to be relevant as biotechnology locations.

Due to the mainly scientific orientation of companies working in the field of biotechnology the general specialisation features of the region can be defined as analogous to the research specialities of the university and non-university facilities located there. The commercial focus is, therefore, in the fields of pharmaceutics and diagnostics (contract research and production, platform technologies) (see also Köhler 1998). In its application to participate in the BioRegio competition, the 'Initiativkreis Bio-Region Rhein–Neckar-Dreieck' (Rhine–Neckar-Triangle BioRegion Action Group), the biotechnology know-how suitable for commercialisation is concentrated on the specialist fields of oncology, the discovery and devel-opment of innovative substances (chemistry, biotechnology), the develop-ment of methods in genetic engineering and immunology, bioinformatics, genome research, cellular biology, therapy and diagnostics for cardio-vascular problems and in the field of medical technology (cf. Initiativkreis 'BioRegion Rhein–Neckar-Dreieck' 1996: 16). By comparison, companies engaged in the areas of 'green biotechnology' (agro-food) and environ-mental biotechnology are relatively under-represented in the Rhine–Neckar Triangle, although this in fact reflects the trend throughout Germany.

A considerable number of production and service-oriented diagnostics firms have settled in the region in the meantime. In spite of a high degree of automation, many of these companies are still increasing their labour force (mainly non-academic employees such as technical assistants). Apart from the diagnostics companies a number of so-called royalty-based pharmaceu-tical companies (Manth 1995) have also settled in the region. These are providers of pharmaceutical basic substances (biopharmaceutical active ingredients and substances) for which pharmaceutical companies obtain licences or the right to use the patents and integrate them in the clinical phases. For regions with a pharmaceuticals industry of national and inter-national significance such as the Rhine–Neckar Triangle, royalty-based pharmaceutical companies present an interesting case from the point of view of regional economics because they raise the regional share in the value-creation chain for medical drugs (from product-oriented R&D on to the production and sales of innovative medicines). A broad spectrum of preparatory measures at a very high standard demanding a high degree of know-how is also contingent upon a corresponding demand and upon trade relations with local (large-scale) industry as partners (customers).

A further area of competence in the Rhine–Neckar Triangle is formed by companies specialising in bioinformatics, BioChip technologies and the development of databank functions. An example is LION Bioscience AG which is involved in gene sequencing with integrated bioinformatics. In the period between 1997 and 1999, the firm succeeded in creating almost 200 highly qualified jobs. However, the company has recently accumulated a net loss of almost 93 million Euro due to the current recession and to reduced spending of the pharmaceutical industry (cf. *Handlesblatt* 2002), and faces a difficult future.

One critical point is that it has not yet been possible to achieve the settlement of a larger number of (quasi) integrated pharmaceuticals companies with their own drugs development departments (based on molecular biology approaches) in the Rhine–Neckar Triangle. The settle-ment of such companies would be an important step on the way to achiev-ing the objective of modernising a regional economy based on life sciences and pharmacy because the value-creation chain (up to confirmation of clinical effectiveness) would be concentrated in the region.

Structure of trade relations and co-operative behaviour

Regional know-how transfer

It is notable that hitherto there have been no or at least few companies established as spin-offs from a university or from local research organisations. Many of the newly established life sciences companies have been set up by founders from research institutions outside the region. In some cases the founders have had experience in the relevant industries and had, at best, informal relations with the local university institutes, research groups and industry. These companies seem to maintain equally intense professional contacts beyond the Rhine–Neckar Triangle as they do within it. This fact permits certain conclusions concerning the interdisciplinary nature of the field of technology and the relatively limited specialist location-building function of close proximity for technology transfer. Apart from this, since 1997 a number of life sciences/pharmaceutical companies have established sales outlets and subsidiaries, as well as a joint venture – a large company in the region and an American pharmaceuticals company.[8]

The Rhine–Neckar Triangle in general and Heidelberg in particular are evidently able to take full advantage of the status as a model biotechnology/life sciences region and draw on financial incentives and other 'pull factors', such as consultant and support institutions, qualified personnel, agglomeration advantages, as well as a high degree of living and leisure quality, to mobilise and commercialise biotechnology know-how from outside the region by establishing new firms.

Intra-industrial co-operation

In contrast with the development of US life sciences locations such as San Diego, Berkeley/San José, Seattle, Durham/Chapel-Hill, Atlanta and Boston which have settled at a greater geographical distance from the traditional chemicals and pharmaceuticals industrial regions of the manufacturing belt in 'new spaces' (Gray and Parker 1998), the Rhine–Neckar Triangle region has always been characterised by the strong presence of the chemicals and pharmaceuticals industries. In the United States the modernisation of the pharmaceuticals and diagnostics industries would seem to succeed in 'mature' locations without any direct geographical contact with the young life sciences industries, without operating their own Research and Development facilities in their respective regions. Co-operation occurs through alliances and networks across great distances (Prevezer 1997: 257). In the Rhine–Neckar-Triangle BioRegion the local chemical and pharmaceutical giants are also involved in numerous co-operative relationships over large distances. The main emphasis still lies on transatlantic co-operation. On the other hand, the increasing importance of young, innovative life sciences companies in the region offers the opportunity for the large established companies to discover opportunities for co-operating at short distances and thus to benefit from geographical proximity.

The considerably extended backdrop of small life sciences companies, of which some are very fast growing, is an important basis for improving co-operation between young life sciences companies and large-scale companies in the region which operate on a global level. Such intra-regional co-operation and business relations are of great significance for developing clusters in biotechnology. We shall, therefore, devote ourselves in the following to the question of the extent to which such co-operation already exists in the region and which are the barriers hindering the further development of co-operative relationships. In this connection, the attitude of local (large-scale) industry towards the newly emerging life sciences companies in the direct vicinity is most interesting. In other words, are co-operations, business relationships and 'strategic alliances' – for instance for joint product developments, research projects or for achieving exclusive customer relations (licence agreements, patent rights) between the local pharmaceuticals and diagnostic industry and the young innovators in the life sciences disciplines – actually being achieved? Or, in spite of existing technological and thematic points of connection, is preference given to the global network and global co-operation?

The life sciences industries in the Rhine–Neckar Triangle are still at an early stage of development. It has already been mentioned that more than half of the life sciences companies located in the Rhine–Neckar Triangle were established after 1995. Inasmuch as one can speak of a biotechnology cluster around Heidelberg and the Rhine–Neckar-Triangle BioRegion, this means that it is still in a relatively early stage of development: practical business relations between the new and the well-established companies in the region are – apart from a few exceptions – still very underdeveloped.[9] It seems as if up to now co-operation agreements for the purpose of joint product developments (application of prototypes) are, on the whole, the exception to the rule. This is astonishing in view of the fact that it may be assumed that the local pharmaceutical companies could easily observe the development of the young life sciences companies in the immediate vicinity and then pick up on the new technologies and integrate them in their process and production structures. It is also remarkable that this is not restricted to the very new, small biotechnology firms but also applies to the better known innovative companies. The following statement by the founder of a new company (interview with the authors) illustrates this well:

> I would describe the attitude of the established firms as generally positive, yet, at the same time, indifferent, for when actual orders come up, the positive interest suddenly dissipates. Of the orders currently being processed, there is not a single one from the region surrounding the company, i.e. none from local or regional industry. I

experience this attitude as one of arrogant indifference rather than being directly adverse.

Large-scale industry tends to seek business relations and co-operative partnerships in the form of alliances with US life sciences companies. The main reason for this is possibly the years of experience of German companies and US life sciences companies, as well as the technological edge due to many years of commercialisation and industrial exploitation. Frequently, references have been made to the fact that the mentalities and ways of thinking characteristic of the executive level of German pharmaceuticals industries are determined by the temporal context. The managing director and founder of one young life sciences company stated that there is a strong tendency towards the 'not invented here' syndrome – anything that had not been discovered and developed by the respective firm itself was first of all blocked out, particularly on executive levels. This attitude was extremely conservative and a real 'innovation inhibitor' in the German pharmaceuticals industry.

Co-operative efforts among the biotechnology firms are limited to an exceptional few. With a high degree of specialisation and complementary technology platforms, joint projects are seldom realised (particularly in the research of active substances). In spite of the frequently selected 'niche' strategy and aggressive patenting strategies, clear-cut competitiveness is still predominant. The present status of commercial interaction in clusters must be seen in the context of a very early stage of development in which the established pharmaceuticals companies are currently still playing the part of neutral observers of the emerging life sciences scene. Common interest is mainly reduced to improving the conditions of life sciences Research and Development in the Rhine–Neckar Triangle and in Germany.

Although Germany has been able to catch up to a certain degree on Great Britain with a boom in founding new companies, German biotechnology companies' relatively smaller proportion in terms of turnover and R&D (in relation to the actual number of companies) indicates the deficits which still exist if the German life sciences industry is compared to the international situation. The second biotechnology report of Ernst and Young (2000) confirms that in the meantime Germany has, on the one hand, even outstripped Britain in terms of the number of biotechnology companies but, on the other, that German biotech firms still lag behind their British and French counterparts with regard to size and maturity. In particular, German biotechnology firms are rather small on average and specialised in niche markets. One may imagine that it is easier for such companies to get established during a period of radical change than during a period of consolidation of a new technological sector or industry. The major risk for such enterprises may be failure due to a lack of links to strong incumbents just when the technological field is about to be consolidated. As experience in the telecommunication sector of those countries having privatised telecommunications, which led to a rise of numerous small private telephone companies, indicates, it is a fear that in the field of industrial biotechnology many of these new enterprises will also disappear in the future. This may also be a significant risk for the biotechnology companies located in the Rhine–Neckar-Triangle BioRegion: as with German biotechnology companies in general, the biotech firms of the Rhine–Neckar Triangle are specialised in technology-based services (such as contract research and research on demand), or production on demand, as well as in so-called platform technologies. In contrast, the proportion of biotechnology firms working primarily in the field of the development of new drugs is relatively weak compared to the corresponding figures on the European and global level (for Germany, see Casper 1999: 21). In addition, among those few enterprises only a third engage in the development of new products, the remaining two-thirds supply the technologies related to it (Ernst and Young 2000). The major part of the development of new products is concentrated in the field of oncology, i.e. research and development of agents for cancer therapy. In the field of platform technologies, there is a dominance of technologies linked to the sequencing and elucidation of the functions of the human genome.

Casper (1999) has interpreted this predominance of enterprises developing platform technologies as an indicator showing the high priority given to incremental innovations in the German bio-industry, and therefore as a variation only of the general orientation typical for the German innovation system. This argument is surprising if one looks at the high innovation dynamics and the short innovation cycles which particularly characterise the field of platform technologies and which subject enterprises to a high innovation pressure, forcing them to launch new products onto the market with relatively short delays.[10] Relations with clients are generally not very stable, since the big clients often change their suppliers for platform technologies. Thus enterprises offering such platform technologies regard themselves increasingly exposed to external, rapidly changing requirements, so that they have great difficulties in evaluating and anticipating the risks. They find themselves in a rather fragile dependency *vis-à-vis* the changing needs of their clients, amongst them especially the big incumbent firms.

In view of these uncertainties, it seems likely that the relatively high number of enterprises offering platform technologies and technology-based services in Germany and in the Rhine–Neckar-Triangle BioRegion is linked to the lagging behind of the biotechnology industry and its weak and fragile starting point. On this view, biotechnology in Germany, on the one hand, has developed relatively late when many fields were already occupied by US firms; on the other hand, projects in the development of therapeutic products would have required a great staying power and much higher stability of the firms, of their core competencies and above all of their relation to hospitals and academic research institutions,[11] but also a certain firm size.[12] In general, the field of therapeutics seems to be characterised by a much higher intensity of relations than the field of platform technologies. In this respect, the Rhine–Neckar-Triangle BioRegion still had some deficits, i.e. the biotechnological networks started to develop later than in the American and British bioregions. The same is true for the establishment and development of a strong regional venture capital industry which may lean on the experiences and competencies necessary for the establishment of young high-tech firms.[13] For example, an important advantage of the Californian biotechnology districts was the existence of an already well-developed venture capital industry which did not only dispose of the necessary financial means, but also of the necessary know-how, based on multiple experiences in other high-tech sectors. Up until now, it has been difficult to forecast whether the strategy of focusing on platform technologies, on technology-based services and on research on demand is promising in the long term. This will depend much on the importance German firms will have for the big global players and if they will be of interest to the latter in their capacity as suppliers.

By contrast with biotechnology regions in other countries which have evolved at a greater physical distance from the traditional pharmaceutical locations, the closeness of the biotechnology and chemicals and pharmaceuticals industry in the Rhine–Neckar-Triangle BioRegion offers the opportunity for the region to develop a specific competence profile to equip it for global competition in life sciences. It could be the future basis for achieving lasting regional value creation and growth effects. It is not, however, possible at present to judge conclusively to what degree the region is able to make use of this opportunity.

Institutional infrastructure supporting development of life sciences

An industry such as biotechnology dependent on the permanent influx of information and on financially sound external investors requires a suitable environment with supporting institutions which are open-minded towards technology and can satisfy the needs of the biotechnology companies. The following describes the most significant dimensions of the institutional environment in the Rhine–Neckar-Triangle BioRegion and demonstrates initial changes regarding an improvement of the situation for industrial biotechnology in the region.

Internationally reputable highly developed basic research

The Rhine–Neckar Triangle exhibits a high concentration of public and private research centres. There are some twenty universities and specialist colleges as well as extensive research capacities outside the universities, both in the private and public sector located in the Rhine–Neckar-Triangle BioRegion. Research activities in the commercial sector are of particular significance. These are particularly well developed in this region and are well above the German average, which is in itself high (Egeln *et al.* 1996: 119). In the university sector and publicly financed non-university research institutions it is conspicuous that by comparison with the rest of Germany there is a far higher proportion of research capacity for legal, economic, social science and medical research. By contrast, engineering disciplines are poorly represented in the region. The main focus in this research infrastructure is on medicine, biosciences and physics. Institutions of international reputation such as the German Cancer Research Centre (DKFZ), the European Molecular Biology Laboratory (EMBL), the Heidelberg Centre of Molecular Biology (ZMBH) and the Max Planck Institute of Medical Research, the Max Planck Institute of Astronomy and the Max Planck Institute of Nuclear Physics are all located in Heidelberg.

The high concentration of bioscience research capacities can be seen from the statistics of the number of researchers at the research institutions working in these fields: almost 3,330 scientists are involved in public universities and publicly financed non-university research institutes in biotechnology research projects. Among them are institutions with an excellent international scientific reputation (see Initiativkreis 'BioRegion Rhein–Neckar-Dreieck' 1996: 7). In addition to these research capacities in public basic research, the chemicals and pharmaceuticals industries maintain considerable research capacities in life sciences. The most intensive research activity in 1996 was carried out by what was then Boehringer Mannheim (today Roche Diagnostics), followed by BASF, Knoll and Merck (see Initiativkreis 'BioRegion Rhein–Neckar-Dreieck' 1996: 9).

Finance institutions and public promotion assistance

By tradition, the venture capital market in Germany is underdeveloped. The state has attempted to compensate for this deficiency in venture capital and the lack of readiness to take risks on the part of private financial services and banks by financing unconventional, i.e. more risky, innovative and technology projects of existing firms and on the part of those which have yet to be formed, by means of assistance/grant programmes and state-subsidised finance instruments. In the past there have been various programmes for supporting the formation of technology-based companies, both at a national level and at the level of the respective federal states. The first promotion assistance programmes were initiated at the national level in the mid-1980s.[14] The Deutsche Ausgleichsbank (German Compensation Bank), the Technologiebeteiligungsgesellschaft (tbg) (Technology Investment Company) of the Deutsche Ausgleichsbank and the Kreditanstalt für Wiederaufbau (KfW) (Credit Institute for Reconstruction) play a central role. The Deutsche Ausgleichsbank offers different programmes for forming new businesses (e.g. Government capital resources aid programme, European Recovery Programme (ERP) scheme for the promotion of new company formations, sleeping partnership interest in new technology companies through the tbg). By contrast, the Kreditanstalt für Wiederaufbau provides refinancing loans for investment companies intending to invest venture capital in young technology companies.

On the *Land* level there is a broad spectrum of programmes in Baden-Württemberg for the promotion and support of company formations (particularly technology-based company formations). These programmes are usually in conjunction with low-interest and long-term loans, easier access to venture capital, bank guarantees, sleeping partnership interests, non-repayable grants, formation consultations, co-operative research projects and the improvement of the general conditions for company founders ('On-campus founder associations', company formation initiatives, etc.).

This promotion system is relatively complicated. The risks are reduced by means of a multi-level system of back-to-back guarantees and they are spread over several institutions. Thus risk connected with a loan is spread over the federal government, the *Land*, the guarantee bank, the borrower's bank and investment bank. Past practice has, however, shown that the finance instruments created by the government have only been able to contribute to a small degree towards eliminating the gaps in financing young companies and pioneering technological projects. In practice, state-subsidised and secured loans for young technology companies tended to be granted to those innovative companies linked with experience-based technology paths and striving towards innovations effecting mainly incremental improvements rather than to those with more radical innovation projects in new fields of technology (Krauss 1997).

In this instance, the BioRegio competition has brought about an improvement in the supply of venture capital for life sciences companies on the local and regional level. For instance, the Rhine–Neckar Triangle prize-winning concept in the BioRegio competition envisaged among other things the formation of a venture capital fund 'Heidelberg Innovation GmbH BioScience Venture KG' (BSV). A first fund was formed in 1997. The fund capital of the company has gradually been extended to some DEM 25 million (part of these funds was refinanced through the Kreditanstalt für Wiederaufbau). Among the limited partners in the fund were the most important industrial companies in the region (although these were in the minority) as well as credit institutes and savings banks operating on a supra-regional level. This Seed Capital Fund – by contrast to the finance institutes operating with state promotion assistance funds – provided active venture capital and worked on a profit-making basis, i.e. it financed itself from the profits of selling shares in the companies when they go up. A second fund with some 113 million euro was formed in 2000 (BSV II).

By contrast to the typical venture capital companies which usually only invest in young companies after the second or third year, the first Heidel-berg Venture Capital Fund (BSV) started investing in new biotechnology companies right from the time before and during formation. This had par-tially to do with the creation of the fund in the course of the BioRegio competition; many of the biotechnology firms established during the BioRegio Programme in the region were still very young. On the other hand, it was the intention of the fund to spread its commitments by also investing in low-risk projects. The possibility of having such early access to capital from outside sources for financing company formation was an enormous relief to the respective biotechnology companies because, as a rule, a positive decision on the part of the BSV venture capital fund to become the lead investor prompted further loan commitments on the part of other investors. Additional possibilities for co-financing are then forth-coming from public sector institutions like the technology investment company (tbg) of the Deutsche Ausgleichsbank or the credit institute for reconstruction (KfW). In practice, the first fund has been extremely selec-tive in its investment decisions so that financing in this way has benefited only a small, select circle of new companies.[15] With the progressive devel-opment of the industrial sector in biotechnology, the geographical limita-tion of the funds' activities to the Rhine–Neckar Triangle is increasingly proving to be a weakness: it meant that the expansion of business was restricted right from the beginning and the cross-border learning process in connection with the support of highly innovative biotechnology companies was more difficult. Although the geographical limitation was originally intended, it hindered the co-operation with potential co-investors outside the region. For this reason, the second fund, BSV II, was designed as a clas-sical venture capital firm, operating without any geographical restrictions.

Promotional concepts as part of industrial policy in Baden-Württemberg

By comparison with other federal *Länder*, there are some special features in Baden-Württemberg's policy for the promotion of life sciences. The variety of approaches and the relatively large number of biotechnology regions – in relation to the size of the *Land* – reflect the polycentric struc-ture of Baden-Württemberg. Apart from the Rhine–Neckar-Triangle BioRegion, Baden-Württemberg has another three BioRegions: the Bio-Region of Ulm, the Stuttgart-Neckar-Alb BioRegion and the BioRegion around Freiburg. This makes it more difficult to implement a concentrated promotion policy for biotechnology clusters. It also causes additional co-ordination requirements for the implementation of promotion policy. A central biotechnology agency (originally located in Karlsruhe in associ-ation with the Fraunhofer Institut ISI and, since 1999, located with the Steinbeis Stiftung in Stuttgart) which provides a broad range of consulting services, is also confronted with the problem of having to take into account the different interests of the respective biotechnology regions in Baden-Württemberg. This makes it really impossible to link the individual BioRegio action groups effectively. Indeed, the four BioRegions are engaged in competition with one another (for instance with respect to the settlement of foreign companies). Therefore promotion on the part of the *Land* is not geared to concentrate resources. It is instead a moderate promotion policy which takes developments in all four bioregions seriously. This limits the possibility of marketing the life sciences region in a uniform manner. Thus the Rhine–Neckar-Triangle BioRegion is confronted with the problem of having to promote cluster formation in the region to a great extent on its own, and activate additional support from outside the region. In addition, the engagement of the other two *Länder* affected apart from Baden-Württemberg varies a lot. For example, the *Land* of Hesse seems to play a clearly less active role in supporting biotechnology in the Rhine–Neckar Triangle than does the *Land* of Rhineland-Palatinate. Since BioRegio promotion activities on the part of the Federal government have actually came to an end and promotion policies have been changed, there is an additional incentive for those active in the region to think about suitable strategies for further promoting biotechnology industry in the Rhine–Neckar-Triangle BioRegion.

There are other institutions in the region, some of which have been in existence since the mid-1980s, which are important for the integration of biotechnology in the region; some new institutions emerged in the course of the BioRegio competition. Of particular significance, for instance, is the Heidelberg Technology Park founded in 1985, offering a favourable infrastructure to company founders since the mid-1980s, which has developed an image as a life sciences park. By contrast with many other technology centres in Baden-Württemberg it has demonstrated a very strong focus on technology (average proportion of biotechnology companies is 70 per cent) and has a special position due to its close relations with the university environment in Heidelberg.

The proximity to the research institutions on the campus of Heidelberg University proved advantageous. The close proximity promoted the early formation of a local biotechnology scene which is characterised by multifarious informal communication with the scientific community. The Technology Park is an important institutional platform for this, of which the BioRegio activity group took advantage. The Technology Park publishes a bi-monthly newsletter, arranges monthly meetings to which the staff of all the firms are invited (TP-Apero) and organises a regular forum in the DKFZ at which one firm is presented each time and which provides an opportunity to get to know the really important individuals in the field of biotechnology in Heidelberg. Some 300 personalities from science, banks, large-scale industry, politics, small and medium-sized companies are invited to these Technology Park Forums which take place about three times a year. During the hour-and-a-half lunch meeting many informal talks take place.

Finally, the BioRegio competition prompted the creation of further institutions. The BioRegio plan for the region included the foundation of a biotechnology centre at Heidelberg (Biotechnologiezentrum Heidelberg BTH) which consists of three legally independent units: 'The Rhine–Neckar-Triangle BioRegion e.V. (registered non-profit association), Heidelberg Innovation GmbH and the aforementioned Seed Capital Fund. This centre was established in the Heidelberg Technology Park. While the Rhine–Neckar-Triangle BioRegion association was responsible for pre-competitive activities, Heidelberg Innovation is located at the interface with the competitive sector, offering services to biotech start-ups as a management company operating the Heidelberg Innovation GmbH BioScience Venture KG Fund and acting as central co-ordinating body for those intending to form companies in the region, closing the circle between pre-competitive basic research and market-oriented company forming.

The Rhine–Neckar-Triangle BioRegion e.V. was founded in October 1996 as a registered non-profit association for the purpose of promoting research and science in the field of biotechnology, after the Rhine–Neckar-Triangle BioRegion was appointed as one of three model regions by the Federal German Ministry of Education, Science, Research and Technology (BMBF) in its BioRegio competition. The region received promotion funds worth a total of DEM 50 million from the BMBF. These funds were intended for a 5-year promotion period (1997 to 2001). However, the Rhine–Neckar-Triangle BioRegion committed almost all the funds in the first 3 years. They were used to support pre-competitive R&D projects in molecular biotechnology, the results of which can, within a clearly defined period, be developed into products suitable for the capital market. The objective of the association was to identify projects worth promoting and to give priority to criteria of scientific quality, degree of innovation and application relevance when evaluating projects. The prerequisite condition for receiving support was the prospect of possible commercialisation in the medium term – preferably by forming companies: the commercialisation of the project results was to be effected in the region and at least 50 per cent of the costs of the project had to be covered by private participation. The 'Committee' (Kuratorium) of the Rhine–Neckar-Triangle BioRegion e.V. was created for the evaluation of the planned projects, an independent body of experts consisting of seven representatives each from science and industry. This committee submitted recommendations determining which projects should be supported by BMBF in the context of the BioRegio promotion. In practice, its decisions formed the basis for BioRegio promotion measures in the Rhine–Neckar-Triangle BioRegion. The association also fulfilled other functions, including accompanying and supporting the projects receiving promotion assistance, making contacts in the region, publicity[16] and, finally, co-operating with existing institutions in order to intensify patenting activities.

The nucleus of the business activities of Heidelberg Innovation consists, by contrast, in various services for company founders. Heidelberg Innovation (HI) offers its customers advice and support in return for a small participating interest in the companies to be formed. The performance specifications of HI includes the identification of promising ideas for projects, the evaluation of the technology involved from the point of view of the customer and of the market, the identification of strategic competitive advantages, support in defining development objectives, support in working out patenting strategies, development of financing strategies on the basis of a jointly conceived business plan and, finally, support by the 'Heidelberg Innovation Frühphasenprogramm EOS' (early phase programme – start-up aid for company forming). Heidelberg Innovation regards itself as co-entrepreneur and is paid for its consulting services in shares in the new company. The company has four main shareholders which are the four large pharmaceuticals companies in the region. This led to a degree of mistrust on the part of potential company founders especially in the initial phase. Now the company's autonomy from the pharmaceutical giants is no longer questioned; the possibility of their gaining access to new know-how has since been clearly precluded. The company received start-up financing amounting to DEM 3.6 million from the BMBF in addition to the shareholder capital.

Concluding remarks

The purpose of the present chapter has been to trace the first steps towards developing the Rhine–Neckar Triangle region from a competence centre for biotechnology basic research into a high-tech life sciences district and to analyse this process. In spite of the high density of research institutions with international reputations, it took a long time for structures for commercialising biotechnology to emerge in the region to any extent worth mentioning. State-financed basic research in Heidelberg certainly had a stimulating effect on applied R&D projects in the private sector. However, this value creation did not take place in the region but generally at distant locations, usually in the US life sciences districts. This points to a characteristic element in biotechnology as a whole, namely the tremendous importance of know-how transfer. Commercialisation of scientific findings happens in places which already dispose of special competence in commercialising biotechnology know-how and where the basic conditions are favourable. In the past there were extreme deficits in this sphere, both in Germany and in the Rhine–Neckar Triangle. Know-how proved to be extremely mobile with the result that the region where new findings and know-how had been generated was not necessarily able to participate in the ensuing value creation. On the other hand, the experience in the USA showed that an important part in the know-how transfer happens in the region itself; it requires short paths and the relatively informal relationship between the parties involved. This applies in particular to the kind of knowledge which is directly linked to a specific person (tacit knowledge).

The Rhine–Neckar-Triangle BioRegion therefore evolved – stimulated by the BioRegio competition – on the basis of the intention of well-known individuals in the field to advance the social integration process of this technology in order to be able to keep the additional value created in life sciences in the region. Despite the favourable start-up conditions, in practice the project to form life sciences clusters in the region met with great difficulties and obstacles. Above all, established companies in related branches of industry, particularly the powerful chemical and pharmaceutical industry in the Rhine–Neckar Triangle, were late in taking an interest in the new technologies and, when they did, they gave preference to US life sciences companies in their attempt to make up lost ground. In the USA, this sector was considerably more advanced in its development which meant that this strategy pursued by the industrial establishment was indeed perfectly rational.

In the meantime there is a considerably greater density of life sciences companies and jobs in biotechnology in the Rhine–Neckar-Triangle BioRegion. However, the region is still in a relatively early stage with regard to the formation of a biotechnology cluster which is integrated in the region. The increase in the number of life sciences companies is an important prerequisite for cluster formation; it does not, however, automatically imply that a cluster will indeed be formed. Although there are a number of potential starting points, in our opinion there are still deficits in the interactive and co-operative relations between the biotechnology companies and the industrial pharmaceutical companies in the region. This is due, on the one hand, to the still insufficient number of companies in spite of the boom in newly formed companies and, on the other hand, to the relative early phase of the technological development of many of the newly formed biotechnology companies. For this reason there is currently a greater tendency towards supra-regional and international co-operative relations.

In sum, the case of the Rhine–Neckar-Triangle BioRegion confirms the great importance of global know-how transfer and international co-operation. The more non-codified know-how plays a role, however, the more in addition a regional component is present. This kind of know-how is similarly not transferable over large distances. This directs the attention more to the co-operative relationships and networks in the region. In addition, especially with regard to the younger and smaller biotech firms, the question arises concerning the possible or necessary support of regional networks, so that new high-tech firms have a chance in the global competition (Krauss 1999c). In this respect, it can be established for the Rhine–Neckar-Triangle BioRegion that within a short time period new intermediary institutions have been developed which particularly favour the integration of the companies in networks and with which the companies co-operate more closely. This is an encouraging development with regard to the development of a cluster in the region. On the other hand, there are still some weaknesses indicating the insufficient cluster development in the region. For example, one could mention the problems in inducing more scientists of the local and regional research institutions to start-up their own biotechnology company and finally, already mentioned, the up-to-now rather low intensity of inter-firm co-operative relationships in the bioregion.

Last but not least, the structure of the life sciences industry in the Rhine–Neckar-Triangle BioRegion shows certain weaknesses in an international comparison. As is the case in Germany as a whole, there is a one-sided emphasis on biotechnology services companies, contract research companies and companies with enabling, i.e. platform technologies. Some companies formed right from the beginning of Bio Regis promotion, which have proved to be extremely dynamic and fast-growing at the end of the 1990s (e.g. Lion BioScience) are now faced with serious difficulties.

The BioRegio competition also made an important contribution towards the general atmosphere of a new beginning in life sciences in the Rhine–Neckar-Triangle BioRegion. Important supporting institutions have emerged and a biotechnology scene is just beginning to develop which has, however, not yet had any impact in terms of viable co-operative relationships between companies in the region. In the meantime the promotion programme for the Rhine–Neckar Triangle is de facto over in view of the fact that the region had exhausted the BioRegio funds after the first 3 years (the other two model regions used up their fund even quicker). This makes no difference to the stimulating effects over the first 3–4 years (including the preparatory phase of the programme). It remains to be seen how cluster formation will continue to develop in the face of changed promotion policies on the federal government level. Since the change of government in 1998 there has been a shift in the emphasis of promotion policy. It seems that there is a shift away from a direct promotion of biotechnology clusters in just a few selected regions. Therefore the Rhine–Neckar-Triangle BioRegion is faced with the challenge of continuing with regional cluster formation in future without external political and financial flanking measures. Now that the BioRegio funds are exhausted, the region must endeavour to press on with the cluster formation process on its own. This is an ambitious task in view of the increasing competitiveness between the German bioregions and the differences in the industrial policies in the responsible Federal *Länder* responsible (and a moderate promotion policy in Baden-Württemberg).

Notes

1 In the meantime Roche decided to upgrade the location of Penzberg by concentrating activities here formerly divided between Tutzing and Penzberg.
2 The BioRegio competition initiated by the BMBF (Federal German Ministry of Education and Research) confirmed three of the four former genetic engineering centres as model biotechnology regions. Only Berlin failed to qualify for the designation as a 'model region' in favour of Jena (now referred to as a BioRegion with 'special status').
3 Similarly, developments in other newly emerging industries are influenced by the polycentric structure of Baden-Württemberg as well. An example is the field of multimedia (Krauss and Wolf 2002).
4 A practical example of links between Heidelberger Zement AG (Heidelberg Cement) and Orpegen was a project for microbiological measures to optimise biological water purification and the monitoring of microbiological interaction in waste water by means of measurement technology. The reasons why Heidelberger Zement AG was so interested in this project was that even today, in the age of plastic drainage pipes, almost all plant and installation through which waste water flows are made of concrete which can be eroded by bacteria corrosive to cement (Industrie- und Handelskammer Rhein–Neckar/Deutsches Krebsforschungszentrum 1995: 45).
5 In the meantime there were even complaints concerning the lack of new, innovative projects. Compared with the amount of capital available there were too few innovative ideas on the part of the company founders (Schitag, Ernst and Young 1998: 24). However, the capital available also depends on macroeconomic factors and the general situation at the stock exchange for young technological companies (e.g. new market, Nasdaq). After the bursting of the Internet bubble, and with increasing capital demands, the situation has again become more difficult for young biotech companies.
6 Baden-Württemberg comprises four (!) different bioregions which is a lot compared to the size of the *Land*: the Rhine–Neckar Triangle, the bioregion Stuttgart–Neckar–Alb, the 'BioValley' around Freiburg and the bioregion Ulm.
7 Compared to its competing bioregions, the local/regional supporting institutions in Heidelberg seem to be rather demanding and thus more selective in their choice of projects and start-ups to finance.
8 These formations are not strictly regarded as new. This does not reflect a valuation on the part of the authors since the amount of foreign direct investment is surely an effective indicator of the quality of the location.
9 This does not, however, mean that a number of these extremely research-oriented biotechnology companies are not already engaged in initial, preparatory talks (also with companies in the region).
10 This calls into question the hypothesis according to which in the field of platform technologies the scientific competencies would be less stable than in firms developing therapeutics. This hypothesis was put forward first by Casper (1999) who affirms that research in the field of platform technologies would, in general, not have the same competency destroying effect as in therapeutic research. Casper (1999: 22) writes: 'Because the platform technologies are generic, scientific competencies are generally much more stable than in therapeutic firms. Unlike most therapeutic research, platform technology research is generally not competency destroying.'
11 As a consequence, the scientific importance of these projects is also higher. For example, scientific publications quote patents in the field of therapeutics much more often than in the field of platform technologies.

12 US biotech firms have a bigger average firm size. However, one should not forget the R&D efforts of the big German companies also engaged in the development of therapeutics, profiting from their great financial muscle and having their own research programs.

13 'Although capital is often described as footloose and fungible, the manner in which venture capital investing takes place is strongly tied to location' (Zook 2000). In fact, 'regional systems of personal contacts and networks through which scarce information is quickly exchanged, flexibility is maintained and resources can be invested expeditiously' prove to be decisive – even in sectors such as information and communication technologies (ICT) (Zook 2000).

14 1983–1988: 'Technology-oriented company forming' Programme TOU, 1989–1994; Venture capital for young technology companies (BJTU) and – since 1995 – Venture capital for small technology companies (BTU).

15 Since Heidelberg Innovation GmbH was founded, of 111 outline concepts for the formation of companies only seven participating interests have been taken out. In all, thirteen firms have been formed with the assistance of Heidelberg Innovation (information material Heidelberg Innovation GmbH, November 1999).

16 Some examples: co-operation in the exhibition 'Gene Worlds' by the *Land* museum for technology and labour in Mannheim, the 'School-Ethics-Technology' programme, lectures on the acceptance of biotechnology and various workshops and congresses.

References

Arbeitskreis Rhein–Neckar-Dreieck e.V. (Working Group, Rhine–Neckar Triangle, registered association) (ed.) (1998) *Das Rhein–Neckar-Dreieck Daten und Fakten*, Mannheim.

Audretsch, D.B. and Stephan, P.E. (1996) 'Company–Scientist Locational Links: The Case of Biotechnology', *American Economic Review*, 86(3): 641–52.

Barnett, R., Clements, Gary J., Grindley, J.N., MacKenzie, N.M., Roos, U. and Yarrow, D. (1998) *Biotechnology in Germany*, Report of an IST Expert Mission, Bonn: British Embassy.

BMFT (Bundesministerium für Forschung und Technologie [Federal German Ministry of Research and Technology]) (ed.) (1993) *Bericht zur Förderung der Genzentren*, Bonn.

Casper, S. (1999) 'National Institutional Frameworks and High Technology Innovation in Germany. The Case of Biotechnology', Discussion Paper FS I 99–306. Berlin: Wissenschaftszentrum für Sozialforschung.

Dolata, U. (1991) 'Forschungsprogramme, Genzentren, Verbundforschung – Vernetzungsstrukturen und Steuerungsmechanismen der bio- und gentechnischen Forschung in der Bundesrepublik', WSI-Mitteilungen, 44(10): 628ff.

—— (1994) 'Nachholende Modernisierung und internationales Innovationsmanagement – Strategien der deutschen Chemie- und Pharmakonzerne', in T. von Schell and H. Mohr, (eds) *Biotechnologie – Gentechnik. Eine Chance für neue Industrien*, Berlin: Springer: 456–80.

—— (1996) *Politische Ökonomie der Gentechnik. Konzernstrategien, Forschungsprogramme, Technologiewettläufe*, Berlin: Sigma.

—— (1999) 'Innovationsnetzwerke in der Biotechnologie?', WSI-Mitteilungen 2/1999: 132–41.

Egeln, J., Erbsland, M., Hügel, A., Schmidt, P. and Seitz, H. (1996) *Der Wirtschaftsstandort 'Rhein–Neckar-Dreieck'. Standortprofil und Unternehmensdynamik*, Baden-Baden: Nomos.

Ernst and Young (2000) *Gründerzeit. Ernst & Youngs zweiter deutscher Biotechnologie-Report 2000*, Stuttgart: Ernst and Young.

Grammel, R. and Iwer, F. (1998) *Mögliche Arbeitsplatzeffekte durch Multimedia in ausgewählten Regionen Baden-Württembergs*, Arbeitsbericht Nr. 81, Akademie für Technikfolgenabschätzung in Baden-Württemberg, Stuttgart, 2. überarbeitete Auflage Februar 1998.

Gray, M. and Parker, E. (1998) 'Industrial change and regional development: the case of the US biotechnology and pharmaceutical industries', in *Environment and Planning*, 30: 1757–74.

Heidenreich, M. and Krauss, G. (1998) 'The Baden-Württemberg Production and Innovation Regime: Past Successes and New Challenges', in H.-J. Braczyk, P. Cooke and M. Heidenreich (eds) [with editorial assistance from Gerhard Krauss] *Regional Innovation Systems: The Role of Governances in a Globalized World*, London: UCL Press: 214–44.

Industrie- und Handelskammer Rhein–Neckar/Deutsches Krebsforschungszentrum (Rhine–Neckar Chamber of Industry and Commerce/German Cancer Research Centre) (eds) (1995) *Biotechnik. Tagungsband zum Technologie-Kongreß 1995*, Darmstadt: Hoppenstedt-Verlag.

Initiativkreis 'BioRegion Rhein–Neckar-Dreieck' ('Rhine–Neckar-Triangle Bio-Region' Action Group) (1996) 'BioRegionen Rhein–Neckar-Dreieck', Antrag zum BioRegio-Wettbewerb, 1.

Köhler, I. (1998) 'Biotechnologie in Deutschland – Aufbruchstimmung in Baden-Württemberg' (Handout to the presentation at the Innovationsbörse Biotechnologie, 9. Juli 1998, Heidelberg).

Krauss, G. (1997) *Technologieorientierte Unternehmensgründungen in Baden-Württemberg*, Arbeitsbericht Nr. 77, Akademie für Technikfolgenabschätzung in Baden-Württemberg, Stuttgart.

—— (1999a) 'Les problèmes d'adaptation d'une économie régionale forte: changement et inerties en Bade-Wurtemberg' [Steering Problems in a Vibrant Regional Economy: Keeping Baden-Württemberg Technology Firms on Track], *Revue d'Économie Régionale et Urbaine* (RERU), 1999/2: 353–76.

—— (1999b) *Technologieorientierte Unternehmensgründungen in einer sich wandelnden Regionalökonomie: Unterstützungsmodelle für die Praxis in Baden-Württemberg*, Arbeitsbericht Nr. 148, Akademie für Technikfolgenabschätzung in Baden-Württemberg, Stuttgart.

—— (1999c) 'Technologieorientierte Unternehmensgründungen – zur Bedeutung regionaler Netzwerke im Zeitalter der Globalisierung', in G. Fuchs, G. Krauss and H.-G. Wolf (eds) *Die Bindungen der Globalisierung: Interorganisationsbeziehungen im regionalen und globalen Wirtschaftsraum*, Marburg: Metropolis-Verlag: 285–308.

Krauss, G. and Wolf, H.-G. (2002) 'Technological Strengths in Mature Sectors – An Impediment or an Asset for Regional Economic Restructuring? The Case of Multimedia and Biotechnology in Baden-Württemberg', *Journal of Technology Transfer* (Special Issue 'Regional Innovation Systems in Europe', edited by P. Cooke, L. Leydesdorff and M. Olazaran) January, 27(1): 39–50.

Manth, S. (1995) 'Die Biotechnologie in der pharmazeutischen Industrie', in M.

Lonsert, K.-J. Preuß and E. Kucher (eds) *Handbuch Pharma-Management*, 2, Wiesbaden: 802–26.

Prevezer, M. (1997) 'The Dynamics of Industrial Clustering in Biotechnology', *Small Business Economics* 9: 255–71.

Schitag, Ernst and Young (1998) *Aufbruchstimmung 1998. Der erste Report der Schitag, Ernst & Young Unternehmensberatung über die Biotechnologie-Industrie in Deutschland*, Stuttgart: Schitag, Ernst and Young.

Strambach, S. (1995) *Wissensintensive unternehmensorientierte Dienstleistungen: Netzwerke und Interaktion – am Beispiel des Rhein–Neckar-Raumes*, Münster: Lit Verlag, Vol. 6.

Theisen, H. (1991) *Bio- und Gentechnologie – Eine politische Herausforderung*, Stuttgart, Berlin, Köln: Kohlhammer.

VRS (Verband Region Stuttgart) (1999) *Triplett 9/99, Biotech-News von A-Z*, Stuttgart.

Zook, M.A. (2000) 'Grounded Capital: Venture Capital's Role in the Clustering of Internet Firms in the US', Paper prepared for the Association of Collegiate Schools of Planning 2000 Conference, Atlanta, GA, 1–5 November 2000.

7 French biotech start-ups and biotech clusters in France

The importance of geographic proximity[1]

Frederic Corolleur, Vincent Mangematin,[2] André Torre and Stephane Lemarié

Based on a survey of French biotech small and medium-sized enterprises (SMEs) (see Annex 1), this chapter examines localisation effects in the biotechnology sector. It consists of two strands of analysis. The first presents a detailed statistical survey of the French biotechnology sector. Among other things, the survey shows that a) localisation effects within France are strong, and b) French firms can be grouped into four general types of firm, ranging from 'type 1' growth-oriented product firms, to 'type 2' niche market players, 'type 3' subsidiaries of larger firms, and 'type 4' firms that have been acquired. Localisation effects differ across these firms, especially across type 1 (international) and type 2 (very localised) firms. The second strand of analysis consists of a review of the localisation and related cluster literature, with implications identified for localisation and knowledge spill-overs within biotech clusters. The relative effects of the proximity of scientific centres compared to public policy on start-ups is examined.

Introduction

Biotechnology can be defined as a set of techniques and knowledge which are related to the use of living organisms in production processes and are the outcome of recent advances in molecular biology (Ducos and Joly 1988). The division of work is at the centre of research on the economics of innovation which accounts for the dynamics of biotechnological knowledge. Each new breakthrough opens onto new hypotheses and sometimes onto a new sub-discipline with research tools, tests and specific competencies, in a process of cumulative discovery. Within this process, academics perform basic research, SMEs explore these new fields of knowledge, and corporations exploit them industrially and commercially (Orsenigo *et al.* 1998, Sharp 1999). Our objective is to analyse the role of geographic proximity in the development of those SMEs. The creation and growth of biotech start-ups and, more generally, high-tech firms, has resulted in the formation of clusters in both the USA and Europe (Feldman 1994, Prevezer 1998, Swann 1999).

Research on the development of biotechnology, carried out in areas of the economics of innovation and the geography of innovation, is based primarily on cases in the USA rather than in Europe. For France, a recent study cán be used to draw up a typology of new biotech firms (Lemarié and Mangematin 2000), thus completing the overview by Ernst and Young (2000). This study shows that on 1 January 1999 France had just over 400 biotechnology SMEs employing 15,000 people, with an estimated turnover of F13 billion. Estimates based on the survey initiated by the French Ministry for Education, Research and Technology are consistent with the information published by Ernst and Young, although they indicate a higher number of firms in France. The average size in terms of the number of employees is nevertheless similar (about forty persons). The majority were founded after 1990 (70 per cent of the sample). Most of the recent firms aim for the pharmaceutical sector. The second sector in terms of the number of firms and employees is agriculture and the agro-food sector. Firms involved in ag-biotech are older than those which aim for the pharmaceutical sector (Lemarié and Mangematin 2000).

Most of these new biotech firms were created in the Ile-de-France region, especially at the Evry Génopole, and close to the main French scientific poles (Lyons, Strasbourg, etc.). From this point of view, the French case resembles the US experience. In the USA the biotechnology sector has developed around centres of scientific excellence (Zucker and Darby 1996, Zucker *et al.* 1998), since the mobility of researchers from academic research centres towards the private sector is a vehicle for the diffusion of knowledge and a powerful incentive for start-ups. Is the constitution of clusters in France similar to the USA? Are the determinants of biotechnology clusters in France the same as those identified for the USA? A review of studies on the determinants of the clustering of productive activities and, more specifically, of innovation, will be proposed in the first part of this chapter. The second part considers the French case in the light of these approaches. The role of institutions and the importance óf the diversity of biotechnology firm models is then discussed in the third part.

How can the clustering of new biotech firms be explained?

Two main categories of analysis are usually applied, based on research conducted in the framework of new economic geography and research on local technological externalities, respectively.

Economic geography and geography of innovation

The first explanation is the one proposed by new economic geográphy (Fujita and Thisse 1997), introducing the possibility of conjoint localisátion of firms in the same space (a town, for example, but rather a region or area of production in the case under consideration here) at the expense of neighbouring or rival spaces. The suggested causes of this polarisation are multiple but we can identify two particularly important ones leading to the establishment of localised increasing returns (Krugman 1991a, 1991b) which maintain a divergent process of localisation of activities: the existence of indivisibilities and the preference for variety. Although the question of indivisibility is hardly relevant for small firms, the instrumentation involved in biotechnology can play a decisive part in the localisation of activities. A start-up cannot invest in heavy equipment that it will use only occasionally. However, these studies focus only on pecuniary externalities, to the exclusion of technological externalities. For P. Krugman, 'knowledge flows are invisible, they leave no paper trail by which they may be measured and tracked' (Krugman 1991a: 53); or else, 'by focusing on pecuniary externalities, we are able to make the analysis much more concrete than if we allowed external economies to arise in some invisible form. (This is particularly true when location is at issue: how far does a technological spillover spill?)' (Krugman 1991b: 485).

Unlike Krugman, Jaffe, Trajtenberg and Henderson analyse pecuniary externalities and their relation to geographic proximity. 'Despite the invisibility of knowledge spillovers, they do leave a paper trail in the form of citations' (Jaffe *et al.* 1993: 26). These three authors, as well as Almeida and Kogut, use patent citations to identify knowledge spillovers and their geographical dimension (Jaffe *et al.* 1993, Almeida and Kogut 1997). Two types of research can be differentiated in the latter type of approach (Feldman 1999).

The first is to try to measure directly the impact of geographic proximity on technological spillovers, which are themselves supposed to enhance innovation performance. Proximity is modelled in terms of distance or geographical coincidence of research units inside the boundaries of a state or a metropolitan area. Despite differences in the modelling and identification of technological spillovers (the patent or innovation identified in the market), the econometric results of Feldman (1994), Audretsch and Feldman (1996a), Jaffe (1989) and Acs *et al.* (1994) all indicate that spillovers are favoured by geographic proximity (for a critical analysis, see Autant-Bernard and Massard 1999).

In the USA, biotech start-ups are localised near poles of academic excellence (Prevezer 1998). More generally, innovation in a given region is closely related to public and private research spending in the region (Feldman 1994). There are no substitution effects between public and private R&D spending. They enhance each other to create areas of expertise (Jaffe *et al.* 1993). Venture capital companies also contribute to the growth of biotechnology clusters. Lerner shows that growth in the number of employees and the sales of start-ups is greater when they are located near venture capital companies. These start-ups also benefit from capital inputs needed for their development of a flow of superior information (Lerner 1996). It is primarily regional public venture capitalists and above all 'business angels' that finance the early stages of SMEs. The main characteristics of these actors is that they are essentially local, they invest small sums and they establish very informal relationships with SMEs (Mason and Harrison 1995).

The second strand of analysis focuses on the role of interactions as sources of knowledge transfers (Zucker and Darby 1996, Zucker *et al.* 1998, Almeida and Kogut 1997, Autant-Bernard and Massard 2000). For Zucker *et al.*, ideas are embodied in individuals who have the skills, knowledge and know-how to engage in technological progress. Their papers analyse the human capital of key individuals rather than the average human capital of the local labour market. Biotech start-ups are localised in regions in which this intellectual capital resides. These star scientists embody knowledge breakthrough techniques that are initially available only at the scientists' laboratory, making it costly for others to obtain and use. These results suggest that the localisation of biotech start-ups and their performance cannot be explained by the presence of universities but by the relationship between renowned academic researchers and biotech firms (Zucker *et al.* 1998). Technological spillovers are no longer abstract, they can be traded (research contracts, licences, etc.). Consequently, the formal institutions that link inventors, capital and markets are important factors explaining the localisation of high-tech firms (Lamoreaux and Sokoloff 1997).

The importance of geographic proximity in question

But if geographic proximity is important for firms' innovation, what are we actually talking about? For economic geography, geographic proximity is a physical distance between actors and is accompanied by transport costs. For the geography of innovation, it is related to the creation of tacit knowledge that firms assimilate. Geographic distance is not the only significant factor here. In order to understand it, it is useful to distinguish and define two concepts: geographic proximity and organisational proximity (Torre and Gilly 2000).

Geographic proximity concerns spatial separation and relations in terms of distance. It consists of more than the reference to natural and physical constraints, clearly inscribed in its definition, since it also encompasses aspects of social construction, such as transport infrastructure, which impact on access time, or financial resources allowing for the use of certain communication technologies. Organisational proximity is based on two types of logic that can be qualified as similitude and affiliation, respectively. With the logic of affiliation, actors belonging to the same area of relations (firm, network, etc.), in which different kinds of interaction take place (e.g. co-operation or circulation of knowledge), are close in organisational terms. With the logic of similitude, actors who resemble one another, i.e. who possess the same area of reference and share the same knowledge, so that the institutional dimension is important, are close in organisational terms. In the first case, membership of the same set is conditioned by the effective nature of co-ordination; in the second, proximity is related to the 'resemblance' of representations and modes of functioning. Far from being antinomic, these two aspects can sometimes be reconciled, particularly when affiliation initially based on horizontal relations of an intra-industrial nature are subsequently concretised in an increase in interdependence between organisations, signifying greater similarity (or institutional proximity) between the players. In the case of biotechnology and many high-tech activities, it is the logic of affiliation that plays an important part, particularly in the circulation of knowledge between organisations – a circulation based on a mode of functioning similar to that of inter-individual relations.

How can this distinction help us to understand high-tech clusters and, more specifically, those of biotechnology and their growth? First, incubators and facilities for assisting and supporting business creation play an essential role in the geography of localisation as presented in spatial economic models. The actors may be geographically close without any relations between them. They will take as much advantage as possible of pecuniary externalities. The localisation of R&D is then the result not of spillovers but of the localisation of production factors. For Simmie (1997), the presence of skilled workers is the only local determinant of the innovative capacity of firms in the Herefordshire region. Another example is the numerous cases of failure of technology parks, technopoles, etc. which, it was hoped, would create *ex nihilo* a dynamic of collective innovation. Second, is this collective dynamic, if it does exist, strengthened or not by the specialisation of the cluster? Not all studies agree on this point. Yet for high-tech activities, unlike traditional activities, it seems that Jacobs-type externalities (diversity) and not Marchal-type externalities (specialisation) have a specific impact on the growth of towns (Paci and Usai 2000). Swann distinguishes the effects of localisation on the entry of new firms and on the growth of incumbents (Swann 1999, see also Prevezer 1998). It appears that while the effect of own-sector strength on growth is positive, the effect on entry can be negative. The effect of other sectors on incumbent growth is negative (though often statistically insignificant), but (in contrast) the effect of other sectors on entry can be positive and fairly significant. But in biotechnology it is the strength of the science base in a cluster that is particularly important in influencing the amount of new entry, although there are a limited number of cross-sectoral effects attracting entry (Swann 1999: 116).

While most of the studies cited highlight the correlation between the R&D efforts of firms or universities situated in the same area, this does not mean that location plays a particular part. Firms' innovation can be affected as much by the R&D of firms or universities located in other regions (Autant-Bernard and Massard 1999). A study by Audretsch and

Stephan (1996) on biotechnology in the USA is illuminating in this respect. It shows that employment of local scientists varies considerably from town to town and from firm to firm. This seems to argue for a more detailed analysis of the characteristics of regions and firms. Their study also concludes that while the founders of firms set up near the university from which they graduated, the companies for which they work as scientific advisers are not essentially local. Finally, it shows that 70 per cent of formal relations between scientists and biotech firms are inter-city relations (Audretsch and Stephan 1996).

Studies on relations between biotech firms and universities are not, however, transposable to the choice of location when firms set up. The analysis is very different at the time of start-up, when the survival and development of the firm depend on the founder's close network of relations, and later when the firm is established and builds sound relations in the same scientific, productive and commercial network. A number of studies illustrate the theory of decreasing importance of geographic proximity in the course of time. The localised character of externalities is explained by the tacit dimension of knowledge and its embodiment in certain persons (not all). Almeida and Kogut share this theory with Zucker *et al.* in a study of patents, their citation and the mobility of patent holders (Almeida and Kogut 1997, Jaffe *et al.* 1993, Audretsch and Feldman 1996b). They claim that there is a substitution of geographic proximity by an organisational proximity detached from the locality. This theory of a natural tendency for knowledge to be codified must nevertheless be qualified. First, it is impossible to codify everything. Codification of existing knowledge paves the way for new combinations of knowledge and hence for new tacit knowledge (Senker 1995). Moreover, if the creation process is quick (thus, if the rate of technological obsolescence is high), it is not profitable to invest in codification. Lastly, expertise at the cutting edge of knowledge is not always mobilised in the same way by firms. Catherine and Corolleur (2000), by analysing business models of biotech firms, show that, depending on their scientific ambition, SMEs will or will not mobilise scientific resources in their geographic environment.

Biotechnology clusters and biotech start-ups in France

Where are biotech start-ups located in France and why? How can biotech clusters be explained in the French case? What part have public institutions played in their emergence? Do all these firms mobilise the resources of their close geographical environment to the same extent?

The importance of public institutions for biotech clusters in France

In France, the development of the biotechnology sector remains concentrated on a few leading regions, as shown in Figure 7.1. While Ile-de-France remains dominant, especially as regards firms created around universities and Genopole Evry, Alsace, Auvergne, Aquitaine, Bretagne, Rhône-Alpes and Midi-Pyrénées are also regions in which biotech firms set up. Firms specialising in genome and drug-development technologies are situated primarily in Ile-de-France, while firms in Aquitaine, Bretagne and Auvergne focus more on agri-food related markets.

Is the geography of new biotech firms related to public R&D externalities (are biotech SMEs set up in regions in which many researchers are present)? Figure 7.2 shows that the localisation of biotech start-ups is neither proportional to the number of researchers in academia in the region nor proportional to the global number of publications in the same area. A first explanation can be found in the specific nature of the French public research system compared to that in the USA. Unlike the US system, where relations between universities and local firms are particularly strong (Mansfield 1995), the intensity of relations appears weak in France. Public research in France is very often situated high upstream and the Paris-Province structure is dominant (Grossetti and Bès 2000). Research contracts

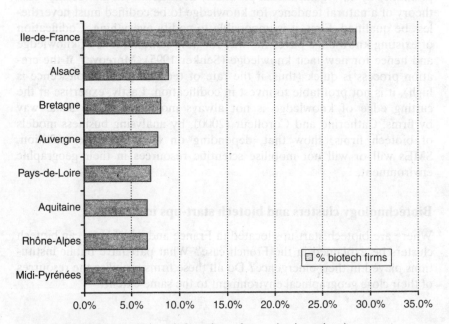

Figure 7.1 Percentage of biotech firms in each area (main regions)

Source: Authors' calculation.

between the public and private sectors and business creation by researchers are in the minority. When they are present, public research externalities appear far more localised in the research phase and less in the innovation phase (Autant-Bernard 2001).[3] Yet over 90 per cent of firms created by researchers are set up in the immediate environment of the laboratory for which they used to work (Grossetti and Bès 2000; and for biotechnology in France: Catherine and Corolleur 2000). Do clusters show a critical mass at which entry starts to take off rapidly? Swann considers that the take-off point for entry in most computer industry sectors is reached when total computer industry employment in the cluster is about 10,000 (Swann 1999). By 1985 Ile-de-France had already grown beyond the critical mass but the other regions had not (Swann 1999.). A priori, one would expect the same to apply to biotechnology. But the regions with the highest proportion of new firms are Auvergne, Rhône-Alpes and Ile-de-France, while firms in Alsace, Bretagne and Centre are generally older. While Ile-de-France attracts new firms, it is not the only one. How can this geography be explained?

Since geographic proximity seems important in the early phases of research (theory of the link between geographic proximity and the nature of the knowledge involved) and the growth of new start-ups does not strictly follow the ranking of regions, should an explanation for the dynamics of biotech clusters not be sought in the intervention of public

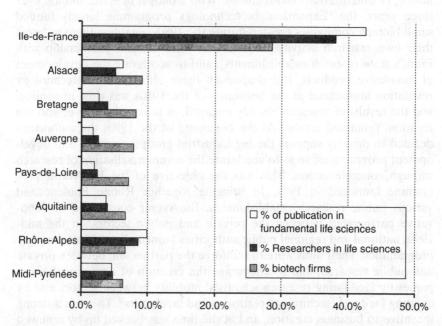

Figure 7.2 Comparison of number of biotech firms and academic research potential, by region (main regions)

Source: Authors' calculation.

actors (laws, innovation incentives, etc.)? Monsan (2000) presents an updated analysis of the recent history of government policy to support biotechnology. At the beginning of the 1980s the aim of French public support for biotechnology was to encourage a number of industrial sectors such as agro-food and seeds. In this way, public funding was used to revitalise groups working in the life sciences and to bring them together, at the same time assisting them to rapidly integrate molecular biology and genetic engineering methodologies. To strengthen relations between public research and industry, biotechnology transfer centres were set up, for example in public sector research (PSR): Institut Pasteur, CNRS (Conseil National de la Recherche Scientifique), INRA (National Institute of Agronomic Research), etc. Subsequently, several of them became research innovation and technological centres (CRITTs, Centres Régional d'Innovation et de Transfert de Technologie)). Lastly, national public policy in favour of biotech was also designed to support start-ups. A number of companies were created using venture capital. These include Transgene (founded in Strasbourg in 1979), Immunotech (Marseille 1982) and BioEurope (Toulouse 1984).

After this initial phase, the major concern of public policy as it was redesigned in 1985 was to preserve the transversal nature of biotechnology while concentrating funds on four priority domains: the food industry, health, IT and international relations. With a budget of €16.5 million over three years, the 'Expansion' biotechnology programme largely funded small biotech companies created during the 1980s, enabling them to boost their own research activity (most often within a close partnership with French state research establishments), and to accelerate the development of innovative products. But despite all these efforts, the biotechnology revolution announced at the beginning of the 1980s was slow in coming, and the results of research already engaged, in terms of turnover and job creation, remained erratic. At the beginning of the 1990s the authorities decided to directly support the big industrial groups' research and development programmes, so as to accelerate the commercialisation of research through concrete action. This was the objective of the BioAvenir programme launched in 1991. In bringing together Rhône Poulenc and various public research establishments, BioAvenir constituted an innovative partnership between the private and public sectors. In the mid-1990s national and regional public authorities launched new biotechnology programmes. Their aims were to reinforce the partnership between private and public research, and to encourage the creation of new growth companies by facilitating research scientists' mobility between sectors and by creating facilities (technology platforms and incubators). This was a strong incentive to business creation, and at the time was backed up by renewed interest in biotechnology from the finance community, in particular for gene therapy, neuro-degenerative disease treatment and genomics. 1996 saw the arrival of the EASDAQ (European Association of Securities

Dealers Automated Quotation), the European financial market for high-growth, high-tech companies, along with that of the Paris Bourse's 'Nouveau Marché'. Both factors contributed to the development of numerous biotech company creation projects.

Different public policy tools have been mobilised at national and regional level. The effects of local public policy can be seen in very dynamic regions such as Auvergne, Alsace and Aquitaine where the science base appears to be weaker than in other regions (like Rhône-Alpes, for example). As shown by Genet (1997), these regions have all invested in a technopole as an incentive for start-ups. The main public structures founded in 1999–2000 (in addition to the Ivry Génopole) are the genopoles in Montpellier, Strasbourg, Paris (Institut Pasteur), Toulouse, Lille, Lyon-Grenoble, Aix-Marseille and Bordeaux, with an annual budget of F10 million. To these can be added the incubators financed by the state and regions. The regional distribution of innovation incentives from ANVAR (Agence National de Valorisation de la Recherche) can be used as a (partial) indicator of differences in regional growth (Table 7.1). At this stage the public structures set up have been defined in such a way as to promote specialisation and complementarity on a national scale.

Table 7.1 Distribution of ANVAR aid by region in 1999

	Number of projects		Total amount of ANVAR grants	
Ile-de-France	42	20%	20.4	23%
Provence-Alpes-Côte d'Azur	32	15%	13.2	15%
Rhône-Alpes	23	11%	9.4	11%
Auvergne	19	9%	9.2	10%
Midi-Pyrénées	13	6%	5.1	6%
Aquitaine	10	5%	2.0	2%
Bretagne	8	4%	1.6	2%
Languedoc-Rousillon	9	4%	4.4	5%
Nord-Pas de Calais	8	4%	2.4	3%
Pays de la Loire	8	4%	1.3	1%
Alsace	7	3%	7.7	9%
Limousin	6	3%	1.4	2%
Picardie	7	3%	1.1	1%
Centre	5	2%	2.2	2%
Haute-Normandie	4	2%	1.8	2%
Poitou-Charentes	5	2%	2.7	3%
Basse-Normandie	2	1%	1.3	1%
Bourgogne	3	1%	0.4	0%
Lorraine	3	1%	1.3	1%
Champagne-Ardenne	1	0%	0.2	0%
		100%		100%

Source: ANVAR 2000 Bilan sectoriel 1999, Pharmacie Biotechnologie, Paris, Direction de la Technologie ANVAR.

Competition between public actors in clusters, to accommodate as many biotech start-ups as possible, is therefore likely to concern a territory-specific offering rather than an undifferentiated public offering (Corolleur and Pecqueur 1996). But while the strategy of public actors is to anchor as many firms as possible in the territory (i.e. to limit firms' nomadism), some firms' interest in a territory is limited to the availability of skilled workers at a low cost, while others seek local partners (laboratories, consultants in intellectual property rights, other biotech firms, etc.).

Recently public policy has supported business creation in the region. It has stimulated new business creation. However, the creation of economic wealth remains strongly localised in Ile-de-France, as shown in Figure 7.3.

Different trajectories on which geographic and organisational proximity have a differing impact

Our study (Lemarié and Mangematin 2000) reveals one successful trajectory (Type 1), representing a minority of cases, and three more disparate trajectories. Some firms have a regular but non-exponential growth of employee numbers and turnover, although they have existed for over 10 years (Type 2); others are affiliated to a parent company (Type 3); and, lastly, large industrial corporations (Type 4) have bought others out.

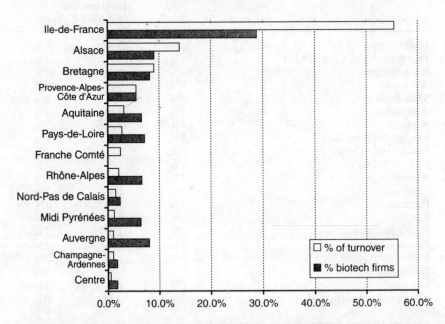

Figure 7.3 Comparison of number of firms and turnover of those firms, by region
Source: Authors' calculation.

These different business models do not mobilise local technico-economic resources equally.

Type 1: Successful start-ups – a small minority of firms

Twenty-eight firms in our sample (14.4 per cent of the 194 respondents), considered to be the flagships of the French biotechnology industry, have grown very fast. Active primarily in the fields of genome research and drug development, their main outlet is the pharmaceuticals market. Whether they were founded about 10 years ago (eleven of them) or before 1980 (twelve of them – close to half), all of them have over fifty employees. Yet these firms employ less than a quarter of all employees in the biotechnology sector. Moreover, only eight of them (i.e. 4.1 per cent) have a turnover of more than F100 million (€5 million) and only six of those are listed on the stock exchange (Biodome, Cerep, Chemunex, Genset, Quantum Appligene, Transgène).

Their development is based primarily on the presence of investors in national and international capital. Venture capital companies, present from the start, have been active in orientating these companies, setting them on a course of rapid growth. By extending the number of subscribers beyond the inner circle, firms are able to benefit from advice, contacts, human capital and an introduction into networks with which they are unfamiliar or which require too much effort to explore. (Fewer than 30 per cent of the 194 respondent firms have a venture capital company among their shareholders.) Moreover, quoting of the firm on the stock exchange enables venture capital firms to sell their shares and withdraw their capital, an indispensable condition for the perpetuation of venture capital financing of biotechnology firms. The presence of venture capital firms in these companies favours the development from essentially domestic organisational proximity (family capital, network of entre-preneurs) to organisational proximity with networks comprising all actors on the biotech scene.

To maintain technological skills, fast-growing firms rely on collabora-tion with French or foreign universities and with public institutions such as the CNRS (National Centre for Scientific Research) or INRA (National Institute for Agricultural Research), rather than basing their development on a product–specific market combination. Collaboration with other firms, especially pharmaceutical companies, enables them to extract value from their technologies. Geographic proximity is clearly of little importance for this type of firm which is situated in an international market for the dif-fusion of its products, and maintains relations with laboratories situated elsewhere. On the other hand, the need to be connected to major commu-nication axes shows the full importance of relations of organisational proxi-mity and the crucial nature of introduction into networks of strong relations. Note, however, that these firms need to be close to centres of excellence to benefit from public research spillovers through interpersonal relations and international exchange maintained by academic laboratories. The quality of a firm's interaction with players in the same geographic area will depend on scientific life in that environment. To attract the best researchers, PhDs and post-doctoral researchers – all potential collaborators – firms are well advised to take advantage of neighbouring centres of academic excellence. This applies to their creation as well as their development.

Type 2: Stable businesses in niches

More than half (53.3 per cent) of biotech employees work in firms that have followed a different development trajectory to that of Type 1 firms. Founded in some instances in the 1970s, generally as limited liability companies (SARL) or limited companies (SA) with private persons only as shareholders, their turnover today is between F10 million (€1.5 million) and F100 million (€15 million). These firms (e.g. Cayla and Anda Biologicals) employ between ten to fifty people, derive a large share of their turnover from export and invest close to 25 per cent of their turnover in research. Active mainly in the pharmaceuticals market, they have a relatively broad technological base maintained both by internal research and by relations with French and foreign universities. These firms, which have been in existence for several years, do not seem to have the intention of becoming leaders in their field on a world-wide scale; they nevertheless represent an alternative development trend for biotech companies.

These companies are characterised by a strong reference to geographic proximity when they seek research or market resources in their immediate environment. In this case, relations with users of products and services are formed on the basis of geographic proximity. Yet they do not, for all that, neglect resources from organisational proximity, as attested by their membership of networks.

Type 3: Firms affiliated to a parent company

One of the strategies of pharmaceutical or seed companies is to create biotechnology firms, either alone or as a joint venture. Biotechnology is in fact a high-risk business whose development requires specific skills. Moreover, small structures are more flexible and easier to adapt to major changes triggered by the production of new scientific knowledge. Finally, investing in a biotechnology enterprise also enables firms to set up in a country with a view to taking advantage of its research 'externalities' and of new markets.

Thus, major French or foreign companies (e.g. Limagrain or Rhône Poulenc, and Monsanto, respectively) have invested in subsidiaries specialising in biotechnology, either to secure a foothold in France (e.g.

BioSepra, Bachem Biochimie and Diagnostica Stago) or to separate biotechnology from the firm's main business (e.g. Syral, Biosem and Limagrain Genetics). These firms, which benefit from the captive market represented by the parent company and from the network of markets to which the latter provides access, have a faster-increasing turnover than that of independent firms. It seems here that geographic proximity plays a relatively minor part in this type of strategy, based above all on the parent company's internal network. Organisational proximity is the most important factor, for geographic incidence is related to location of the parent company.

Type 4: Firms which are sold

In the last type of trajectory, firms are bought out by industrial groups after proving themselves. Included in this category are firms such as Appligene (founded in 1985, with an 80 per cent takeover by the US company Oncor in 1995, and Appligene Oncor then bought out in 1999 by Canadian Quantum), Systemix (founded in 1988, bought out by Sandoz in 1992) and Agrogene (founded in 1989 and progressively bought out by Limagrain before takeover by Perkin Elmer), which differ from subsidiaries created *ex nihilo* (Type 3) in so far as they are initially independent. Takeovers can be explained by problems encountered by some SMEs (difficulty in gaining access to the market, incomplete technological base) and by the purchaser's intentions. The takeover must be considered as a step in the development of the SME and not as a sign of failure. The purchaser's intention is either to complete its technological base by adding the SME's portfolio of patents or technological competency, or to use the SME to facilitate its commercial growth. In the latter case, seldom mentioned, the purchaser is often a foreign group. The SME then acts as a bridgehead in France to transfer technologies or products developed by the parent company.

A takeover generally leads to significant changes in biotech SMEs, for these firms were initially created to support an independent activity that ends up having to serve the interests of its main shareholder. If the SME was bought to be a bridgehead in Europe or France (e.g. Oncor's takeover of Appligene or Perkin Elmer's buy-out of Agrogene), its research activities will probably be scaled down to ensure there is no duplication with the parent company's R&D effort. In some cases problems arise due to a culture shock between different companies or sectors, necessitating a sufficiently long period of transition before the benefits of such restructuring can be reaped.

We cannot talk here of proximity, whether geographic or organisational, for the aim is of a totally different nature. On the other hand, the location of the firm plays an important role since it is often a Trojan horse enabling a bigger firm to penetrate a geographic market to which it does not otherwise have access.

Conclusion

Based on a statistical analysis of the regional location and growth of biotech SMEs in France, this chapter considers the dynamics of localisation of firms when they set up, and the influence of geographic environment on their development. At the time of creation, geographic proximity with the initial networks of the entrepreneur (often from the public or private research community) impacts strongly on the firm's location. Geographic proximity enables the firm to establish itself soundly in its local environment, and organisational and geographic proximity overlap. This is one of the reasons why the impact of regional public policy in favour of business creation is so strong. As the firm grows, organisational proximity dominates and the firm moves away from geographic proximity since its market and field of reference are often international.

As in traditional sectors, certain elements influence biotech firms' choice of locality. Local infrastructure (incubators, support activities, innovation missions, etc.) plays a key part in firms' location. For some firms with technological needs that they cannot meet on their own, the existence of a technology platform is essential. For these firms, whose development is science-based, proximity to high-quality academic research is important. Such research provides a favourable cultural and scientific environment to attract able researchers likely to co-operate with the firm and thus enhance its scientific potential and reputation.

Even if, in high-tech sectors with an international profile, the importance of geographic proximity decreases as the firm grows, localisation in a dynamic scientific environment suited to the emergence of new activities is essential at the time of creation. Regional policies thus have a strong impact on a firm's initial location, simultaneously creating self-reinforcing effects on a given geographic area and clusters of firms.

While policies in favour of business creation seem to combine harmoniously on the different levels of public intervention (municipal, regional and national), the problem of firms' survival after 2 or 3 years is a very real one in an industry characterised by rapid technological change. Further studies will need to examine the development of firms in each region, in order to evaluate the impact of each factor (public policy in favour of start-ups and geographic spillovers). Others will also need to examine the linkages between the scientific reputation and the development of firms, by region.

In France there is diversity in the modes of development of biotech SMEs, adapted to the projects of their directors and shareholders. The path of 'success', where the firm tries to grow as fast as possible and aims at becoming world leader in its sector and in the stock market, is not the only possible one for biotech firms. It is probable, however, that from their creation firms in the biotech sector prepare their future and growth trajectory which will depend on the amount of initial investments, the networks to which they have access, the partnerships they form and whether or not they choose to appeal to outside investors. Policies supporting innovation and high-tech SMEs have to take this into account, or they could set viable firms on paths that prove to be no more than a mirage

Annex 1

On the initiative of the MENRT Technology Division (Biotechnology group)[4] a survey was made of firms performing biotechnology research (see Table 7.2). Biotechnology firms were considered to be those that develop or use industrial technologies derived from life science and technology (and sometimes materials) using the properties of living organisms for producing goods and services (definition proposed by the Industry Ministry, 'Les 100 technologies clés à l'horizon 2000').

The survey consisted of several stages:

1 compilation of list of organisations (firms, economic interest groups and associations) engaged in biotechnology research, from available sources;
2 validation of list and addition of information, by local experts;
3 definition of list of 478 target organisations, irrespective of size or status (SA, not for profit organisations);
4 administration of the questionnaire;
5 processing of data and compilation of a directory.

221 answers were registered but remained largely incomplete. In order to obtain a representative sample, the data base thus obtained was enhanced with various other available data bases: base constituted by the INRA/SERD team, the France Biotech base, the Genetic Engineering Directory,

Table 7.2 Data collected by means of the questionnaire

- Identity of the firm and the top managers, with position
- Main technologies developed and implemented by the firm (to be ticked off on a list of 33 technologies)
- Main areas of activity (markets) in which the firm is active (to be ticked off on a list of 28 markets)
- Turnover, R&D spending, net and effective income for past 3 years
- Patents owned and exploited by the firm
- Quality control in the firm
- Effective and hoped for partnerships for research, production and commercialisation

Infogreffe and Diane. Missing information was thus obtained and certain firms were added to the base when all the required information was available.

In order to standardise the answers, only registered companies (SA (Société Anonyme), SARL (Société Anonyme à Responsabilité Limitée), SNC (Société en Nom Collectif)) were selected. To ensure the relevance of comparisons with information published by Ernst and Young (1999 Report), we analysed only those firms with under 500 employees. Finally, we excluded the rare biotech firms created before 1960. The base used in our analysis consisted of 194 firms, for which full information was available. Several indications allow us to consider the analysed sample as representative: over 60 per cent of the firms in the France Biotech directory and 90 per cent of the firms present in the Genetic Engineering Directory answered the questionnaire. When we analysed the base of 600 firms to which the questionnaire was sent, fewer than 450 corresponded to the selected criteria. We can therefore consider that the sample analysed corresponds to roughly half of the biotech firms active in France.

Notes

1 We would like to thank Gerhard Fuchs and an anonymous referee for their helpful comments. I would also like to thank the participants of the ENESAD seminary in Dijon in March 2000. Usual caveats apply.
2 Corresponding author.
3 This result was obtained for the 1990s by measuring the geography of public R&D spillovers over the R&D and patents of firms (Autant-Bernard 2000). It contradicts the results of Mansfield for the USA, where geographic proximity is equally important for both applied research and basic research (Mansfield 1995).
4 A steering committee consisting of Pascale Auroy (ARD), Christine Bagnaro (ANVAR), Patrice Blanchet (DTA/2, MENRT), Marie José Dudézert (DTA/2, MENRT), Anne Sophie Godon (Arthur Andersen) and Vincent Mangematin (INRA/SERD) met under the chairmanship of Jean Alexis Grimaud in 1998–1999 to plan and conduct the survey.

References

Acs, Z.-J., Audretsch, D.B. and Feldmann, M.-P. (1994) 'R&D Spillovers and Innovative Activity, *Managerial and Decision Economics*, 15(2): 131–8.
Almedia, P. and Kogut, B. (1997) 'The Exploration of Technological Diversity and the Geographic Localisation of Innovation', *Small Business Economics*, 9: 21–31.
Audretsch, D. and Feldman, M. (1996a) 'R&D Spillovers and the Geography of Innovation and Production', *American Economic Review*, 86(3): 630–40.
—— (1996b) 'Innovation clusters and the industry life cycle', *Review of Industrial Organization*, 11: 253–73.
Audretsch, D. and Stephan, P. (1996) 'Company Scientist Locational Links: the case of Biotechnology', *American Economic Review*, 86(3): 641–52.
Autant-Bernard, C. and Massard, N. (1999) 'Econométrie des Externalités Tech-

nologiques et Géographie de l'Innovation: une analyse critique', *Economie Appliquée*, 4.

—— (2001) 'Science and knowledge flows: evidence from the French case', *Research Policy*, 20: 1069–78.

Catherine, D. and Corolleur, F. (2000) 'PME biotech et géographie de l'innovation, des fondateurs à leur modèle d'enterprise', 36th Colloquium of ASRDLF, Crans-Montana Switzerland, 6–9 September 2000.

Corolleur, F. and Pecqueur, B. (1996) 'Local economic policy in France in the 1980s', in C. Demaziere and P. Wilson (ed.) *Local Economic Development in Europe and the Americas*, London, New York: Mansell Publishing Limited: 54–69.

Ducos C. and Joly, P-B. (1988) *Les biotechnologies*, Repères No. 61, Paris: Editions la Découverte.

Ernst and Young (2000) *European Biotech 99*, London: Ernst Young International.

Feldman, M. (1994) *The Geography of Innovation*, Boston: Kluwer Academic Publishers.

—— (1999) 'The New Economics of Innovation, Spillover and Agglomeration: Review of Empirical Studies', *Economics of Innovation and New Technology*, 8(1): 5–25.

Fujita, M. and Thisse, J.F. (1997) 'Economie géographique. Problèmes anciens et nouvelles perspectives', *Annales d'Economie et Statistiques*, 45: 37–87.

Genet, C. (1997) 'Quelles conditions pour la formation des biotechnopoles?', *Revue d'Economie Régionale et Urbaine*, 3: 405–24.

Grossetti, M. and Bès, M.-P. (2000) *Organisations et individus en interaction: une étude de cas sur les coopérations entre entreprises et laboratoires de recherche*, 5th Workshop on economics with endogenous interacting agents, Marseille, 15–17 June 2000.

Jaffe, A. (1989) 'Real effects of academic research', *The American Economic Review*, 79(5): 957–70.

Jaffe, A., Trajtenberg, M. and Henderson, R. (1993) 'Geographic localisation of knowledge spillovers as evidence by patent citations', *Quarterly Journal of Economics*, 108(3): 577–98.

Krugman, P. (1991a) *Geography and Trade*, 4th edn, Leuven: University Press, Leuven, Belgium; MIT Press, Cambridge, MA, London, England.

—— (1991b) 'Increasing returns and economic geography', *Journal of Political Economy*, 99(3): 483–99.

Lamoureaux, N.R. and Sokoloff, K.L. (1997) 'Location and technological change in the American glass industry during the late 19 and early 20 centuries', *NBER Working Paper* 5938.

Lemarié, S. and Mangematin, V. (2000) 'Biotech firms in France', *Biofutur*, Special Issue: 32–42.

Lemarié, S., de Looze, M.A. and Mangematin, V. (2000b) 'Dynamics of innovation and strategies of development of SMEs in biotechnology: the role of size, technology and market', *Scientometrics*, 47(3): 541–60.

Lerner, J. (1996) 'The government as venture capitalist: the long run impact of the SBIR programme', *National Bureau of Economic Research*, Working Paper 5753.

Mansfield, E. (1995) 'Academic research underlying industrial innovations:

sources, characteristics, and financing', *The Review of Economics and Statistics*, Vol. LXXVII, No. 1: 55–65.

Mason, C.M. and Harrison, R.T. (1995) 'Closing the regional equity gap: the role of informal venture capital', *Small Business Economics*, 7(2): 153–72.

Monsan, P. (2000) 'Twenty Years of Biotech in France', *Biofutur*, Special Issue: 27–30.

Orsenigo, L., Pammolli, F., Riccaboni, M., Bonaccorsi, A. and Turchetti, G. (1998) 'The evolution of knowledge and the dynamics of an industry network', *Journal of Management and Governance*, 1: 147–75.

Paci, R. and Usai, S. (2000) 'Technological enclaves and industrial districts. An analysis of the regional distribution of innovative activity in Europe', *Regional Studies*, 34(2).

Prevezer, M.D. (1998) 'Clustering in Biotechnology in the USA', in P.E. Swann *et al.* (eds) *The Dynamics of Industrial Clustering in Biotechnology*, Oxford: Oxford University Press: 124–93.

Senker, J. (1995) 'Tacit Knowledge and Models of Innovation', *Industrial and Corporate Change*, 4(2): 425–47.

Sharp, M. (1999) 'The science of nations: European multinationals and American biotechnology', *International Journal of Biotechnology*, 1(1): 132–62.

Simmie, J. (1997) 'Innovation in the high-technology knowledge economy of a core metropolitan region. Evidence from Hertfordshire', *Séminaire du programme CNRS. Les enjeux de l'innovation*, December 1997.

Swann, G.M.P. (1999) 'Innovation and size of industrial clusters in Europe', in A. Gambardella and F. Malerba (eds) *The Organization of Economic Innovation in Europe*, Cambridge: Cambridge University Press: 103–24.

Torre, A. and Gilly, J.P. (2000) 'On the analytical dimension of proximity dynamics', *Regional Studies*, 34(2), April 2000: 169–80.

Zucker, L.G. and Darby, M.R. (1996) 'Star Scientists and institutional transformation: patterns of invention and innovation in the formation of the biotechnology industry', *Proceedings of the National Academy of Science*, 93: 12709–16.

Zucker, L.G., Darby, M.R. and, Armstrong, J. (1998) 'Geographically localized knowledge: spillovers or markets?' *Economic Inquiry*, (36): 65–86.

8 Success and failure in the development of biotechnology clusters

The case of Lombardy

Stefano Breschi, Francesco Lissoni and Luigi Orsenigo

Introduction

This chapter discusses the development of the biotechnology industry in an Italian region, Lombardy. More specifically, it asks why significant innovative and commercial activities in biotechnology did not emerge in what might have been considered at the outset a promising area for the growth of this industry, and why in very recent years some timid symptoms of dynamism seem to be appearing.

As a case study about a failure, rather than a success story, it is difficult to draw firm conclusions. In a sense, the problem is overdetermined. There are too many possible candidate variables that might explain why innovative activities in biotechnology did not take off and the available data do not allow any serious statistical test.

As a consequence, the chapter is largely speculative. However, we shall try to make progress in turning speculation into a substantial account, based on a theory-driven interpretation of the determinants of the patterns of innovative activities in specific geographical areas.

There is now considerable empirical evidence that innovative activities tend indeed to cluster in specific geographic areas, at different levels of aggregation (Audretsch and Feldman 1996, Feldman 1994, Swann *et al.* 1998, Ellison and Glaeser 1999, Henderson 1999).

The case of biotechnology is extreme and puzzling, in this respect, from a variety of perspectives. It is very well known that the biotechnology industry is largely an American phenomenon and that other countries have been lagging behind for over two decades. Despite some recent encouraging signals of dynamism in some European countries and in Japan, the American leadership is still undisputed. Even within the USA, the development of biotechnology has been characterised by high degrees of regional concentration. In Europe, too, innovative activities in biotechnology tend to agglomerate into specific areas. So, what are the factors that explain different performances in 'national biotech'? And what are the factors leading to agglomeration in the case of biotechnology?

After an overview of the patterns of the development of biotechnology in Italy (second section), the specific case of the biggest biotechnology cluster in Italy – Lombardy – will be described (third section). Then, we shall briefly touch upon two main conceptual issues which have attracted the attention of many analysts in recent years and which drive this chapter too, namely:

a   What are the factors that might explain the lagging behind of the Italian (and more generally, European) biotechnology industry vis-à-vis the United States (fourth section)?
b   Do innovative activities tend to cluster in specific geographical areas? If the answer is positive, what are the determinants of these processes of agglomeration, at least in the case of Lombardy (fifth section)?

The background: the development of biotechnology in Italy

In Italy, as in other European countries, innovative activities in biotechnology lagged significantly behind the USA and proceeded along different lines. Structural weaknesses in the industrial base, in the research system and at the institutional level hindered the development of biotechnology.

The main difference, of course, is the virtual absence of the phenomenon of specialised biotechnology start-ups, even as compared to other European countries. No reliable figure of the number of new biotechnology firms in Italy is available, but a rough estimate would suggest that they are around less than two dozen. Moreover, the few Italian start-ups do not resemble the American prototype in many respects. Most of them are not involved in drug research or development but are instead either intermediaries commercialising products developed elsewhere, or in the provision of instrumentation and/or reagents. Finally, some of these companies (especially the most significant ones) have been founded as spin-offs of larger pharmaceutical companies undergoing processes of restructuring rather than as university spin-offs. However, the major distinctive feature of the Italian case is the delay with which innovative activities got started and the limited size and scope of such efforts, even within the large chemical and pharmaceutical (and agro-food) companies. Even today, Italy has to be considered a backward country in biotechnology. Just to give a rough idea, it is worth noting that the number of Italian patent applications to the European Patent Office totals only 163 in the whole period from 1978 to 1996.

In the absence of extensive new firm creation, most of the innovation in biotechnology in Italy – as in other countries of mainland Europe – has occurred within established firms and public research centres. The main actors in the development of biotechnology in Italy were the large chemical firms. The beginning of research activities, as well as the emergence of public policy, was the background to the formation of a 'biotechnology lobby', who stimulated the interest of industry and above all of the government. By the early 1980s, the two largest Italian chemical groups – ENI (Ente Nazionale Idrocarburi) and Montedison – had already started some small research activities and had considered the possibility of some more systematic effort. However, such plans resulted only in the establishment of two small research agreements with Italian academic laboratories. Besides ENI and Montedison, only a handful of medium-sized pharmaceutical companies engaged in innovative activities, whilst the absence of any research tradition in the food industry and in agriculture prevented any significant effort in those directions.

Around the chemical industry, however, a biotechnology lobby gathered and organised. Scientists were the first to perceive the potentialities of biotechnology and took an active role in eliciting both industrial and public interest in the new emerging techniques. Yet they had traditionally few linkages with industry and their pressure achieved results only when they succeeded in involving the Association of the Chemical Industry (Federchimica). Federchimica was perhaps the single most influential institution in the development of Italian biotechnology. In 1986, it published the first major report on biotechnology and from then on it lobbied for getting public support. Subsequently, Federchimica spun off other initiatives, particularly the Italian Biotechnology Industrial Association, although its main result was to elicit and contribute to the design of government intervention.

The weakness of government support is a further distinguishing feature of the Italian case. Before 1986, public support for biotechnology was very small and unco-ordinated. It flowed mainly to universities through the National Research Council's (CNR) 'Finalised Projects', but research funding was small and it was spread over many diverse and very general projects, without any clearly defined priority. Industry was only marginally involved in these projects. Industrial research was funded through the two existing schemes supporting applied research, but again no specific priority was attributed to biotechnology.

As in most countries, the Italian government agencies knew very little about biotechnology and, given the uncertainty surrounding its future developments, they were not able to devise any specific policy. In contrast to other experiences, though, the Italian administrative apparatus also lacked the experience, the competencies and the structures for dealing with the problems of formulation and implementation of a set of policies in high-tech industries (Orsenigo 1989). Thus, the existence of biotechnology was not even perceived until the mid 1980s, under the pressure of the biotechnology lobby and the example set by other countries.

Attempts to co-ordinate interventions and to devise a coherent strategy started only in the second half of the 1980s, when a National Committee for Biotechnology was established at the Ministry for Scientific and Technological Research (MURST). The Committee comprised the scientists and the industrialists of the original biotechnology lobby and eventually designed the National Plan for Biotechnology, which was passed by the Parliament in 1987.

The plan was aimed at supporting applied research in different fields (especially biomedical research), while support for basic research and industry–university collaboration was provided through new programs launched by the CNR. Other initiatives were taken to stimulate research conducted in the public research centres like ENEA (Ente Nazionale per le Energie Alternative)`and the CNR. In the following years other programs were launched by the CNR, by MURST and by other Ministries. It is very difficult to evaluate the effective size of the financial resources devoted to the support of (basic and applied) research and to the promotion of industry–university collaboration, let alone the impact of these projects. An extremely rough estimate would suggest that in the period from 1987 to 1996 the total funding amounted to a figure around L1,000–1,200 billion. An analysis of the National Research Plans on biotechnology launched by the Ministry of University and Scientific and Technological Research in the period from 1989 to 1997 suggests, however, that only a small group of universities and an even smaller group of companies were involved in these projects, with a very limited scientific output (only 1 patent extended outside Italy) and little interaction between universities and the companies (Cancogni 1998).

In addition to these initiatives, the development of biotechnology in Italy was characterised by the mushrooming of local collaborative initiatives between public and private agents at the local level, through the establishment of science parks, research consortia, venture capital funds, etc. However, the scope and the impact of these efforts remained on the whole quite limited.

Thus, despite these efforts, very few firms engaged in significant research activities and their innovativeness was far lower than that of the major European competitors. Very few firms account for a large proportion of biotechnology patents, and innovation in biotechnology rests essentially on the activities of a small group of large/medium-sized established companies. As a consequence, Italian performance as a whole remains far behind that of Germany, France, UK, Switzerland, and also of Sweden and Denmark (Table 8.1).[1]

Still in the 1980s, the main actors were the two large Italian chemical groups, ENI and Montedison. As far as Montedison is concerned, research capabilities in biotechnology were present in the laboratories of its pharmaceutical subsidiary (Farmitalia-Carlo Erba, at that time the largest and most prestigious Italian pharmaceutical company) and in the central laboratories of the group (Istituto di Ricerche Donegani). In the late 1980s, Montedison expanded its biotechnology research through acquisitions and through the development of a network of collaborations with domestic universities and American laboratories and specialised biotechnology firms.

Table 8.1 Major biotechnology innovators in Italy

Institution	Number of EPO patent*	% of total Italian patents*
1978–90		
EniRicerche	12	25.0
Sclavo	7	14.6
Farmitalia Carlo Erba	6	12.5
1990–6		
EniRicerche	16	14.7
Biocine	10	9.2
Pharmacia & AMP Upjohn	9	8.3
Consiglio Nazionale delle Ricerche	9	8.3

Source: Authors' calculation of the EPO-CESPRI Database (Centre on the Processes of Innovation and Internationalisation, Bocconi University, Milan, Italy).

Note
*Patent applications at the European Patent Office.

As for ENI, a significant biotechnology group was created within EniRicerche (the research laboratories of the group). Moreover, ENI owned Sclavo, a medium-sized company located in Siena, considered to be among the world leaders in vaccine production.

Finally, a subsidiary of the Fiat group, Sorin, active in the production of medical devices, started research on the development of diagnostic kits based on the use of monoclonal antibodies and assays.

Since the beginning of the 1990s, however, even these initiatives have been drastically downsized. The Italian chemical and pharmaceutical industries underwent a deep crisis. The Italian chemical and pharmaceutical companies were already structurally weak, small by international standards and their commitment to innovative activities was certainly not comparable to that of their international competitors. The major Italian chemical and pharmaceutical companies were acquired by foreign corporations (more than 70 per cent of total pharmaceutical sales on the Italian market are now generated by foreign-owned firms and by subsidiaries of large multinationals). Moreover, a series of scandals linked to the spread of a bribery system in the processes of setting drug prices, severely hit the whole industry. Finally, cost containment policies by the Government implied a further shock to the profits and the strategies of the pharmaceutical companies operating in Italy.

As a consequence, investments in biotechnology R&D were drastically reduced. For example, the pharmaceutical division of Montedison – Farmitalia Carlo Erba – was eventually acquired by Pharmacia and its research activities were subject to substantial restructuring. Similarly

Sclavo (now called Biocine), after a series of break-ups and vicissitudes, was acquired by Chiron. Many research projects were discontinued and – given the overall weakness of Italian research capabilities – only few initiatives were launched or maintained by the foreign research headquarters to compensate for the decrease in domestic investments.

The development of biotechnology in Lombardy

The history of the development of biotechnology in Lombardy coincides to a very large extent with the history of Italian biotechnology as a whole. Indeed, since its inception, innovative activities in this area have been strongly concentrated in a few regions, Lombardy being by far the single most important centre, followed by Tuscany and – in the 1990s – by Latium. Lombardy accounts for almost half (43.9 per cent) of the patents applied for to the European Patent Office in the period from 1979 to 1996 and its contribution has been only slightly declining in the period from 1990 to 1996 (falling to 39.4 per cent). All in all, Lombardy, Latium and Tuscany contribute around 80 per cent of total Italian patenting activities[2] and over the past few years the overall degree of spatial concentration of innovative activities in biotechnology has changed very little.[3]

The agglomeration of innovative activities in Lombardy – and more specifically in the area around Milan – might be simply explained by the fact that Milan has the strongest concentration of research laboratories, both academic and industrial, and it is by far the most important financial centre of Italy.

Milan is traditionally one of the major centres of academic research in medicine and in biology. Whilst other universities had perhaps the best research teams and the more advanced 'schools', yet in Milan could be found a very strong concentration of units and researchers in different disciplines.

Lombardy has traditionally hosted a large majority of the chemical and pharmaceutical companies, especially their headquarters and their research laboratories.[4] More generally, Lombardy consistently shows a very strong technological specialisation in chemicals and pharmaceuticals, whichever indicator is used (R&D expenditures, patents, number of researchers, etc.).

At the beginning of the 1990s, Lombardy hosted 49 per cent of the Italian firms active in biotechnology, 36.3 per cent of the researchers, and 42.6 per cent of the research laboratories. Similarly, Lombardy attracted 29 per cent of the public funds made available by the National Research Council's 'Finalised Project' on Biotechnology. It is also worth noting that, respectively, more than three-quarters and around 60 per cent of all the collaborations among firms – both at the national and international level – and universities and companies involved in biotechnology are located in Lombardy (Orsenigo 1991).

Against this background, a series of initiatives was taken to further develop biotechnology research and commercial activities, primarily through the creation of science parks or – more generally – aggregations of academic and industrial researchers to promote collaborative research and act as incubators for academic spin-offs.

The first initiative was the so-called 'Biopolo', a consortium between a few pharmaceutical companies and academics of the Faculties of Biology, Chemistry and Agricultural Sciences, with the participation – under various headings – of the local authorities. The Biopolo was an offspring of the original 'biotechnology lobby' and was promoted and stimulated by a group of professors of the State University of Milan since the late 1980s. Its main area of interest was the applications of biotechnology to the agro-food industry and environment.

In practice, the Biopolo took off very slowly, as a consequence of the scandals in the pharmaceutical industry, political meddling and academic politics. Its main activity consisted in supporting the creation of a specific field denominated 'biotechnology' within the Faculty of Sciences of the State Milan University and collaboration between university and industry was essentially focused on teaching activities and training. Only recently, with the creation of the second state University of Milan in 1998 – resulting from the splitting of the previous institution – the Biopolo has started operating in a more systematic way. With the creation of the second University, in fact, a Faculty of Biotechnology was set up which is beginning to act as a centre of aggregation for research.

A second initiative, the S. Raffaele Science Park, was more successful. The Science Park was launched in 1993 under the impetus of the head of the S. Raffaele hospital, a private institution created and managed by a charismatic (and highly controversial) priest/entrepreneur, Don Luigi Verzè. The San Raffaele Hospital was conceived and developed to put a high priority on research – particularly on biotechnology and in general on molecular biology – and it quickly became a leading scientific centre in the biomedical area in Italy, with solid relationships with the international community and high-quality standards and reputation. Around the S. Raffaele Hospital, DIBIT (Department of Biological and Technological Research) and subsequently the S. Raffaele Science Park were formed, initially without any public funding. Now, the science park hosts sixty-three research units, including a few laboratories of the National Research Council, of the Polytechnic of Milan and, since last year, of the new University 'Vita e Salute' (another initiative of Don Verzè, with Faculties of Medicine and Psychology, and conceived as a highly prestigious and selective institution). A number of important international pharmaceutical companies and a couple of new start-ups (which, however, are not yet completely operative) participate in the S. Raffaele Science Park, with specialised laboratories in a large variety of research areas. Moreover, the S. Raffaele Science Park hosts a number of laboratories funded by initiatives like Telethon and by other private foundations.

Although the S. Raffaele Science Park has among its main objectives the promotion of and assistance to spin-offs, with the provision of various types of services (scientific, technological, logistical, financial and administrative services), no really important result has been achieved so far in this area.

In fact, the most important and notable examples of new biotechnology companies in Lombardy are not university spin-offs, but industrial spin-offs, born out of the processes of restructuring some large pharmaceutical companies.

One of these cases was Lepetit, leader in antibiotics research and production. After being acquired by Marion Merrel Dow, its laboratories had become one the major research centres in this field. After a series of vicissitudes, however, Lepetit was finally acquired by HMR (Hoechst-Marion-Roussel) and the lab was closed. At this stage, a group of researchers took the initiative to launch a new company, Biosearch Italia, trying to maintain and exploit the accumulated know-how. With the support of venture capitalists (3i-Investor in Industry), the new company was founded with the aim of being quoted in the newly created 'Nuovo Mercato' (the equivalent of the Neuer Markt or the Nouveau Marché) in the year 2000. Its main research lines are focused on antibiotics, but new areas have also been opened in anti-tumorals and genomics, in collaboration with the former parent company, now Aventis.

A similar story is that of Newron. Here, once again, a group of researchers from the Milan-based R&D laboratories of Pharmacia and Upjohn (formerly Farmitalia – Carlo Erba), closed after the change of property, decided to continue their research with funding from 3i in the area of the central nervous system. So far, Newron has been renting some spaces and services from Biosearch Italy, but is expected to be quoted on the Nuovo Mercato in 3 years' time.

NovusPharma is a further example, being born from the restructuring processes of the Boehringer Mannheim branch operating in the area of oncology. After the acquisition from Hoffman La Roche, the laboratories were closed. In this case, three European venture capital firms (the Italian branch of 3i, Atlas Ventures (NL) e Sofinnova (F)) supported the initiative of some researchers to create their own company. NovusPharma has already developed collaborations with the National Institute on Tumours, the European Institute of Oncology and the Faculty of Biotechnology of the second University of Milan and maintains an agreement with Roche. NovusPharma has ambitious growth targets and quotation on the Stock Exchange is expected in 2 years' time.

Factors explaining the (slow) development of biotechnology in Italy and the case of Lombardy

To a large extent, explanations of the feeble development of biotechnology in Italy, of the clustering of innovative activities in Lombardy (and a few other areas), and of the specific evolution of the industry in Lombardy tend to coincide. We would also advance the hypothesis that the Italian case is just an extreme instantiation of a more general European experience.

To deal with these questions, however, two different issues must be distinguished. First, why did NBFs not flourish in Europe? Second, why were European large established companies – in general terms – slower than their American counterparts in adopting biotechnology – more precisely molecular biology?

Factors hindering the development of new biotechnology companies

It is now widely recognised that in the United States a combination of factors made it possible for small, newly founded firms to take advantage of the opportunity created by biotechnology. In Europe (although to a lesser extent in the UK) many of these factors were not in place. Let us briefly examine the role of these factors in the case of Europe, and Italy in particular.

Strength of the local scientific base

It is widely recognised that the very strong state of American academic molecular biology played an important role in both facilitating the proliferation of start-ups (Sharp 1985, Orsenigo 1989, Zucker *et al.* 1997). The strength of the local science base may also be responsible; within Europe, for the relative British advantage and the delay of France and Germany. There seems to be no doubt about the superiority of the American and British scientific systems in the field of molecular biology, and it is tempting to suggest that the strength of the local science base provides an easy explanation for regional differences in the speed with which biotechnology developed.

In Italy, it is widely acknowledged that the level and the scope of basic research in molecular biology was not very high. Indeed, some research groups conducting state-of-the-art research were present in the early 1980s, especially in fields like immunology. Naples and Pavia were particularly important in this respect. In Naples, IIGB (International Institute of Genetics and Biophysics), which was directed for a few years during the 1960s by James Watson, was an internationally renowned research centre that spun off successive generations of high-quality researchers, and clusters of research groups spread all over Italy. Similarly, Pavia constituted another pole of excellence, where Italian studies in genetics were practically born thanks to the work of Buzzati Traverso and where, later on, an important National Research Council group was created and developed. Milan and Rome had also some excellent research groups, whilst Genoa had a tradition of research in immunology and IST (Institute for Research on Tumours), a spin-off of the National Institute for Cancer Research, was created. Padua, finally, had developed significant competencies in the field of the chemistry of proteins.

Other research initiatives were developed within public research centres (like the CNR's groups or ENEA[5]) and by private institutions. For example, the Italian Association for Cancer Research (mainly a funding agency) introduced a new, competitive approach to the funding of scientific research in Italy. The National Institute for Cancer Research and its offspring IST (Institute for Research on Tumors in Genoa) operated at the frontier of knowledge in experimental oncology and immunology and had a dense network of relationships with American and British laboratories. Moreover, since the mid-1980s both institutions started a systematic attempt to slow down the brain drain process that was hitting the domestic research system, by recruiting expatriated Italian researchers. The Mario Negri Institute for Pharmacological Research, which was initially located in Bergamo and then opened up various branches in other locations, was another centre of excellence in research.

In sum, while some good research centres existed, on the whole Italian research in molecular biology and in other disciplines relevant to biotechnology was lagging behind most of the major European countries. Above all, research was concentrated in a few heterogeneous clusters, with little communication and co-ordination except personal and informal relationships among the individual researchers. Over the years, the level and scope of basic research have significantly improved, thanks also to the activities and the international contacts of a younger generation of researchers who studied and worked initially in the USA and other countries, but they still lag significantly behind the main European countries in terms of absolute amounts of funding, organisational efficiency and overall quality of the research.

The strength of the local knowledge base also goes a long way to account for the agglomeration of innovative biotechnological activities in a few clusters in Italy. However, some qualifications are needed. First, as we have seen, Milan did not necessarily have the best scientific research in absolute terms as compared to other Italian locations. Second, centres which had poles of excellence in scientific research did not become important biotechnology clusters, e.g. Naples. This would suggest, at this stage, that not only the absolute quality of science, but also the existence of critical thresholds in the 'quantity' of good science were necessary conditions for the emergence of clusters.

Industry–university relations

An explanation based only on the strength of the local scientific base might seem unsatisfying to the degree that academic science is rapidly published and thus, in principle, rapidly available across regions and across the world. However, even in this extreme case of a science-based technology, in the early years of the industry the exploitation of 'biotechnology' required the mastery of a considerable body of tacit knowledge that could not be easily acquired from literature (Zucker *et al.* 1997, Pisano 1996, Orsenigo 1989).

Thus, it has often been suggested that the flexibility of the American academic system, the high-mobility characteristics of the scientific labour market, the willingness to exploit the results of academic research commercially[6] and, in general, the social, institutional and legal context that made it relatively straightforward for leading academic scientists to become deeply involved with commercial firms were also major factors in the health of the new industry.

In contrast, links between the academy and industry – particularly the ability to freely exchange personnel – appear to have been much weaker in Europe. Indeed, the efforts of several European governments were targeted precisely towards the strengthening of industry–university collaboration.

Thus, one observes a mushrooming of initiatives all across Europe aiming at establishing stronger links between industry and universities and to encourage a more entrepreneurial attitude of the universities. Policies have practically been targeted mainly at the setting up of specific organisational devices to manage technology transfer, like science and technology parks or other agencies for technology transfer. These initiatives have taken a wide variety of forms and show a mixed record in their performance.

In the case of Italy, the structure and standards governing the academic system certainly did not favour the entrepreneurial exploitation of university-based research. Interactions between industry and university had been traditionally weak and in any case largely informal and based on personal – rather than institutional – relations.

This state of affairs has changed very slowly over the years and it has been only very recently that a different attitude has started to emerge. In a survey carried out in 1994 among the academic researchers participating in the National Plan for Biotechnology – a programme launched by the Ministry of University and Scientific and Technological Research (MURST) to sustain biotechnology research and industry–university collaboration – a large fraction of the respondents to the questionnaire declared themselves willing to engage more directly in the commercial exploitation of their research. However, administrative rules and the lack of appropriate organisational structures within the universities were quoted as the main factor hindering such developments (Cesaroni *et al.* 1995). A more recent study on industry–university relations in Italy (Orsenigo and Cancogni 1999) confirmed that, despite a renewed dynamism in this field, only a few universities have developed any systematic organisational structure to deal with relationships with industry and with the commercial exploitation of scientific research. More than 60 per cent of the universities do not even have standard contract typologies, let alone dedicated technology transfer offices.

Thus, the traditional separation between academia and industry, and the organisational deficiencies within universities make it very difficult to commercialise academic research. However, it has to be stressed that, given the weakness of scientific research in general, the absence of appropriate 'transfer mechanisms' appears to have played a relatively minor role so far. To put it provocatively, transfer mechanisms are largely irrelevant if there is nothing to be transferred. Moreover, the development of organisational structures supporting technology transfer appears to be largely dependent on the existence of a strong research base.

Access to capital

It is commonly believed that the lack of venture capital restricted the start-up activity of biotechnology firms outside the USA. True, venture capital played an enormous role in fueling the growth of the new biotechnology-based firms (or 'NBFs'). However, at least in Europe, there have been many other sources of funds available to prospective start-ups (usually through government programmes). In addition, the results of several surveys suggest that financial constraints did not constitute the main obstacle for the founding of new biotechnology firms in Europe (Senker *et al.* 1998). In addition, although venture capital played a critical role in the founding of US biotechnology firms, collaborations between the new firms and the larger established firms provided a potentially even more important source of capital. Yet large European companies tended to collaborate relatively more with US biotechnology firms than with prospective European start-ups.[7] Even in the absence of other institutional barriers to entrepreneurial ventures, start-ups in Europe might have been crowded out by the large number of US-based firms anxious to trade non-US marketing rights for capital (Henderson *et al.* 1999). Given the number of US NBFs in search of capital, European firms had little incentive to invest in local biotechnology firms.

As a partial support for this interpretation, we recall that in Italy several initiatives by both domestic and foreign investors to launch venture capital funds were attempted in the 1990s, with little success so far. These funds, if anything, ended up investing in new biotechnology companies outside Italy. Conversely, some of the few successful Italian NBFs have been funded by foreign venture capital firms. Thus, the failed development of venture capital in Italy seems to depend less on the lack of investors and funds than on the paucity of supply of promising start-ups based on solid scientific research.

Intellectual property rights

It is widely acknowledged that the establishment of clearly defined property rights also played a major role in making possible the explosion of new company formations in the USA, since the new firms, by definition, had few complementary assets that would have enabled them to appropriate returns from the new science in the absence of strong patent rights (Teece 1986).

In the USA, a very tight appropriability regime in the biotechnology industry emerged quite quickly. In 1980, the Congress approved the so-called Bayh–Dole Act, which gave universities (and other non-profit institutions, as well as small businesses) the right to retain the property rights to inventions deriving from federally-funded research.[8] In 1980, the US Supreme Court ruled in favour of granting patent protection to living things (Diamond v. Chakrabarty), and in the same year the second reformulation of the Cohen and Boyer patent for the rDNA process was approved. In the subsequent years, a number of patents were granted establishing the right for very broad claims (Merges and Nelson 1994). Finally, a one-year grace period was introduced for filing a patent after the publication of the invention.

In Italy, as in Europe as a whole, the grace period introduced in the USA is not available: any discovery that has been published is not patentable. Moreover, the interpretation has prevailed that naturally occurring entities, whether cloned or uncloned, cannot be patented. As a consequence, the scope for broad claims on patents is greatly reduced and usually process rather than product patents are granted. A draft directive from the Commission that attempted to strengthen the protection offered to biotechnology was approved by the European Parliament only in 1998, and an earlier version was rejected in 1994. Still, considerable controversy surrounds this issue.

While it is clear that stronger intellectual property protection is not unambiguously advantageous, it is, however, highly plausible that at least in the early days of the industry the USA reaped an advantage from its relatively stronger regime.

A regulatory climate that did not restrict genetic experimentation

Opposition to genetic engineering research by the 'Green' parties is often quoted as an important factor hindering the development of biotechnology, especially in Germany and in other Northern European countries. Public opposition to biotechnology is also said to have been a factor behind the decision of some companies to establish research laboratories in the USA. In Italy, opposition from these quarters was not, however, an important factor, at least until last year, when systematic opposition to genetically modified food started to develop among consumers.

Factors hindering the adoption of biotechnology among large established firms

A further important feature of the patterns of development of European biotechnology is the delayed response of many large established companies to adopt the new techniques as compared to American (and to some extent British) companies. The relevance of this factor can hardly be underestimated. Given the low rate of creation of new start-ups, the development of biotechnology in Europe rested on the activities of large companies. The delay in the adoption of molecular biology within large corporations was therefore an essential factor explaining the European sluggishness. Moreover, in the absence of vibrant research activity by large firms, new prospective start-ups lacked an essential source of survival and growth, through the establishment of collaborative agreements. As mentioned previously, in the absence of such competencies, large companies would turn to the American scientific and technological base to tap and absorb the new requisite competencies during their catching-up process. Thus, in Europe a vicious circle between the relative backwardness of large firms and low rate of formation of new start-ups was created.

Firms' size, market structure and the competitive environment in Europe

The rate of adoption of molecular biology by established companies varied widely across the world and across firms. Within Europe some large British and Swiss firms were able to adopt the technology rather quickly. Other firms that had smaller research organisations, that were more local in scope, or that were more orientated towards the exploitation of well-established research trajectories,[9] found the transition more difficult (Henderson and Cockburn 1994, Gambardella 1995). Thus, many of the smaller American companies, and almost all of the established French, Italian, German and Japanese companies appear to have been slower to adopt the new technologies.

The relative strength of the local science base appears to be again an important part of the explanation. American and UK science was more advanced than mainland Europe: hence the slow diffusion of the new techniques to European pharmaceutical firms. This explanation is not the whole story, however. For example, many Swiss companies established strong connections with the US scientific system, suggesting that geographic proximity as such played a much less important role in the diffusion of molecular biology.

A second possible explanation is that diffusion was shaped by the relative size and structure of the various national pharmaceutical industries. The pre-existence of a strong pharmaceutical national industry, with some large internationalised companies, may have been a fundamental prerequisite for the rapid adoption of molecular biology. In many European countries (particularly in Italy), the industry was highly fragmented into relatively small companies engaged essentially in the marketing of licensed products and in the development of minor products for the domestic markets. However, size or global reach may have been a necessary condition, but the delay of the largest German companies to adopt these techniques suggest that it was not sufficient.

Thus, the most plausible explanation is that other institutional variables were also important. A possible candidate is the stringency of the regulatory environment. There is now widespread recognition that the introduction of the Kefauver–Harris Amendments had a significant impact in inducing a deep transformation of the US pharmaceutical industry, particularly through raising the cost and complexity of R&D. Partly as a result many US firms were forced to upgrade their scientific capability.

Similarly, Thomas (1994) has suggested that the European country whose leading firms did move more rapidly to adopt the new techniques – Britain – also appears to have actively encouraged a 'harsher' competitive environment. Ever since the 1960s, the British system encouraged the entry of highly skilled foreign pharmaceutical firms, and a stringent regulatory environment also facilitated a more rapid trend towards the adoption of institutional practices typical of the American and Swiss companies: in particular, product strategies based on high-priced patented molecules, strong linkages with universities and aggressive marketing strategies focused on local doctors. The resulting change in the competitive environment in the home market induced British firms to pursue strategies aiming less at the fragmentation of innovative efforts into numerous minor products, than at the concentration on few important products that could diffuse widely into the global market. By the 1970s, the ensuing transformations of British firms had led to their increasing expansion into the world markets.[10]

The diffusion of the new technologies varied, however, not only across regions, but also across firms. Most firms that rapidly adopted the new techniques were large multinational or global companies, with a strong presence, at least as research is concerned, in the USA and generally on the international markets. Zucker and Darby (1995) present some evidence that size alone is a reasonable predictor of adoption, at least in the USA. Henderson (1994) and Henderson and Cockburn (1996) have shown that those firms that adopted molecular biology faster and more efficiently had also already adopted the techniques of 'rational' drug discovery. By and large these were larger firms that had early developed a 'taste' for science and that were able to integrate the new knowledge within the firms. In turn, this was accomplished by a series of organisational changes directed towards building and sustaining tight links to the public research community, essentially through the successful adoption of particular, academic-like forms of organisation of research (Cockburn, *et al.* 1997, Henderson *et al.* 1999).

Here other institutional factors appear to have been a necessary, albeit not a sufficient condition.

First, it is likely that the Anglo-Saxon forms of corporate governance made it easier for companies to 'hire and fire' personnel or rapidly cut non-performing assets, as compared to firms located in 'stakeholder' economies such as Germany. In addition to the problem of cutting established research competencies, European companies faced the risk of giving long-term employment to biologists before biology was proven to be successful over the long run.[11]

Second, to the extent that the adoption of the new techniques and of the associated academic-like forms of organisation of research within companies was faster in companies that had early developed a 'taste for science', it is tempting to suggest that the origin of the American advantage in the use of biotechnology lies in the proximity and availability of first-rate scientific research in universities and in the closer integration between industry and the academic community, as compared to other countries. One might also speculate that this was – at least to some extent – the result of the stronger scientific base of the American medical culture and – relatedly – of the adoption of tight scientific procedures in clinical trials. Through this mechanism, American companies might have to develop earlier and stronger relationships with the biomedical community and with molecular biologists in particular. Segregation of the research system from both medical practice and from close contact with commercial firms (as in France and possibly in Germany) has been highlighted as a major factor hindering the transition to molecular biology in these two countries (see for instance Thomas 1994, Henderson et al. 1999, McKelvey and Orsenigo 2001).

Clustering

The previous observations might bear some relevance for an understanding of the causes of the formation of (and of the failure to develop) innovative clusters in high-technology industry and in biotechnology in particular.

With specific reference to the case of Italy and Lombardy, it is quite clear that most of the factors that account for the dominance of the US industry were simply not in place. Italy lacked a strong scientific base, its industrial base was weak and there was little interaction between industry and universities. Moreover, financial and regulatory constraints have plausibly hindered the development of biotechnology. Against this background, it is then not particularly surprising that innovative activities tended anyhow to cluster in those regions where at least some of these conditions were present. If anything – as mentioned above – Lombardy (and in part Tuscany in pharmaceuticals) had a stronger industrial base and it was a relatively big centre of academic research.

But are these factors sufficient or only necessary conditions for cluster-ing to occur? And which other forces might explain the phenomenon? The question is particularly important in the case of biotechnology, which is usually considered as a strong science-based technology and as such – at least in principle – in large part abstract and codified knowledge (Arora and Gambardella 1994). Under these circumstances, knowledge should be in principle available to everybody. So, what forces led to the agglomera-tion of biotechnology activities in specific clusters?

Part of the answer lies in the observation that mastery of biotechnology required (and still requires) a lot of complementary tacit knowledge. To the extent that the transmission of tacit knowledge is facilitated by geo-graphic proximity (Jaffe *et al.* 1993, Audretsch and Feldman 1996, Swann *et al.* 1998), clustering may be a likely outcome. However, in the case of biotechnology other authors have suggested that the US start-ups were not simply the result of geographic proximity (Zucker *et al.* 1997, 1998). To put it in a different way, certainly geographical proximity is not a sufficient condition for the development of clusters. So, what other factors might be responsible for the observed patterns? And is clustering a necessary con-dition for the development of biotechnology?

Recently, international trade theorists and industrial economists have rediscovered what urban and regional economists have long taken for granted about this issue. For example, Henderson (1986) lists four sources of location externalities, three of which come directly from Marshall and can be found more or less unaltered in Krugman (1991):

a   Economies of intra-industry specialisation: a localised industry can support a greater number of specialised local suppliers of industry-specific intermediate inputs and services, thus obtaining a greater variety at a lower cost;
b   Labour market economies: a localised industry attracts and creates a pool of workers with similar skills, which benefits both the workers and their employers;
c   Ease of communication among firms: information about new tech-nologies, goods and processes seem to flow more easily among agents located within the same area, thanks to social bonds that foster recip-rocal trust and frequent face-to-face contacts. Therefore adoption, dif-fusion and innovation seem faster and more intense in geographical clusters than in scattered locations. That is, some 'knowledge spill-overs' exist, which are geographically bounded;
d   Public intermediate inputs: local authorities may place a stronger than usual effort in providing them as soon as they recognise the import-ance of a specific industry for the welfare of the local communities.

All these agglomeration forces can play a role in defining a cluster of innovation. Definitely, points a), b) and to a lesser extent d) played a role in the case of Lombardy. Thus, localised innovation advantages may arise even in the absence of agglomeration force c). However, this is precisely the force that has attracted the attention of most economists and fascinated many policymakers, especially in the case of biotechnology and with specific reference to university–industry relationships.

The role of geographically bounded knowledge spill-overs is linked to tacitness. Tacitness implies that personal contacts, imitation and frequent interactions are necessary tools for knowledge transmission, and ones which are clearly available at a lower cost for firms located within the same city or region (Swann and Prevezer 1998). Regional economists have built upon such observations, and added many socio-economic features to the need for agglomeration. In particular, they have pointed out that the transmission of tacit knowledge requires mutual trust, a sharing of language and culture, as well as intense non-business relations. Thus social networks, such as those one can find in areas with a homogeneous social background, appear to be key carriers of tacit knowledge (Breschi and Lissoni 2000).

However, very little is known about the precise ways by which knowledge is actually transferred among people located in the same geographic area. The usual story assumes that by being near to universities and other innovative firms, employees of local firms will hear of important discoveries first and thus be able to utilise them before others are aware of their existence.

Some authors (Zucker et al. 1997, 1998) have argued that the standard notion of geographically localised knowledge spill-overs does not seem to apply to the case of biotechnology industry, at least in the phase of its emergence. Rather, they argue that discoveries in this technological area are characterised by high degrees of natural excludability, i.e. that the techniques for their replication are not widely known and anyone wishing to build on new knowledge must gain access to the research team or laboratory setting having that know-how. In these circumstances, the discovering scientists ('superstars') tend to enter into contractual arrangements with existing firms (contract or ownership) or start their own firm in order to extract the supra-normal returns from the fruits of their intellectual human capital. Moreover, the scientists work with or create a new firm within commuting distance of home or university (where they tend to retain affiliation), thus creating localised effects of university research.

These authors show that the innovative performance of biotechnology firms is positively associated to the total number of articles by local university 'star' scientists. However, when the number of articles written by university stars is broken down into those written in collaboration with firm scientists ('linked') and the remaining ('untied'), the coefficient on articles written by local university stars not in collaboration with the firm loses its significance and nearly vanishes in magnitude. Previous evidence on the existence of indiscriminate localised knowledge spill-overs seems therefore to have resulted from a specification error, i.e. the inability to control for the actual relationships linking individual scientists to individual firms.

These results suggest some conjectures:

a   At least in the early phases of new industries, knowledge is not 'in the air', but is embodied in individual scientists and research teams. Social ties and personal contacts are not sufficient to gain access to naturally excludable knowledge. This requires deep involvement in the research process and bench-level scientific collaboration. If anything, this result tends to support the idea that one must invest resources not simply to search for new knowledge, but to build the competencies to absorb the knowledge developed by others and to understand the highly context-specific 'codes' into which knowledge is translated.

b   Naturally excludable and rivalrous knowledge does not spill over, but people (teams) embodying knowledge move (locally) across organisations in order to exploit the value of their knowledge. In other terms, localised effects of university and industry research are most likely to result primarily from a combination of appropriability of tacit non-replicable knowledge and low geographical as well as organisational mobility of researchers.

It is also worth mentioning that the assumption that inventors and firms operating in a specific industry and in close spatial proximity to each other will be more innovative than those who are geographically isolated because of the greater likelihood that they will share (tacit) knowledge has been criticised by Lamoreaux and Sokoloff (1997). In summary, they show that:

i   Concentration of firms and production in a given area is not *per se* a necessary and sufficient condition to determine high rates of innovative activity. To put it in slightly different terms, static externalities related to the current scale or size of an industry in a given city do not necessarily generate better (local) information flows to the advantage of innovative activities. What seems to matter more is the accumulated stock of knowledge (dynamic externalities) in a diversity of industries as well as the levels and types of human capital in a region. Regions that first emerge as centres of innovative activity in a certain industry tend to maintain their advantage over time.

ii   Industries may move across regional and national borders without a corresponding re-location of inventive activity. Inventive activity is 'stickier' than production. Of course, it remains to be seen why it is so. On the one hand, there is the possibility that the locational stickiness of inventive activity derives from the reluctance or lack of incentives to migrate by people with knowledge and experience in an industry. On the other hand, a possible explanation could relate to the richness of general technological know-how in higher-order regions that serve as an effective substitute for specific knowledge and allows new applications to be found across a wide range of industries.

iii   Institutions matter for regional innovation, but in a different way than frequently claimed by many regional economists. These latter tend to stress the role played by 'soft' institutions like trust, norms, codes of communication, conventions, in facilitating the process of information sharing among firms and individuals. According to another perspective, institutions are also important because they help to build those 'bridging' market mechanisms that mediate relations among inventors, suppliers of capital and those who are willing to commercially develop or exploit new technologies.

Finally, empirical evidence has been recently collected to show that linkages bounded by proximity are not always key to innovation (Echeverri-Carroll and Brennan 1999). The results obtained show quite convincingly that local sources of knowledge are key in determining success in the development of new products and processes only in areas with a large accumulation of knowledge (e.g. Silicon Valley). On the contrary, innovations in firms located in cities with a relatively small accumulation of knowledge depend on the relationships with universities and other high-technology firms (suppliers and customers) located elsewhere, especially in higher-order urban centres. More specifically, the results of this study permit one to draw a number of important conclusions:

a   Local boundaries play a fundamental role for the recruitment of a skilled workforce and technical personnel. The presence of other firms working on similar or related things is important not only as a direct source of engineers and scientists, but also because of the indirect effect of reducing the likelihood that a skilled worker will suffer a long period of unemployment. In other words, local areas are important also for non-knowledge-related agglomeration economies.

b   The most dynamic and innovative firms look for knowledge embodied in engineers and scientists wherever they are available, and not necessarily constrained in this by geographical barriers. The question on the importance of intellectual human capital (engineers and scientists) developed within the metropolitan area was given very low rates by fast innovators on average, whereas they scored very high on the question of the availability of frequent flights connecting to other high-tech regions (i.e. Silicon Valley).

c   Local knowledge sources are relatively less important for firms located in lower-order regions. For these firms, local universities are viewed as suppliers of a skilled workforce, rather than loci of innovations or sources of product ideas or spill-over effects. In order to sustain high rates of innovation they must develop linkages with actors (universities and other high-tech firms) located in higher-order regions (see also Lyons 1995).[12]

Trying to draw some conclusions from this discussion, it would appear that clustering may be the outcome of different factors, but mainly:

1 The existence of a strong critical mass of scientific knowledge, in absolute terms: in other words, excellence in scientific research is a basic precondition for attracting innovative activities. Without this, firms (incumbents and/or prospective entrepreneurs) might look for other locations for tapping the relevant knowledge. Moreover, diversity is also important. Insofar as innovation rests on the integration of different fragments of knowledge, the presence of a diversified scientific base becomes a key issue;

2 The existence of a strong and diversified industrial base, with accumulated capabilities and organisational structures enabling them to actually participate in the network of cognitive and social relationships that are necessary to get access to, to absorb, integrate the new knowledge and, on these bases, to engage in successful innovative activities;

3 The existence of specific and often formal organisational devices (including markets for know-how) that allow flows of knowledge to take place.

Conclusion

In this chapter, we have argued that the sluggishness of the development of biotechnology in Italy was due to the lack of most of the basic preconditions for the take-off of innovative activities in this field, as it concerns the scientific and industrial base, the organisational structures linking science to industry, venture capital and intellectual property rights.

Innovative activities clustered, but did not take off, in those regions, primarily Lombardy, where at least some of these preconditions were in part present: mainly as regards the availability of good science and a solid industrial base. Such conditions were, however, not sufficiently developed. As a consequence, biotechnology did not take off.

Finally, we have also argued that clustering is a likely, but certainly not sufficient, condition for the development of innovation in biotechnology and perhaps not even a necessary condition. A cluster may develop if all the above-mentioned preconditions are in place and if 'hard' organisational devices for sustaining intense knowledge flows are created.

These observations might have some implications for policies. Indeed, in recent years European biotechnology seems to have found a new dynamism, and even in Italy and in Lombardy some interesting developments are taking place.

One interpretation of this dynamism might be that policies might – at last – have begun to exert some impact. In many countries, measures have long been taken to introduce within Europe some (or parts of) of the typical American institutional features which have been crucial to the development of new biotechnology start-ups. Thus, policies have been targeted at fostering venture capital, at developing financial markets tailored for new high-risk companies, at promoting the commercialisation of academic research and the mobility between academia and commercial activities. This is certainly the case of Germany and perhaps of France, too. In other countries, however, the effect of policies seems to have been much smaller. And even in the German case, the effects of BioRegio have been widely different across regions. This, in turn, may be the outcome of different policy designs and/or of other structural conditions. In general, there seemed to be minimum critical thresholds that policies have to overcome before they can have some impact, and that in any case interventions aimed at modifying institutions and deeply ingrained forms of behaviour take time.

So, changes in other structural conditions may have played an important role. A primary candidate is to be looked at in a general process of maturation and catching-up in the scientific, technological and organisational base of European biotechnology, mainly as it concerns basic research in universities and in large established companies. As argued in the chapter, the strength and width of the knowledge base, both in universities and in industry, and its integration in efficient organisational forms, was and remains perhaps the single most important factor in explaining performance in biotechnology. Thus, the increasing diffusion of molecular biology in the general training of doctors and in the medical practice, an increased integration of research and teaching, the widening and the increasing integration of the research base in Europe produces now state-of-the-art knowledge that can be exploited by NBFs, at least in specific niches, and by large corporations which are now in the position to express a qualified demand for such research and services.[13]

To be sure, the gap with the USA is far from being filled. Moreover, the institutional structure of most European countries remains profoundly different from the American one. Thus, the future of the new European NBFs and of the patterns of evolution of the biotechnology industry remains to be seen. However, some tentative implications might be drawn from this case.

First, policies can and do have effects, especially if they overcome some critical threshold and they are 'integrated', i.e. they act simultaneously on all the relevant variables. Second, however, policies take time before exerting their effects. Third, the development of a strong research base and of strong technological competencies remains a crucial precondition for industrial dynamism and also for the efficacy of other policy initiatives aiming at inducing institutional and cultural changes: the creation of appropriate incentive mechanisms is clearly an important issue, but incentives without competencies may be totally ineffective or even dangerous.

Notes

1 Table 8.1: Another indicator of the infrequent involvement of Italian industry in biotechnology is the participation in the National Association for the Development of Biotechnology (Assobiotec), the trade association created within the Chemical Industrial Association in 1986. The total number of participating firms peaked to only fifty-eight in 1992 and subsequently it has been declining. Clearly, not all the firms involved in biotechnology participate in the Association and over the last few years divergences within the Association have led some companies to resign their membership. On the other hand, very few of these companies do actually perform research, but are mainly involved in the commercialisation of products and services generated elsewhere. An independent survey on the Italian biotechnology industry carried out in 1989 showed that out of the 134 companies identified by Federchimica as being involved in biotechnology research, only twenty of them had actually in place some ongoing research. The total R&D expenditure of these companies was estimated to be around L200 billion, including also expenditures not directly linked to research proper, like salaries paid to all the employees in specialised firms (Orsenigo 1991).

2 The Tuscany clusters reflect the strong position of Siena, where there is a considerable tradition in biomedical scientific research at the university and where Biocine (formerly Sclavo) is located. Conversely, Latium is the location of the headquarters of several multinational companies and thanks to public subsidies several research laboratories have been opened in Pomezia, just outside Rome.

3 From this perspective, the Italian case would seem to support the hypothesis that innovative activities (especially in new technologies) tend to exhibit strong tendencies towards agglomeration in a few geographical areas and that spatial concentration tends to persist over long periods of time. In the present case, however, this observation might be simply the outcome of a small numbers problem and – more generally – of the absolute low level of innovative activities in this field in Italy. In other words, spatial concentration might result here not so much from the working of specific agglomeration forces, but simply from the sporadic nature of innovative activities.

4 Federchimica was located in Milan. Montedison had its headquarters in Milan and its main research laboratories (Istituto Donegani) were located in the neighbourhood (although in a different region, Piemont). Similarly, the main research laboratories of ENI, EniRicerche was located just in the outskirts of Milan.

5 ENEA was the agency for research on nuclear technologies. Its mission changed several times after the decision to stop nuclear research in Italy and successively became an agency for research in alternative energy sources and a centre for co-ordinating technology transfer.

6 This willingness has been strengthened since the late 1970s with the passage of the Bayh–Dole Act.

7 Indeed, most NBFs' strategies emphasised licensing products rights outside the USA to foreign partners. Thus to an even greater extent than many established US pharmaceutical firms, European firms were well positioned as partners for US NBFs.

8 The 1984 passage' of public Law 98-620 expanded the rights of universities further.

9 In short, those firms that had not adopted the techniques of 'rational' or 'guided' drug discovery.

10 The Japanese experience also looks in many respects like that pursued in Europe outside Switzerland and the UK.

166 S. Breschi, F. Lissoni and L. Orsenigo

11 We owe this observation to an anonymous referee. A similar argument is suggested by Casper (1999).

12 In a related vein, Suarez-Villa and Walrod (1997) have supported the idea that not locating in a spatial cluster may actually hold advantages, by allowing firms to safeguard their privacy and to introduce new products earlier than their competitors.

13 It could also be noted that the take-off of the European start-ups has been taking place in conjunction with the emergence of new technological trajectories based on generic techniques. Certainly in Germany, but not in Italy, most new start-ups are indeed active in these areas (Casper 1999). This may not have occurred purely by chance, because these techniques have characteristics that make them relatively easier to develop within the European technological and institutional environment. First, it is intriguing to think that these techniques represent in a way a sort of revenge of the old chemical-based research paradigm in pharmaceuticals. Their function is essentially to allow for the fast screening of thousands of potentially promising compounds, as it happened – at an infinitely lower speed – at the times of 'random screening' before the molecular biology revolution in pharmaceutical research. To the extent that the 'culture' of the European industry has remained more closely linked to the old paradigm, it should not come as too big a surprise that it is in these areas that new start-ups have more chances to be born and prosper. Second, the new companies embodying competencies in these fields are profoundly different in their nature from the other types of NBF. Precisely because they are based on generic, transversal techniques, their core competencies are less unstable and technical change is less competence-destroying for them. Moreover, they can interact with a large variety of different agents and have in principle a much larger market. Similarly, lead times are much shorter, because sales are usually on a contract basis and immediate. As a consequence, their risk profile is also comparatively lower and access to capital comparatively easier (Casper 1999).

References

Arora, A. and Gambardella, A. (1994) 'The Changing Technology of Technological Change: General and Abstract Knowledge and the Division of Innovative Labour', *Research Policy*, 23: 523–32.

Audretsch, D. and Feldman, M. (1996) 'R&D Spillovers and the Geography of Innovation and Production', *American Economic Review*, 86(3): 630–40.

Breschi, S. and Lissoni, F. (2000) 'Geographical boundaries of sectoral systems', progetto TSER *ESSY – Sectoral Systems in Europe: Innovation, Competitiveness, and Growth*, deliverable No. 5, IV Framework Programme, European Commission-DG XII.

Cancogni, E. (1998) *Relazioni pericolose. I rapporti università-industria in Italia*, dissertation, Milan: Bocconi University.

Casper, S. (1999) 'National institutional framework and high-technology innovation in Germany: the case of biotechnology', Wissenschaftszentrum, Berlin: mimeo.

Cesaroni, F., Cioppi, M. and Gambardella, A. (1995) 'Pure, Willing and Entrepreneur: Industrial Transferability and Italian Scientists in Molecular Biology', in P. David and E. Steinmueller (eds) *A Productive Tension: University–Industry Research Collaborations in the Era of Knowledge-Based Economic Development*, Stanford: Stanford University Press.

Cockburn, I., Henderson, R. and Stern, S. (1997) 'Fixed Effects and the Diffusion of Organizational Practice in Pharmaceutical Research', MIT Mimeo.

Echeverri-Carroll, E.L. and Brennan, W. (1999) 'Are innovation networks bounded by proximity?', in M. Fischer, L. Suarez-Villa and Michael Steiner (eds) *Innovation, Networks and Localities*, Springer Verlag: Berlin: 28–49.

Ellison, G. and Glaeser, E.L. (1999) 'The geographic concentration of industry: Does natural advantage explain agglomeration?', *American Economic Review* 89(2): 311–16.

Feldman, M. (1994) *The Geography of Innovation*, Boston: Kluwer.

Gambardella, A. (1995) *Science and Innovation in the US Pharmaceutical Industry*, Cambridge: Cambridge University Press.

Henderson, J.V. (1986) 'The Efficiency of Resource Usage and City Size', *Journal of Urban Economics*, 19: 47–70.

—— (1999) 'Marshall's Scale Economies', NBER Working Paper 7358.

Henderson, R. (1994) 'The Evolution of Integrative Competence: Innovation in Cardiovascular Drug Discovery', *Industrial and Corporate Change*, 3(3): 607–30.

Henderson, R. and Cockburn, I. (1994) 'Measuring Competence? Exploring Firm Effects in Pharmaceutical Research', *Strategic Management Journal*, 15 (special issue): 63–84.

—— (1996) 'Scale, Scope and Spillovers: The Determinants of Research Productivity in Drug Discovery', *Rand Journal of Economics*, 27(1): 32–59.

Henderson, R., Orsenigo, L. and Pisano, G. (1999) 'The Pharmaceutical Industry and the Revolution in Molecular Biology: Exploring the Interactions Between Scientific, Institutional and Organizational Change', in D. Mowery and R. Nelson (eds) *The Sources of Industrial Advantages*, Cambridge: Cambridge University Press: 267–311.

Jaffe, A.B., Trajtenberg, M. and Henderson, R. (1993) 'Geographic Localization of Knowledge Spillovers as Evidenced by Patent Citations', *Quarterly Journal of Economics*, August 1993: 578–98.

Krugman, P. (1991) *Geography and Trade*, Cambridge, MA: MIT Press.

Lamoreaux, N.R. and Sokoloff, K.L. (1997) 'Location and technological change in the American glass industry during the late nineteenth and early twentieth centuries', NBER Working Paper 5938.

Lyons, D. (1995) 'Agglomeration economies among high technology firms in advanced production areas: the case of Denver/Boulder', *Regional Studies*, 29(3): 265–78.

McKelvey, M. and Orsenigo, L. (2001) 'Pharmaceuticals as a sectoral system of innovation', TSER *ESSY-Sectoral Systems in Europe: Innovation, Competitiveness, and Growth*, deliverable No. 4, IV Framework Programme, European Commission-DG XII.

Merges, R. and Nelson, R. (1994) 'On Limiting or Encouraging Rivalry in Technical Progress: The Effect of Patent Scope Decisions', *Journal of Economic Behavior and Organization*, 25: 1–24.

Orsenigo, L. (1989) *The Emergence of Biotechnology. Institutions and Markets in Industrial Innovation*, London: Pinter Publishers.

—— (1991) 'Archipelago Europe – Islands of Innovation. The case of Italy, in Commission of the European Communities', FAST – MONITOR Project, FOP 243, Prospective Dossier N.1: Science, Technology and Economic Cohesion in the Community, 20–21, Bruxelles.

Orsenigo, L. and Cancogni, E. (1999) 'Le relazioni università-industria in Italia', in C. Antonelli (ed.) *Conoscenza tecnologica. Nuovi paradigmi dell' innovazione-specificità italiana*, Edizione Agnelli: Torino.

Pisano,'G. (1996) 'The Governance of Innovation: Vertical Integration and Collaborative Arrangements in the Biotechnology Industry', *Research Policy* 20: 237–49.

Senker, J., Joly, P.B. and Reinhard, M. (1998) 'Biotechnology and Europe's chemical/pharmaceutical multinationals', in J. Senker (ed.) *Biotechnology and Competitive Advantage*, Aldershot: Edward Elgar: 110–29.

Sharp, M. (1985) 'The New Biotechnology: European Governments in Search of a Strategy', Sussex European Papers, Brighton: University of Sussex.

Suarez-Villa, L. and Walrod, W. (1997) 'Operational strategy, R&D and Intra-metropolitan clustering in a polycentric structure: the advanced electronics industries of the Los-Angeles basin', *Urban Studies*, 34(9): 1343–80.

Swann, P. and Prevezer, M. (1998) 'Introduction', in P. Swann, M. Prevezer and D. Stout (eds) *The Dynamics of Industrial Clustering: International Comparisons in Computing and Biotechnology*, Oxford: Oxford University Press: 52–76.

Swann, P., Prevezer, M. and Stout, D. (eds) (1998) *The Dynamics of Industrial Clustering*, Oxford: Oxford University Press.

Teece, D.J. (1986) 'Profiting from Technological Innovation: Implications for Integration, Collaboration, Licensing and Public Policy', *Research Policy*, 15(6): 285–305.

Thomas, L.G. (1994) 'III, Implicit Industrial Policy: The Triumph of Britain and the Failure of France in Global Pharmaceuticals', *Industrial and Corporate Change*, 3(2): 451–89.

Zucker, L. and Darby, M.R. (1995) 'Present at the Revolution: Transformation of Technical Identity for a large incumbent pharmaceutical firm after the biotechnological breakthrough', NBER Working paper 5243.

—— (1995a) 'Costly Information in Firm Transformation, Exit, or Persistent Failure', NBER Working paper 5577.

Zucker, L., Darby, M.R. and Brewer, M. (1997) 'Intellectual Human Capital and the Birth of U.S. Biotechnology Enterprises', *American Economic Review*, 87(3): 290–306.

Zucker L., Darby, M.R. and Armstrong, J. (1998) 'Geographically localised knowledge: spillovers or markets?', *Economic Inquiry*, 36 (January): 65–86.

9 Dutch cluster policy and the character of regional concentration of biotech firms

Christien Enzing[1]

Although the Dutch breeding ground contained some very excellent growth factors – a strong science base being set up from the early 1980s onwards, a tight network between academia and history and a very well-conceived economic cluster policy since the early 1990s – the growth rates of new biotech companies was considerably lower compared to elsewhere in the world. In fact, two separate subsystems in the Dutch biotech industry have been developed: a relatively few number of high tech start-ups localised in knowledge intensive areas and a number of large and medium-sized companies in traditional industrial sectors that are active in biotech-nology.

In this chapter we will present the specific characteristics of biotechno-logy development in the Netherlands and of Dutch biotechnology policy in the period 1980–99 in more detail. We will analyse why the Netherlands has such a small number of biotech start-ups and is lagging behind in this respect. In a number of regions of the Netherlands from the early 1990s, local organisations set up (bio)science parks with new bio-business and foreign biotech companies. These regional developments will be presented in detail. Conclusions will be drawn on the specific characteristics of the Dutch biotech innovation system as the arena where the creation of new biotech start ups, after a quick start in the 1980s, came to a halt.

Setting the Dutch biotech scene

With its sixteen million inhabitants, the Netherlands is one of the smaller EU member states. It has a strong agricultural and food sector; the (petro) chemical sector is the second biggest. Since the late 1970s the Dutch government has pursued a policy of stimulating innovation in high-technology areas. Nevertheless, the total public spending on R&D is relatively low compared to other EU member states. In 1994, the Gross Expenditures on Research and Development (GERD) as a percentage of the Gross Domestic Product (GNP) was 2.03 per cent. It increased to 2.04 per cent in 1997, but declined to 1.94 per cent in 1998. GERD by industry as percentage of GDP declined from 1.1 per cent in 1997 to 1.05 per cent in 1998. Governmental expenditures as percentage of GDP also declined in this period: from 0.35 per cent to 0.34 per cent. These figures are still below the average OECD (Organization for European Cooperation and Development) level but above the average EU level.

Because of its socially and politically stable character and its geographical position in Europe, the Netherlands is a very open and internationally oriented country. In 1995, almost 6,300 foreign companies, including biotech companies, have located their European activities in the Netherlands. But Dutch biotechnology firms are also export-oriented and some are international market leaders. Almost 90 per cent of the Dutch biotechnology companies have one or more permanent bases abroad (Two Rivers 1997; Ministry of Economic Affairs 1994).

Even since the late 1970s, when the first biotechnological (then: recombinant DNA) research was carried out, the debate on biotechnology has been very intensive in the Netherlands. The Dutch government has facilitated a number of public debates about specific issues such as genetic modification of animals, cloning and xenotransplantation.

Biotechnological research, development and production activities have been subject to legislation since the early 1980s. The Dutch legal framework covers the total field of biotechnology, including the ethical aspects of animal biotechnology. The framework is considered to be quite strict. At the beginning of the 1990s, industry, government and public issue groups have set up a permanent dialogue – the so-called 'Informal Consent' – in which mutual goals are formulated. Labelling of food products with genetically modified products is a very hot issue, especially since GM-soy and -maize has been brought by ships from the USA to the Netherlands. For that reason a new broad public debate on the ethical and social aspects of biotechnology and food was held in 2001.

Due to its size, most people and organisations active in the field of biotechnology in the Netherlands know each other. Networking is also a rather integrated part of most governmental R&D schemes. In 1993 the Ministry of Economic Affairs gave this an extra stimulus by publishing *Biotechnology in The Netherlands: The Network Approach*. In this publication – a co-production with the Netherlands Society for Biotechnology (NBV) – information is filed about governmental organisations, R&D programmes, universities, research institutes, polytechnic/institutes for higher education, organisations for technology transfer, professional organisations, interest groups, information sources, international organisations and members of the NBV. The industry is not included in the publication, but NIABA, the Dutch Industrial and Agricultural Biotechnology Association (set up in 1988) regularly publishes a list of its members and a free newspaper.

Twenty years of Dutch biotech policy

Since the late 1970s, biotechnology has been subject to government policy in the Netherlands. Specific instruments were designed and organisations were set up for the stimulation of biotechnological research and its industrial application. In 1979, the 'Innovatienota' (Innovation Paper) was sent to the Dutch Houses of Parliament by the Minister of Science, in co-operation with the Ministers of Economic Affairs and of Education and Sciences. In this Paper, technological innovation was presented to the Dutch Parliament as the major answer to the social-economic challenges of the late 1970s: slow-down of national economic growth, structural high unemployment, weakening of national competitiveness, rising prices of production resources, etc. The central goal of the new policy was the reinforcement of innovation activities within industry and R&D organisations and a better allocation and use of available technological knowledge.

Several instruments were introduced to support this policy, such as instrument that was introduced was the Innovation Oriented Research Programme (IOP). IOPs aim at developing basic scientific and technical knowledge in specific areas relevant to Dutch industry. The area of the first IOP was biotechnology. In order to prepare and manage the IOP-b, the Programme Committee Biotechnology (PCB) was set up in 1981. The PCB appeared to be one of the most influential actors in biotechnology activities on the policy level in the early and mid 1980s.

Whereas in the early 1980s, science and technology policy was mainly oriented towards a reinforcement of the science base, in the mid 1980s the Dutch government reformulated its policy. The Technology Policy Committee, chaired by Prof. Walter Zegveld (the so-called Zegveld Committee), elaborated this new policy. One of the recommendations of the Zegveld Committee was to expand the IOP-schemes to other technologies and to stimulate the involvement of industry in technology research activities (Ministry of Economic Affairs 1984a). As a result, the policy regarding biotechnological R&D was intensified and became more market-oriented (Ministry of Economic Affairs 1984b). On the basis of the existing IOP-b scheme, mainly focusing on industrial biotechnology, additional programmes on medical, environmental and agricultural biotechnology were introduced.

Another aspect which gained importance in the mid 1980s was the policy of increasing the (positive) awareness in society in general and in industry in particular of the need for innovation (Ministry of Economic Affairs 1986). Several campaigns were financed and organisations were set up to support this policy such as the Foundation for 'Informing the Public on Science and Technology' (PWT).

In 1987, the Ministry of Economic Affairs introduced the 'Programmatische Bedrijfsgerichte Technologie Stimulering' (Programmatic Industry Oriented Technology Stimulation). This co-operative scheme started in

1987 as a specific biotech scheme (PBTS-b), succeeded by other specific technologies (i.e. information technology, medical technology). In 1997 it was transformed into a generic scheme: BTS. The goal of the BTS is to stimulate market-oriented R&D activities within enterprises. Together with the IOP-b scheme, the PBTS-b proved to be the major instruments for the stimulation of biotechnological R&D during the 1980s and the beginning of the 1990s (Enzing 1993).

Technology transfer and networking

Also in 1987, the report *Wissel tussen Kennis en Markt* (Exchange between Knowledge and Market) was presented to the Dutch government by the Advisory Committee on Technology Policy Reinforcement, chaired by Wisse Dekker, a former Philips CEO. The Dekker Committee strongly recommended a stronger focus on technology transfer through a reinforcement of the relation between public research organisations and industry. In particular the diffusion of knowledge towards the smaller and medium-sized enterprises should have a high priority. The implementation of the Dekker report led to a number of activities. An advisory network of twenty innovation centres throughout the country was set up in 1989 for the support of innovation in SMEs (ICNN), the public awareness campaigns were intensified and public research organisations were forced to intensify the market orientation of their research activities.

The conclusions and recommendations by the Dekker Committee had a major impact on biotechnology policy in the following years. In 1988, the national biotechnology programme mentioned two major targets: the reinforcement of the biotechnology R&D activities in those firms that do not yet have a strong position in this field in the Netherlands and the intensification of the involvement of firms in the Dutch network of biotechnology R&D-infrastructure (Ministry of Economic Affairs 1988). In order to implement these targets the Dutch organisation for Applied Scientific Research (TNO) and the Ministry of Economic Affairs initiated a marketing campaign on biotechnology transfer towards SMEs. The Ministry also financially supported the initiation of the Dutch Industrial and Agricultural Biotechnology Association (NIABA).

In 1994, the Minister of Economic Affairs presented the biotechnology policy for the second half of the 1990s: *Biotechnology policy: from research to market*. The central theme was the facilitation of the transition of the results of biotechnology research into marketable products. Table 9.1 shows the political goals as formulated in this document.

Table 9.1 Biotechnology policy goals for the late 1990s

1	*Reinforcement of the existing networks between the knowledge infrastructure and biotechnology industry.* Instruments are the Dutch Association of Biotechnological Research Schools (ABON) and the public–private co-operation projects NOBIS (bioremediation) and Mibiton (public–private partnerships in expensive biotechnology instruments and facilities).
2	*Reinforcement of the participation in European research programmes by Dutch firms and research organisations.* EG-Liaison, associated to Senter, is the responsible actor for implementing this policy.
3	*Enlargement of the industrial base and reinforcement of the relations between firms and research organisations.* Instruments are the PBTS-biotechnology scheme, the 'Technisch Ontwikkelings Krediet' (Technological Development Fund) and the 'Wet Bevordering Speur- en Ontwikkelingswerk' (Law on Research and Development activities).
4	*Stimulation of consultation between producers of new biotechnological products and consumer and environmental organisations.* Instruments are publicity campaigns for raising public awareness and starting public debates on specific biotechnology subjects.
5	*Development by the different involved ministries of a transparent regulatory policy towards the admittance of biotechnology.* By adopting a rather anticipatory attitude, the Ministries developed regulations that were far ahead of EU regulations and those in the other member states.

Source: Ministry of Economic Affairs (1994).

Industrial cluster policy

This focus on networking in Dutch innovation policy gained new dimensions when the cluster concept was introduced. After the competitive advantage of the Netherlands was analysed on the basis of the methodology of Michael Porter (1990), the 'cluster'-concept became very popular in the Netherlands (Jacobs *et al.* 1990).

Although several definitions of clusters were in use, they combine a number of dimensions:

- geographical: the geographical (regional, national or even international) clustering of a number of elements in a production network, or a set of connected networks (industrial district literature);
- horizontal (the classical branch classification) and vertical (the production chain, industrial column user–producer–supplier interaction or 'fillières') (Hakansson 1987, von Hippel 1988, Lundvall 1988);
- lateral: the connection with 'related' sectors with whom specific competences can be shared and which lead to 'economies of scope', for instance car and aerospace industry, consumer electronics and entertainment industry, agro-chemical, seed and pharmaceutical industry (Porter 1990);
- technological (partly an extension of the former): general technologies as link between sectors (Nooteboom 1993);

- relation with the relevant R&D infrastructure: education and research – national system of innovation (Kline and Rosenberg 1986, Imai 1992);
- quality of the network: it is not only about the fact that companies work together, but also about how they work together: conservative versus constructive networks (Kay 1993, Piore and Sabel 1984).

The multi-factoral character of clusters and of cluster dimensions was a very fruitful source for companies as well as governments for future innovative activities. In the paper on 'Industry Policy for the Nineties' (1993), the Dutch government introduced the cluster concept in its innovation policy. The most important elements were: innovative supply and contract out relations to central companies, relations with public funded R&D organisations and educational institutions in regional grouping.

In the Netherlands the cluster concept was mainly used for a defensive industrial policy ('save the existing clusters'), but also for a more offensive technological industrial policy ('create new and reinforce existing clusters') as well as for a so-called 'third phase' in Dutch industrial policy: knowledge intensification of traditionally strong clusters like agro/food, transport, building, seaports and airports, etc. (Jacobs and De Man 1995).

The cluster concept proved to be a very useful concept for transforming the old-fashioned industrial policy – characterised by large lump sums to traditional industry that had to be consolidated – into a more modern industrial policy. A large number of projects was set up in order to stimulate the creation of strong innovative clusters and networks in the market around 'central' companies, in particular the middle-sized giants like DAF (trucks), Océ (copiers) and Fokker (aerospace). Already existing instruments involving forms of public/private or private/private co-operation, were – from the moment the cluster concept was introduced – considered to be important means for the implementation of the cluster policy. But new instruments for the stimulation of public/private co-operation were also introduced in the mid 1990s, such as the so-called Technological Top Institutes. In these institutes large industrial firms, academic research groups and research organisations work together in research programmes that are defined (and partly financed) by large industrial firms. Together with countries like Denmark, Scotland and the United States, the Netherlands is considered to be leading in the field of cluster-based policies (OECD 1999). This was the situation at the end of the 1990s; the cluster concept was the dominant view on innovation policy with a dominant role for existing large firms.

Regional biotech clusters: a bottom-up view on biotech start-ups

There is extensive evidence on the geographic location of innovative activities, knowledge spillover and industrial competitiveness (Jaffé *et al.* 1993, Feldman 1994) showing that the growth of new industries has a strong local character. Specific studies on biotech clusters in knowledge-intensive areas (Audretsch and Stephan 1996, Prevezer 1997, Swann *et al.* 1998) illustrate the formation and development of regionally -based biotech clusters. Of course the Netherlands, for its very small size could be considered as a region and its industrial biotech activities considered as belonging to one cluster.

Table 9.2 shows the size of the regional biotech clusters: the number of companies in the ten main research centres in the Netherlands (universities and public-funded research institutes). For the remaining companies a simple geographical division into northern, middle and southern Nether-lands is made. If we take a close look at the geographical diversity of biotech activities in the Netherlands, a number of hot spots can be observed. There are two very active groups of public and private entre-preneurs who have already been successful in setting up bioscience parks which host foreign and local biotech companies: the BioScience Park in Leiden and the Science Park in Groningen (in the north of the Nether-lands). Amsterdam is a good third, with the specific position as the central capital of the Netherlands which attracts people and business anyway. Finally there are a number of university towns that have more recently become active in the field of biotechnology and where biotech companies – in most cases start-ups – are located, i.e. Wageningen and Maastricht (see Box 9.1 for a brief 'tour de horizon' of the main regional biotech clusters).

Box 9.1: Regional clusters of biotech firms in the Netherlands

BioScience Park Leiden and Delft
The BioScience Park Leiden was one of the first science parks in the Nether-lands. Already in the beginning of the 1980s, due to very active and entre-preneurial staff at the University of Leiden (Prof. Dr. Schilperoort, also chairman of the PCB), of the Maatschappij voor Industriële Producten (a risk capital organisation set up by the Dutch government) and the Mayor of the City of Leiden, the BioScience Park Leiden was set up. They were very successful in attracting US biotech companies to their Park (Centocor, Amgen and Genzyme) and also several start-ups have their home base in the Park. The Leiden BioScience Park has a strong medical and pharmaceu-tical profile, mainly due to the strong public R&D infrastructure in this region: the University Hospital of Leiden, the human medical and biophar-maceutical research groups of the University of Leiden which are part of

Top Research School on Drugs Research and the TNO Institute of Preventive Healthcare. The science park also locates a number of agro biotech companies such as Mogen (now Zeneca) and the agro-pharmaceutical company Pharming. There is close co-operation in biotechnology research between the Universities of Leiden and Delft and for that reason we have included the Delft region in the Leiden biotech cluster. This extensive region around Leiden (including Delft and Zoetermeer) holds some 'old' seed companies, some new start-ups specialised in biotech instruments and two major companies in the food and ingredients industry: Gist brocades (now part of DSM) for food ingredients and Numico (former Nutricia) for infant and clinical food products located in Zoetermeer. However, these major companies do not have specific regional roots, but a national and international network of research institutes and companies with whom they work together.

North Netherlands: Biomed City

Also in the Northern region of the Netherlands, Groningen, an entrepreneurial spirit led to the foundation of what is now called 'BioMed City'. In BioMed City offices and laboratory space is available at four locations within a short distance from the University Hospital and the University of Groningen. The MediTech centre functions as a business incubator and focuses on Biomedical Technology. The Zernike Science Park (after Frits Zernike, Nobel Prize winner for Physics and professor at this university) locates 25 innovative companies and has facilities for high-tech production. It functions as a Bio-Science Business Laboratory Park focusing on the commercialisation of biotechnological and biochemical research. There are now facilities for medium-sized companies under construction. The third location is DSM Biological, the central facility of the DSM's biopharma division, and also set up for contract manufacturing of bio-pharmaceuticals. The fourth location of BioMed City is Eemspoort with space for large production plants. BioMed City was founded in 1996 in order to better communicate the profile of Groningen as a preferred location for biomedical and pharmaceutical companies. It was a joint effort of the University Hospital and the University of Groningen, the City Council and the Investment and Development Company for the Northern Netherlands (NOM). Nowadays approx. 100 biomedical and pharmaceutical companies are located in the northern part of the Netherlands, including some foreign companies like Cordis Europe, Yamanouchi Europe. The first initiatives for a Science Park in Groningen had already been taken in the late 1980s, and among the persons who were very active at that time were a number of entrepreneurial university professors who either came from the United States or had worked there for a considerable period of time.

Amsterdam Science Park

A third regional biotech cluster can be observed in the Amsterdam region. In this region a considerable number of firms developing and/or using biotechnology have been identified. Although the science base in this city is relatively broad (two universities, both with academic hospitals, the Royal Tropics Institute, the Dutch Cancer Institute and affiliated Anthonie van

Leeuwenhoek Hospital, the Central Laboratory of the Blood Bank, the inter-university Ophthalmology Institute and the Dutch Institute for Brain Research) and a location is available with services for new companies to settle, the number of university spin-offs is very small. The Community Council of Amsterdam is now developing strategies for stimulating new business development in biotechnology and a special committee has worked on a SWOT analysis of Amsterdam as a region for bio-business. In the meanwhile, in the Watergraafsmeer polder (WTCW area), a 30 million guilder programme (financed by the national government) is running to set up facilities and create optimal conditions for (start-up) high-tech firms, including life sciences/biotechnology and bio-informatics: The Amsterdam Science Park. This is an initiative of the University of Amsterdam, the National Organisation for Scientific Research (the national Dutch Research Council), the Rabobank and the Council of Amsterdam.

Other knowledge-based regions: Wageningen, Nijmegen, Enschede and Maastricht

For the other regions with a high-quality knowledge infrastructure, a good overview of the factors that play a role in biotech business development is not available. Almost each university has a technology transfer bureau and almost every local Council has been facilitating a high-tech business park close to the university campus. From the four knowledge-based regions left, Wageningen should especially be mentioned because of its high density of agro and food research: the Wageningen University and Research Centre (WURC) that hosts the former Agricultural University and the research institutes of the Ministry of Agriculture, Nature Conservation and Fisheries. Also close to Wageningen is the Dutch Institute for Diary Research (NIZO) in Ede and the TNO Institute for Food and Nutrition Research (TNO–Voeding) in Zeist. Nevertheless, the number of (start-up) biotech firms in the Wageningen region is rather limited. It is more correct to consider Wageningen as a national centre for agro and food research. It hosts the Top Technological Institute on Food Research in which the research organisations mentioned (WURC, NIZO and TNO–Food Research) and 12 leading companies in the food industry participate. Unilever plays a central role in this Top Research Institute. In the context of increasing internationalisation, especially of giants such as Unilever, the creation of this institute must be considered as a means to keep the Unilever R&D facilities in the Netherlands. Numico has recently moved its R&D facilities (from Zoetermeer) to Wageningen.

In the southern part of the Netherlands, the University and University Hospital of the city of Maastricht are a growth medium for a number of biotech start-ups. At this moment approx. 4 biotech start-ups have been identified in this region. Recently the regional development agencies of Maastricht, Aken (Germany) and Liège (Belgium) have set up Ineurope, a partnership for Life Sciences with the objective to attract small and medium-sized companies to this Euroregio. In the last 5 years around 150 international companies have settled in this Euroregio, including a considerable number in the life science field; more should follow. It is to be expected that, similar to other cities with university hospitals, Rotterdam would also show a number of biomedical/biopharmaceutical start-ups. This is not the case. In this region we have identified some seed, plant breeding and instrumental companies and Unilever Research in Vlaardingen. The latter is one of the main biotech firms in the Netherlands, but it does not function as a feeding ground or incubator for new biotech start-ups in the region.

In 1999 the City of Lelystad (province Flevoland) decided to set up a BioScience Park of 45 hectares, that opened in July 2001 and is financially supported by EU funds. At least 1,300–1,800 people should be working there in a 'Pharma Park' (human and veterinary healthcare companies) and an 'Eco Park' (ecological agriculture)

The organisations most responsible for the regional biotech activities are local Councils, entrepreneurial professors and technology transfer bureaus set up in the early 1980s. Currently the so-called regional development agencies are playing an active role in regional business development. In five regions (including the provinces of Friesland, Groningen en Drenthe, Overijssel, Gelderland, Brabant en Limburg) these regional development agencies, together with local and national investment agencies create new employment by stimulating the regional economy. They provide advice on subsidies, invest venture capital in promising companies, initiate development projects and act as an intermediary between industry and government.

However, the bulk of Dutch companies that are active in biotech are not geographically closely connected to the location of one of the biotech research centres in the Netherlands; this includes most of the big and medium-sized companies in traditional sectors with biotech activities.

State-of-the-art: a strong science base but a lack of new business development in biotechnology

After almost 25 years from the start of the first biotechnology activities in the Netherlands, it can be concluded that there is a very strong biotechnology science base in the public and private sector, with a volume of 8,000 ftes (full-time equivalents). Peer reviews show that the quality of Dutch biotechnology research is rather high (Benedictus and Enzing 1998a, 1998b, KNAW 1999). In 1999, approximately 155 companies are involved in biotech research, development and/or production and they cover all major biotechnological application areas: agro-industry, fine chemistry, food and feed industry, pharmaceutical industry, human/animal health, environment and instruments. Some of these companies are world market leaders: Unilever, Numico, Organon (AKZO-Nobel), DSM, Avebe. Approximately sixty of these companies are dedicated biotech firms

Table 9.2 Regional clustering of biotech companies in the Netherlands

University town/ region	(Bio) Science or University Business Park	Research Centres	Number of companies
Amsterdam	Watergraafsmeer, Amsterdam Science Park	University of Amsterdam, Free University of Amsterdam, both with academic hospitals, the Royal Tropics Institute, the Dutch Cancer Institute and affiliated Anthonie van Leeuwenhoek Hospital, the Central Laboratory of the Blood Bank, the inter-university Ophthalmology Institute and the Dutch Institute for Brain Research	18
Delft	Business Park	Technical University Delft	9
Enschede	Business Park	(technical) University Twente	2
Groningen	BioMed City, BioScience Park	University and Academic Hospital Groningen	21
Leiden	BioScience Park	University and Academic Hospital Leiden, TNO Preventive Healthcare	23
Maastricht		University and Academic Hospital of Maastricht	3
Nijmegen		University and Academic Hospital of Maastricht	4
Rotterdam		University and (Academic) Dijkzicht Ziekenhuis	6
Utrecht		University and Academic Hospital of Utrecht	12
Wageningen	Agribusiness Park	Wageningen University and Research Centre, Dutch Institute for Dairy Research (NIZO in Ede)	7
Other companies in the northern part of the Netherlands			16
Other companies in the middle part of the Netherlands			14
Other companies in southern part of the Netherlands			20
Total			**155**

Source: Database TNO-STB (December 1999).

operating predominantly in the fields of diagnostics and therapeutics, plant biotechnology and environmental biotechnology. Approximately 900 ftes are employed in the biotechnological SMEs, of which 500 are in biotechnology related positions in R&D (NIABA 1999, Ernst and Young 1999).

In the period from 1981 to 1998 huge investments have been made by the Dutch public and private sector (Table 9.4). In the period from 1981 to 1993 the Dutch government stimulated biotechnology with more than 400 million guilders (178.6 million ECU) and in the period from 1994 to 1998 it spent – mostly through generic technology schemes – another 155 million ECU on biotechnology (Enzing *et al.* 1999). The share of Dutch scientists in EU programmes (FP 3, 4 and 5) has been and is rather high. The average participation of Dutch scientists in EU R&D programmes is approximately 12.5 per cent, which is in absolute figures two times the 'just retour' of the Dutch contribution to the EU.

Considering the process of new biotech business development in Europe, a growth can be observed in numbers as well as in size. However, the Dutch share in these figures is relatively low. In 1999 1,178 so-called emerging life sciences companies (ELISCOs) were wanted; only 60 of these are located in the Netherlands. These Dutch companies represent approximately 2 per cent of the total workforce of the 1,178 West European ELISCOs – 45,823 ftes (Ernst and Young 1999).

There is only one conclusion: the Netherlands is very much lagging behind in the field of new biotech business development, especially if we take into account the rich pool of biotech knowledge that has been created in this country during the last two decades. The Netherlands is ranked in 7th position after the UK, Germany, France, Israel, Sweden and Switzerland; if it comes to young start-ups the Netherlands can be found in 10th position after Belgium, Denmark and Finland. Whereas the investments of European participation companies in young biotech companies almost doubled in 1998 – from 1.6 to 3.5 billion guilders – investments in Dutch biotech companies rose with a figure of 12 per cent, a rather modest share compared to an average of 40 per cent in Europe.

Table 9.3 State-of-the-art of biotechnology/life sciences in the Netherlands

Stimulation of biotechnology/life science innovation projects		
• Government	ca. 765 million guilders	
• Industry	ca. 510 million guilders	
• Total (1981–1998)	ca. 1.275 million guilders	
Dutch share in EU FP Life Science programmes (3, 4 and 5)		ca. 12.5%
Dutch high biotech start-ups	ca. 60 companies	ca. 900 ftes
Dutch market share in EU	ca. 5% (companies)	ca. 2% (ftes)

Source: NIABA (1999), Ernst and Young (1999).

However, in the beginning of the 1990s approximately forty biotech start-ups had been established in the Netherlands. The Netherlands was very successful at that time and ranked in second position after the United Kingdom. For a combination of reasons, the dynamics in business development faded out and in 1999 the figures of Ernst and Young show that the number of small high biotech start-ups is somewhere around sixty (Ernst and Young 1999).

Analysis of slowly developing Dutch new bio-business development in a regional context

The Netherlands has some very excellent ingredients for successful biotechnology clusters: a strong science base set up from the early 1980s onwards, a tight network between academia and industry and a very well conceived economic cluster policy since the early 1990s. However, the three did not mix; no specific policy was made either to stimulate (regional) biotech cluster formation or to target new business development (rather then serving incumbents). All in all, the number of biotech start-ups is rather low and the formation of regional clusters has just started.

How should we understand this? Are there specific characteristics of the Dutch Biotechnology Innovation System responsible for this lagging behind? We have identified the following six key factors and will discuss them in detail. The first set of four factors deal with the specific character of Dutch innovation policies, the other two with the specific character of the Dutch business community.

Cluster policy favours the existing industrial structure

Although Dutch technology policymakers were very much aware of the economic importance of regional clustering and the role of small companies in industrial development, this did not lead to new instruments in this respect. In Dutch (bio)technology policy there is a very strong focus on national winners and their central role in new economic development. This already started in the mid 1980s when companies such as Gist brocades and Unilever received enormous sums of money for doing biotech R&D. Another example is the Technical Top Institute on Food Sciences organised around six medium and big companies in the life sciences. In the business plan of the institute no role for new start-ups or spin-offs is mentioned. A similar process of stimulating existing companies can also be observed in the national cluster policy: groups of companies always with one big central company and related research institutes were stimulated to work together. In the period 1980–99 there were no national or regional programmes in the Netherlands that had as their goal to stimulate regional biotech activities or biotech start-up companies.

Market-oriented technology policy

In the 1980s biotechnology development was stimulated by specific biotechnology programmes, but since the beginning of the 1990s biotechnology was mostly stimulated by general R&D and innovation schemes. In the period from 1994 to 1998 the Netherlands belonged, together with Austria and Iceland, to the group of countries that had a decreasing number of specific biotechnology programmes. In this period the spending of the Dutch government on specific biotechnology programmes was in absolute as well as relative figures the lowest in Europe. Except for Greece and Portugal, all other European member states considered biotechnology as an important area in R&D policy that had to be stimulated by specific and voluminous R&D programmes (Enzing *et al.* 1999). One of the main reasons was, as already discussed, that market-oriented technology development became the dominant concept in the Dutch R&D policy. Criteria, such as commercial applications and for some programmes sustainable development, played an important role in the selection of the projects.

Participation of companies in research programmes and the existence of conditions for intellectual property rights were rather common measures included in the Dutch R&D programmes. This policy favoured the participation of existing companies. Companies that already have a settled position are much better equipped to formulate their research ideas and potential markets than just-started companies.

Weak development of local and regional policies for stimulation start-ups

The local presence of laboratory facilities, management assistance, pilot plant facilities, DNA libraries, gene banks, etc. are a common feature of the most successful centres of life sciences start-up activities (Swann *et al.* 1998). Another related aspect is the importance of 'role models'. The incubator is a focal centre of entrepreneurial activities and, except for technology transfer and managerial advice, also a transfer point of entrepreneurial spirit in the region. As we concluded these facilities were only available in a few localities in the Netherlands. In 1999 only in three regions (Leiden, Groningen and Amsterdam) local facilities such as incubators that are a breeding ground for new start-ups, existed.

Regulation

The Netherlands has no general biotechnology legislation which encompasses all the legal aspects of the use of biotechnology. On the contrary, rules concerning biotechnology activities are integrated in the existing regulations. In the early 1990s, Dutch regulation was ahead of many European and non-European countries, specifically with the Dutch Decree on Novel Foods (1993) and also with the environmental regulations set up in the early 1980s. Important drivers for the establishment of biotechnology regulations in the Netherlands were the public debate on the health and safety aspects of biotechnology and the intensive financing schemes for biotechnological R&D during the 1980s and 1990s, resulting in projects reaching the phases of product development and market introduction (Enzing 1995).

Although the well-developed regulations give some clarity to entrepreneurs about what to expect with respect to the legislative aspects of their biotechnology activities in the Netherlands, representatives from industry think that the Netherlands is too quick with ethical considerations and, consequently, with legal regulations; it is far ahead of European trends. Industry representatives also say that in general Dutch legislation concerning biotechnology is considered an extra hindrance for start-up companies.

There is only one white spot on the judge's black robe: the patenting of biotechnological findings. The attitude of the Dutch Government, under pressure from Parliament, has always been one of opposition to the patenting of plants or animals. During the many years of debate on a European level about a directive on patenting biotechnological inventions, the Netherlands has made many efforts to make their objections known to the other European member states. Early in 1998, awaiting European legislation, a new Dutch law was even approved concerning a prohibition of the patenting of animals and plants. But with the approval by the European Parliament and the European Council of Ministers of the directive on patenting biotechnology discoveries in the mid-1998s, the Netherlands were forced to alter current legislation and allow the legal protection of biotechnological research results. Within the Council of Ministers, only the Netherlands voted against the directive. One of the main arguments of the Dutch Government is that the directive would grant a patent 'for life' and, as a consequence, would stimulate so-called 'bio-piracy'. Though the Dutch Government did not at first appeal, under pressure from Parliament a procedure was started in the European Court of Justice in Luxembourg (Two Rivers 1999). The Dutch biotechnology industry, represented by the NIABA, is absolutely in favour of such a directive and is of the opinion that if the directive is not implemented the basis for young start-up companies will be completely lost.

Investment capital

The Dutch market for venture capital is relatively well developed. One of the world's most successful biotechnology venture capitalists, Atlas Venture, has its home base in the Netherlands. In 1995, the amount of available capital represented 0.6 per cent of the Dutch GNP. Of the total amount of venture capital in the Netherlands, a major part is provided by several investment banks (30 per cent) and pension funds (10 per cent). Only 1 per cent is provided by industry. Most venture capital firms in the Netherlands (approximately sixty) are associated with the NVP, the Dutch association of venture capital firms. In the 1990s, the amount invested by venture capital firms increased significantly from 550 million florin in 1990 to 1,680 million florin in 1997. Approximately 200 million florin was invested as seed and start capital. The total investments made by venture capital firms amounted to almost 5,000 million florin in 1997. About 84 million florin was invested in biotechnology companies (NVP website).

However, when attempting to make use of external financial resources for the first time, Dutch firms encounter a number of difficulties. First, providers of capital have difficulties in assessing future revenues and risks of new products and services. Venture capitalists are also reluctant to regard immaterial assets, in which most start-up firms invest, as a security for financing investments. Second, venture capitalists regard the presence of high-quality management capabilities in start-up firms as an essential condition for providing financial resources. If there are any doubts about management capabilities, financing is refused. Approximately 95 per cent of the requests for venture capital are rejected, mostly because of a probable lack of management capabilities. Dutch informal investors use the same criterion. When informal investors provide financial resources, they also provide management support. As a consequence of the existing difficulties, relatively many Dutch firms tend to postpone or even cancel their investment projects. Dutch venture capital firms tend to turn away from investments that involve a high risk factor, like the segment of innovative start-up firms. Only 15 per cent of the total venture capital investments in the Netherlands are for start-up firms. A consequence is that the availability of small financial investments is diminishing. In 1995, only nine of the forty-three associated members of the NVP invested amounts less than 0.2 million florin per project. In contrast to the venture capital firms, informal investors concentrate on small-scale investment projects, and consequently in new and expanding young firms. They invest approximately 34 per cent of their capital portfolio into starters (Ministry of Economic Affairs 1998).

In October 1996, the Ministry of Economic Affairs, in co-operation with regional industrial development agencies and venture capital firms, initiated three so-called TechnoStarters Funds: a TechnoStarters for the Southern and Eastern Netherlands, a TechnoStarters Fund for the Northern and Eastern Netherlands and a Technology and Industry Fund for Amsterdam and the province of North-Holland (TIFAN). The funds provide risk-bearing capital to start-up firms with high-technology products and also give additional management support. The Ministry of Economic Affairs provides 3 million florin per fund and the other partners 8 million florin, resulting in a total amount of 33 million florin. The funds provide financial support in exchange for participation in the firms, mainly by means of shares. Since the official start, early in 1997, approximately ten start-up biotechnology firms have applied for funding, but all have been refused, mainly due to a lack of commercial viability. In order to get financial support by the TechnoStarters Funds, starting firms are expected to realise a return on sales within 1 year. Most of the applying biotechnology firms are still in the phase of research and development, and therefore are not expected to meet this criterion.

For a good business plan, presented by communicative business people and focused on attractive market developments, it is possible to attract venture funds. The financial bottle-neck in the Netherlands is in the availability of seed capital for financing the first commercial activities before venture capital is invested, such as the financing of development activities of the design and first steps in a patenting strategy. At the end of 1999 only one Dutch biotech start-up, Pharming, has gone public through an IPO; two are in the preparation phase.

Entrepreneurial culture

Particularly in the field of new business development there is a weakness in the Dutch innovation system. The factor that has been analysed as the most crucial in the backlog of the Dutch biotech industry is the lack of entrepreneurial – risk-taking – culture in the Netherlands. The academic mentality is characterised by a great reluctance to take (financial) risks. In the Netherlands only 10.2 per cent of the working population are entrepreneurs. This figure is below the EU average and the US average (both 11.4 per cent). Also the number of fast-growing companies is rather low in the Netherlands. About 6 per cent of the medium-sized companies in the Netherlands are in this category, in the USA this figure is 25 per cent. Because three-quarters of all new jobs are created by start-up firms and grow-up firms, the stimulation of this type of activity has a high priority in Dutch economic policy (Ministry of Economic Affairs 1999a). There are also hardly any incentives for academics to become entrepreneurs: good researchers are always offered good jobs in public-funded research institutes or in industry. In the academic world there is hardly any information available about the do's and don'ts of a profitable technology transfer, let alone of setting up one's own business.

For academics who become entrepreneurs it is very important to retain links with the academic world. A recent study showed that 70 per cent of the academic founders of 101 US biotech companies maintained full-time employment with their academic institutions (Audretsch and Stephan 1999). In the Netherlands this is far from the case and until recently was even discouraged by the government authorities. Professors or advanced postdoctoral academics are not encouraged to start up new companies: returning when things go poorly is not a serious option. Also some Dutch university administrators take very stringent negotiation positions when it comes to agreements on patents and licensing of research results, throwing up barriers for academics who want to undertake entrepreneurial activities.

Only a very few scientists from universities or research institutes have started a new company. A relatively large number of biotech start-ups have been set up by persons who have been located in the USA for a period of time and bring with them the culture of setting up their own business. The conclusion was similar in other studies, e.g. migration as an important factor for success of new business development (Niosi forthcoming).

Conclusions

The development structure of the biotech industry in the Netherlands does not show the same pattern as the US or UK biotech industry with a dominant role of new start-ups and small firms in the first stage of development and with a growing number of strategic alliances between these specialised biotech firms and big life sciences multinationals (Orsenigo 1989, Zucker *et al.* 1997).

Considering the growth and actual structure of the Dutch biotech industry, it seems that there have been two processes, almost parallel. On the one hand, we can conclude that in the Netherlands the character of local/regional biotech clusters is mainly determined by the growth and development of biotech start-ups and some successful medium-sized biotech companies in bioscience or business parks close to university and research institutes. In these regional clusters, the big multinational companies do not play a role of any importance.

On the other hand, we can also conclude that in the process of growth and development of the Dutch biotech industry, the role of start-ups has been almost zero. Considering the size of biotech activities in terms of turnover and employment, the biotech activities in the Dutch industry were and are most concentrated in large (multinational) companies (Unilever, DSM/Gist-brocades, AKZO-Nobel, Numico Campina Melkunie, FCDF).

The existence of these two different subsystems in the Dutch biotech industry refers to what Nooteboom (1999) presented as a mix of two systems of governance: the 'exit' and 'voice' systems (stereotypically the US versus the German style). On the one hand, a few small entrepreneurial companies have started and grown in a more or less similar fashion to their counterparts in the biotech areas in the USA. On the other hand, we have the incumbents that adopt biotechnology as one of the technologies to strengthen their market position and have strategic alliances in such new promising fields as genomics all over the world. This dual system, piloting companies into their own specific contexts around the concept of trust, could move in the direction of a 'third-way' system (Nooteboom 1999) when after a certain period new Dutch policies for biotech start-ups have materialised.

At the end of the 1990s a sense of urgency was felt in the Netherlands that extra measures had to be taken in order to stimulate commercialisation of biotech R&D, especially through biotechnological entrepreneurship. In the 1970s and 1980s a number of excellent Dutch academics moved to the USA and Canada and some of them are now very successful entrepreneurs. It was feared that, because the Netherlands had such a wealthy pool of biotech knowledge and other European countries had successes in their bioregions (Germany, UK, Belgium), a new brain-drain might start, but this time to other European countries.

For that reason the Dutch national government first ordered an international comparative analysis of seven biotechnology regions in the world. These regions (Boston-USA, Cambridge-UK, Quebec-Canada, Munich-Germany, Belgium, the Netherlands and southern Sweden) were benchmarked using the factors: science base, culture, capital, environment, incubators, management and dynamics. The benchmark showed that The Netherlands, as well as Belgium and southern Sweden, is rather underdeveloped. The need for home-grown entrepreneurs and a change of political attitude towards the industry as a whole was considered to be vital if the sector is to survive competitively for the future (Moret *et al.* 1998: 50). This led to the next phase in Dutch biotech policy. In 1999 the Ministry of Economic Affairs published the Life Sciences Action Plan, a scheme to stimulate life sciences start-up with a budget of 100 million florin for a period of 5 years (Ministry of Economic Affairs 1999b).

A new episode started.

Notes

1 TNO Strategy, Technology and Policy, Delft, the Netherlands.

References

Assouline, G., Chataway, J. and Genet, C. (1996) 'Réseaux et dynamiques locales', *Biofutur* 157, June 1996: 17.
Audretsch, D.B. and Stephan, P. (1996) 'Company–Scientist Locational Links: The case of Biotechnology', *American Economic Review*, 86(3): 641–52.

—— (1999) 'How and Why Does Knowledge Spill Over in Biotechnology?', in D.B. Audretsch and R. Thurik (eds) *Innovation, Industry, Evolution and Employment*, Cambridge: Cambridge University Press: 216–29.

Benedictus, J.N. and Enzing, C.M. (1998a) *Moleculaire en reproductiebiologie bij dieren, Sterkte Zwakte analyse (Animal Molecular and Reproduction Biology: a Strength–weaknesses analysis)*, NRLO-rapport nr. 98/35, Den Haag.

—— (1998b) *Moleculaire Plantenbiotechnologie, Sterkte Zwakte analyse (Molecular Plant Biotechnology: a Strength–weaknesses analysis)*, NRLO-rapport nr. 98/39, Den Haag.

Enzing, C.M. (1993) *Twaalf jaar biotechnologiebeleid (Twelve years of Biotechnology Policy)*, report written for the Ministry of Economic Affairs, TNO-STB, Apeldoorn.

—— (1995) *Overzicht van wetgeving, maatregelen en activiteiten van de overheid betreffende biotechnologie (Overview of legal regulation and other governmental activities concerning biotechnology)*, report written for the Rathenau Instituut, TNO-STB, Apeldoorn.

Enzing, C.M., Benedictus, J.N., Engelen-Smeets, E., Senker, J.M., Martin, P.A., Reiss, T., Schmidt, H., Assouline, G., Joly, P.B. and Nesta, L. (1999) *Inventory and analysis of biotech programmes and related activities in all countries participating in the EU FP4 Biotechnology Programma 1994–1998, Analytical Report*, TNO-STB/SPRU (UK)/ISI-FhG (BRD)/QAP Decision and INRA (Fr), published by the EU Publication Office under the title: *Inventory of Public Biotechnology R&D in Europe* (EUR 18886/1–3).

Enzing, C.M. and Kern, S. (forthcoming) *European Biotechnology Innovation System: National report of The Netherlands*, TNO-STB, Delft.

Ernst and Young (1999) *European Life Sciences 99. Sixth Annual report. Communicating value*, London: Ernst and Young International.

Feldman, M (1994) *The Geography of Innovation*, Boston: Kluwer.

Hakansson, H. (1987) *Industrial Technological Development: a network approach*, London: Croom Helm.

Hippel, E. von (1998) *The Sources of Innovation*, New York: Oxford University Press.

Imai, K. (1992) 'A note on the structural evolution of innovation systems', paper for the workshop 'Systems of Innovation', Bologna, Italy, 5–6 October 1992.

Jacobs, D., Boekholt, P. and Zegveld, W. (1990) *De economische kracht van Nederland. The competitive advantage of the Netherlands*, Den Haag: SMO-Boek.

Jacobs, D. and de Man, A.P. (eds) (1995) *Clusters en concurrentiekracht. Naar een nieuwe praktijk in het Nederlandse bedrijfsleven?*, TNO-STB i.s.m. EUR, Bedrijfskunde, Alphen a/d Rijn, Samsom.

Jaffe, A.B., Trajtenberg, M. and Henderson, R. (1993) 'Geographic Localisation of Knowledge Spillovers as evidenced by patent citations', *Quarterly Journal of Economics* 63(3): 577–98.

Kay, J. (1993) *Foundations of Corporate Success*, Oxford: Oxford University Press.

Kline, S.J. and Rosenberg, N. (1986) 'An overview of Innovation', in R. Landau and N. Rosenberg (eds) *The Positive Sum Strategy: Harnessing Technology for Economic Growth*, National Academy of Engineering, Washington, D.C.: The National Academy Press: 275–306.

KNAW (1999) *Bio-Exact: Mondiale trends en nationale positie in biochemie en bio-fysica*, Verkenningen, Amsterdam, Koninklijke Nederlandse Akademie van Wetenschappen.

Lundvall, B.A. (1988) 'Innovation as an interactive process: from user–producer interaction to the national system of innovation', in G. Dosi *et al. Technical Change and Economic Theory* 1988: 349–69.

Ministry of Economic Affairs (1984a) *Project Technologiebeleid Rapport: Naar een op de marktsector gericht technologiebeleid*, Report of the Zegveld Committee, Den Haag.

—— (1984b) *Beleidsoverzicht Technologie 1984–1985*, Den Haag.

—— (1987) *Wissel tussen kennis en markt*, Report of the Advisory Committee for the Extension of the Technology Policy (Commissie Dekker), Den Haag.

—— (1988) *Beleidsoverzicht Technologie (1988–9)*, Den Haag.

—— (1993) *Biotechnology in The Netherlands: The Network Approach*, a co-production with the Netherlands Society for Biotechnology, Den Haag.

—— (1994) *Biotechnologiebeleid: Van onderzoek naar markt*, Den Haag.

—— (1997) *Kansen door synergie*, Den Haag.

—— (1998) Note on 'The knowledge protection and exploitation policy of universities', Den Haag.

—— (1999a) Note on 'The entrepreneurial society', presented by the State Secretary of Economic Affairs, September 1999.

—— (1999b) *Actieplan voor starters op het gebied van Life Sciences*, Letter to the Dutch parliament, 26 May 1999.

Ministry of Science Policy (1979) *Innovatie: het overheidsbeleid inzake technologische vernieuwing in de Nederlandse samenleving (Innovatienota)*, Den Haag.

Moret, Ernst and Young (1998) *Strategies for accelerating technology commercialisation in Life sciences: An international comparative analysis of seven bioscience regions*, Den Haag.

NIABA (1999) *Biotechnologie Nieuws*, 12(5), November 1999.

Niosi, J. (forthcoming) *Canada's National System of Innovation*, Montreal: McGill-Queen's University Press.

Nooteboom, B. (1993) 'Een aanzet tot industriebeleid (I)/(II)', in *ESB*, 17-3-1993: 240–9.

—— (1999) 'Innovation and inter-firm linkages: new implications for policy', *Research Policy*, 28 (8): 793–805.

OECD (1999) *Cluster analysis and Cluster based policy making in OECD countries*, Paris.

Orsenigo, L. (1989) *The Emergence of Biotechnology Institutions and Markets in Industrial Innovation*, London: Pinter Publishers.

Piore, M. and Sabel, C. (1984) *The Second Industrial Divide. Possibilities for Prosperity*, New York: Basic Books.

Porter, M. (1990) *The Competitive Advantage of Nations*, New York, Free Press.

Prevezer, M. (1997) 'The Dynamics of Industrial Clustering in Biotechnology', *Small Business Economics*, 9(3), June: 255–71.

Swann, P., Prevezer, M. and Stout, D. (1998) *The Dynamics of Industrial Change*, Oxford: Oxford University Press.

Two Rivers (1997) *Holland Biotechnology, The future is here and now*, Haarlem.

—— (1999) *Holland biotechnology, Moving into the age of biodiscovery*, Haarlem.

Zucker, L., Darby, M. and Brewer, M. (1997) 'Intellectual Human Capital and the Birth of U.S. Biotechnology Enterprises', *National Bureau of Economics Research Working Paper 4653*, Cambridge: MA.

10 The fourth pillar?

An assessment of the situation of Finnish biotechnology

Gerd Schienstock and Pasi Tulkki

Abstract

The success in constructing a flourishing information and telecommunication cluster has encouraged Finland to seek equal possibilities in other knowledge-intensive industrial branches. Currently, biotechnology is seen as an auspicious business area. As in other parts of Europe, Finnish biotechnology concentrates mainly on pharmaceutical industries. More than 70 per cent of the human resources of Finnish biotechnology industries is located in that industrial area.

Despite large investments and financing, modern biotechnology industries are still a marginal industrial branch in the Finnish economy. Its turnover in 1999 was only 1 per cent of the total GNP. The wide spectrum of Finnish higher education and the close relations of co-operation between universities and industries can open up promising prospects. Finland's technology-affirmative attitudinal climate works in the same direction. This progress can be delayed by a lack of highly skilled human resources, which is already a problem in the IT sector. The small size and minor experience in global markets have also limited the success of the Finnish firms.

Introduction

Finland is largely known as a country of forest industries. Until the end of the 1950s, about 90 per cent of exports from Finnish industry came from the forest or wood processing industry. In the 1960s, this figure decreased to nearly 70 per cent, but the forest cluster, constituted by forestry, mechanical forest industry, chemical forest industry, and several related supplier and customer industries, was still by far the biggest exporter in Finland. The share of the metal industry at that time was about 13 per cent. During the following decades, the metal industry improved its position as an export industry, mainly due to the increasing trade with the Soviet Union. Nowadays the share of the forest cluster in the Finnish export industry is still 31 per cent, but the share of metal industry increased to 45 per cent. Half of the metal industry's export consists of the products of the new information and telecommunication sector. During the 1990s, Finland was able to develop the IT industry as the third pillar of its exports beside the old wood processing industry and the traditional metal industry.

Indisputably, Nokia is the dominating company in the Finnish IT sector. The share of Nokia in the recent export boom of Finnish industry became so large that fear of a 'Finnish Nokia dependence' was expressed. On the other hand, the high standard of expertise and know-how created by Nokia can be viewed as a base for constructing other high-technology clusters. Both arguments are mentioned when the need for a fourth pillar for the Finnish export industry is being discussed. In this debate, biotechnology is seen as a promising new growth area to which Finnish public attention is now very strongly drawn. There is great hope that the success story of the IT sector, which for good reason can be considered the result of national planning (Science and Technology Policy Council of Finland 2000) can be repeated in the biotech sector. The progress made in the IT branch can be explained by a close co-operation between industry, public R&D research institutes and the education system. Business enterprises in the sector have invested heavily in R&D and at the same time about half of all the national research input is used in or for the benefit of this single branch. And in higher education, about 35 per cent of all the university and polytechnic graduates have an education in IT or neighbouring fields. Certainly, there are other industries which are seen as possible candidates for future growth, such as the content industry and the new media industry. However, biotechnology seems to be the first choice in political as well as public debate when the advancement of a new growth area is discussed. One indicator of the fact that biotechnology is given highest priority is the increasing financial support for research in this sector.

The Finnish view of biotechnology

In Finnish publications, the interpretation that biotechnology represents a new type of technology predominates. Up to now clustering of biotechnology takes place mainly within existing industries such as the agro-food industry, pharmaceutical industry, and wood processing and chemical pulp industry, as well as in the debilitated waste management industry. The way Kreiner and Schoulz (1993: 189–209) have described the 'pre-clusterical' situation of biotechnology industries also applies to Finland:

> In a loose sense, we may talk about a biotech community, since across all differences, all the competing classifications being applied and used, they identify themselves in certain situations and contexts as working in biotech.

One sign of the development of an independent biotechnology cluster, however, is the foundation of the Finnish Bioindustries (FIB) organisation. The majority of the companies in this field are now members of this association (including some foreign members), which are mostly micro enterprises; whether biotechnology will ever become an industrial cluster of its own, however, is controversial. So far, biotechnology is de facto a new method used by various industries in research, development and production, and in many different industrial clusters. In this respect, it is comparable to telecommunication technologies. The complex nature of biotechnology makes it difficult to assess its economic impacts (Ahola and Kuisma 1998). Nevertheless, it is possible to identify the focus domains of modern biotechnology (see Figure 10.1).

In Finland, modern biotechnology is mainly applied in the pharmaceutical industry, biomedicine and bioremediation. Exploitation of modern biotechnology in the agro-food industry, and the forestry and chemical pulp industry is just taking off. Research and development work with biocatalysts and enzymes seems to produce some promising results. Many of these biocatalysts can be used in the processes of the agro-food industry and the chemical pulp industry. The waste management industry in Finland is rather underdeveloped, although some applications based on modern biotechnology are currently being researched.

Some conceptual aspects

For a long time, the scientific debate on the development of new technologies and new industries based upon them has been dominated by the controversy between the 'knowledge or technology-push approach' and the

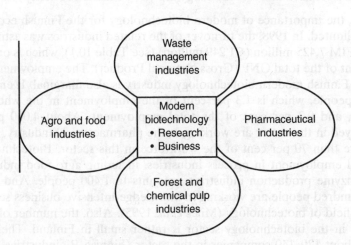

Figure 10.1 The focus domains of modern biotechnology

Source: Pasi Tulkki.

Note: See TEKES (1998) 'Technology and Future' (Teknologia ja tulevaisuus): 95.

'market-pull approach'. Nowadays there is a widespread agreement that both factors, newly created knowledge and the market, are important for the development of new technologies and industries. There is also, however, a third factor which must be mentioned here: the closeness of the existing knowledge stock within firms to the newly emerging knowledge (Nelson and Winter 1982, Lovio 1993, Malerba 2000).

Concerning the knowledge or technology aspect, not only the amount and the quality of research plays an important role, but the co-operation of knowledge producers, mainly universities, with industries is also decisive, since successful innovation processes depend upon an inclusive and rapid knowledge flow between these two parts of the idea–innovation chain. Furthermore, companies need to have an absorptive capacity to be able to use the new knowledge produced in the university. Their knowledge stock must be compatible with the newly produced knowledge, as learning in companies takes place in a cumulative way.

Regarding the market aspect, close co-operation between producers and users is crucially important for firms in order for them to be able to develop products for which market demand exists. In this respect, small countries with closely networked small and medium-sized firms may even have some advantage; but, in the long run, the development of new technologies that can become the basis for new industries depends upon the access to international markets through global players. In the following, we will discuss the extent to which the emerging biotechnology sector in Finland can rely on such favourable preconditions.

The importance of biotechnology for the Finnish economy

So far, the importance of modern biotechnology for the Finnish economy is still limited. In 1998, the turnover of the related industries was estimated to be FIM 7,425 million (€1,249 million) (see Table 10.1), which is only 1.1 per cent of the total GNP (Gross National Product). The employment rate of the Finnish modern biotechnology industry is also marginal. It employs 5,610 people, which is 1.3 per cent of the employment in the whole industry, and 0.3 per cent of the total employment. About 4,000 people employed in the sector are working in the pharmaceutical industry, which is more than 70 per cent of the workforce in this sector. Biotechnology-related employment in process industries, including agro-food industries and enzyme production industries, amounts to 1,400 people. And about one hundred people are working in knowledge-intensive business services in the field of biotechnology (Miles *et al.* 1995). Also, the number of companies in the biotechnology sector is rather small in Finland. There are only about 120–140 companies in the sector (Finnish Bioindustries 2000), while the total number of companies in the Finnish economy is about 210,000. Most of the companies in this field are very small, employing less than ten people.

Table 10.1 Total volume of modern biotechnology in Finland in 1998

Branch	Number of companies	Turnover (FIM million)	Personnel
Drugs	17	4,310	2,640
Diagnostics	28	1,220	1,390
Biomaterials	8	45	60
Food and forage	10	1,410	1,060
Industrial enzymes	3	325	290
Agro	7	10	30
Biotech-KIBS (Knowledge-intensive business services)	16	70	110
Others	3	35	30
Total	**92***	**7,425**	**5,610**

Source: Finnish Bioindustries FIB (2000).

Note
*The member companies of FIB.

Up to now, modern biotechnology has had no significance in Finnish export statistics. In 1997, the value of exports of high-tech pharmaceuticals was only FIM 140 million (€23.5 million), and the value of exports of high-tech chemicals was FIM 310 million (€52.2 million). The combined value of exports of both high-tech industries was only 1.3 per cent of the total high-tech exports in Finland. Export of electronics and telecommunication, on the other hand, the strongest high-tech sector in Finland, had a value of FIM 22,760 million (€3,800 million) (White 1998).

The number of patents can also be seen as a good indicator of competitiveness. Here we can see a dramatic increase in all patent categories. Table 10.2 indicates the leading role of the pharmaceutical industry in biotechnology.

The distribution of venture capital investments represents another good indicator in addressing the importance of a particular industry. In Finland, the total value of venture capital investments in 1997 was FIM 5,850 million (€984 million), of which two-thirds were investments from the private sector. The venture capital investments in biotechnology were FIM 25 million (€4.2 million), which is only 0.4 per cent of total investments.

Despite the marginal position of modern biotechnology in the Finnish economy, there are high expectations concerning the future development of this new sector and its contribution to the Finnish economy and to Finnish exports. These expectations are supported by the results of a survey analysis conducted in Finland in 1996. According to this survey, one-fifth of the Finnish population accepts the GMO (genetically modified organism) food without reservation. Finnish people also associate some advantages with modern biotechnology. In an EU survey, two-thirds of

Table 10.2 Patents allocated in biotechnology to Finns in Finland, in Europe (EPO) and in USA, 1989–98

	1989	1990	1991	1992	1993	1994	1995	1996	1997	1998	Total
Total	55	75	79	90	76	98	103	142	98	128	*944*
Drugs	48	67	70	74	66	83	82	118	79	101	*788*
Patents allocated in Finland	31	46	39	45	32	40	42	64	24	46	409
Patents allocated in Europe	4	11	11	9	19	28	20	28	22	25	177
Patents allocated in USA	13	10	20	20	15	15	20	26	33	30	202
Other biotechnology	7	8	9	16	10	15	21	24	19	27	*156*
Patents allocated in Finland	4	2	1	6	2	4	3	4	1	3	30
Patents allocated in Europe	1	1	5	7	7	10	7	12	10	10	70
Patents allocated in USA	2	5	3	3	1	1	11	8	8	14	56

Source: National Board of Patents and Registration in Finland (1999).

Finns were optimistic concerning the implications and consequences of modern biotechnology, while on average only 50 per cent of the EU citizens had an optimistic view of biotechnology (EU 1997). The share of optimistic people was biggest in Finland compared to all other EU countries, a fact that can be seen as an important supportive environmental factor which may open up great prospects to biotechnology in Finland.

We must be cautious, however, not to become too optimistic concerning the future of biotechnology in this country. A company survey conducted in 1997 shows that Finland, together with other Nordic countries, Austria, Switzerland, Germany and Greece, is considered as having a less supportive environment for investments in and use of biotechnology. The following elements were considered as the most important influencing factors: market conditions, consumer acceptance, intellectual property, regulatory framework, entrepreneurship, the science base, availability of equity capital, skilled staff, availability of suppliers and fiscal policy (EU 1997).

Constructing the biotechnology competence

Biotechnology is very much dependent on formal education, as – according to Lundvall (1999) – knowledge in this field is highly codified. This is reflected in the fact that Finland has certainly invested heavily in biotechnological education in the last 15 years. Since the mid 1980s, bio-engineers have been educated at the Helsinki University of Technology. In 1998, a master's programme in biotechnology was established at the University of Turku. In 2000, sixty new students started their studies in a new training programme in biotechnology at the University of Kuopio. In the Science Park of Viikki in Helsinki, about 3,000 students study different subjects of biotechnology and life sciences (Halme 1996). Finnish polytechnics too offer training programmes in biotechnology. However, the number of biotech students is not yet comparable with the number of engineering students, for example. On the university level, about 500 students start their studies in biotechnology each year, while about 3,500 start their engineering education.[1]

Furthermore, fourteen graduate schools have been established at Finnish universities supporting research in various areas of life sciences (Makarov 1999). Five of them are situated in Helsinki, four in Turku, two in Kuopio and one in Oulu, Tampere and Joensuu respectively (see Table 10.3). The location of graduate schools reveals something of the anticipated location of Finnish biotechnology industries; the major regions of the future biotech industries seem to be the Helsinki and Turku regions. The graduate schools are mainly integrated in regional biotechnology centres of expertise.

Table 10.3 Biotechnology graduate schools in Finland

University	Graduate schools
University of Helsinki	• The Biomedical Graduate School • The Graduate School in Neurobiology • The Finnish Graduate School on Applied Bioscience • The Graduate School in Biotechnology • Viikki Graduate School in Biosciences
University of Turku	• The Turku Graduate School of Biomedical Sciences • The Finnish Graduate School in Musculo-Skeletal Problems • Biological Interactions Graduate School
Åbo Academi (Turku)	• The Graduate School of Informational and Structural Biology
University of Oulu	• Biocenter Oulu Graduate School
University of Joensuu	• The Graduate School in Forest Sciences
University of Kuopio	• A.I. Virtanen Graduate School

Source: Pasi Tulkki.

New outlook in the pharmaceutical industry

In Finnish industrial policy discourse, biotechnology is mainly associated with the pharmaceutical industry (e.g. Jalkanen 1998). The leading role of the pharmaceutical industry can be explained to some extent by the fact that the workforce in this sector is traditionally highly skilled with many academics, having a degree in medicine or technical sciences, working in R&D departments. The fact that private ownership dominates in this industry while it does not in other biotechnology fields may be seen as an important factor as well (Rannikko and Tulkki 1999: 39–40). Public opinion is also supportive; because of the careful clinical testing system and the regulations in medical industries, people accept biotechnological solutions in drugs more easily than in other product branches (Jauho and Niva 1999).

The crisis of the pharmaceutical industry at the beginning of the 1990s may also have contributed to the dominance of medicine in Finnish biotechnology. Many companies in the industry changed their strategies and abandoned their biotechnological research and development activities. As a consequence of this, many highly educated employees in companies' R&D laboratories lost their jobs and began to start their own small R&D firms. The founding of the new centres of expertise also strengthened the development; in these new centres there was a proper support structure available for small R&D enterprises.

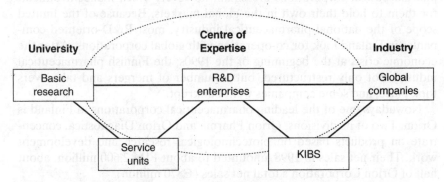

Figure 10.2 Basic structure of the university–industry biotechnology network in the area of pharmaceutical industries

Source: Pasi Tulkki.

Today the new university-affiliated biocentres – or the Centres of Biotechnological Expertise – have an important role to play in the research and development activities of the pharmaceutical industry. The BioCity centre in Turku, Biocenter in Oulu and the A.I. Virtanen Institute in Kuopio all work in the field of medical and diagnostical research. They have strong links to pharmaceutical industries, but they have also been criticised for excessive use of limited resources. These Centres of Expertise take in a lot of small firms, spin-offs either from universities or larger pharmaceutical companies.

The founding of the Centres of Biotechnological Expertise has changed the structure of the Finnish pharmaceutical industry significantly (see Figure 10.2). Previously, only a few large national companies having their own research units existed. Now a network of small R&D-based firms situated in the university-affiliated Biotech Centres of Expertise has become a key actor in this biotechnology sector. These enterprises can be divided into three different types. Firms belonging to the first type concentrate on research and development activities, while the second group of companies specialises in knowledge-intensive business services, and the third type of companies can be characterised as technology support-producing enterprises. Some global pharmaceutical companies also have smaller units in Finland and in Finnish biocentres. In addition to enterprises, the Centres of Expertise also host university institutes and private research institutes.

The Turku area in the south-west of Finland has attracted a remarkable number of Finnish pharmaceutical companies. To further develop this industrial agglomeration, the city of Turku has made large investments in modern biotechnology. The reason for the city's heavy investment in biotechnology is that it did not participate in the rapid development of the Finnish information and telecommunication technology. Finnish pharmaceutical corporations are small, however, which makes it difficult for them to hold their own in the global markets. Because of the limited scope of the national pharmaceutical industry, most R&D-oriented companies in Finland look for co-operation with global corporations. After the economic crisis at the beginning of the 1990s, the Finnish pharmaceutical industry not only restructured, but a number of mergers and take-overs took place, and some companies went bankrupt.

Nowadays one of the leading pharmaceutical corporations in Finland is Orion. Two of its divisions, Orion Pharma and Orion Diagnostica, concentrate on products based on biotechnological research and development work. Their net sales in 1998 amounted to about FIM 2,600 million, about half of Orion Corporation's total net sales (€870 million).

Orion Pharma is engaged in the research, development, production and marketing of pharmaceuticals and drug substances, as well as drug-related products for the prevention and treatment of diseases. Their product portfolio encompasses all elementary therapy groups, including veterinary drugs. International operations account for approximately half of the total net sales (FIM 2,400 million). The growth of the business is increasingly based on drugs resulting from the company's own pharmaceutical research activity. Orion has several drugs manufacturing plants in Finland, and one in Denmark.

The focus of Orion's pharmaceutical research is on neurology, asthma, menopausal disorders, cancer and heart failure. In special fields, R&D activity comprises all phases of pharmaceutical research, from basic research in Finland to multinational clinical trials. R&D expenditure amounts to about 16 per cent of net sales of pharmaceutical reparations, and around 730 persons are engaged in R&D activities. Orion Pharma collaborates with bio-centres in Kuopio, Turku and Helsinki.

Orion Diagnostica is a division relying on biomedical research in its tests for diagnosing diseases. Its core competence is in infectious disease diagnostics, specific protein and hormone assays, and bone markers. International markets account for almost 80 per cent of the operations, most importantly Scandinavia, Central Europe, the USA and Japan. The division also has subsidiaries in the Nordic countries. Orion Diagnostica co-operates with scientific institutes and company units in Medipolis in Oulu.

The agro-food industry

Conservatism and less favourable attitudes towards technological development are the main reasons for the low innovation capacity of the Finnish agro-food industry in the field of biotechnology (Salo *et al.* 1998: 36–7) Moreover, exaggerated expectations concerning return on investment, the fear of technological risk and the lack of skills and competence in modern biotechnology can be seen as significant factors that have hampered biotechnology-related R&D activities in the Finnish agro-food industry.

The delayed social and economical transformation in Finland contributed to the high status of farmers in Finland. In Finnish agro-food industry, the farmers, their unions and their co-operatives represent the only relevant group that has an influence on techno-economic development. Most of the agro-food industrial mills, creameries, slaughterhouses and food factories have been owned by the farmers' production co-operatives. The share of privately owned companies in the food industry is very limited and they are rather small by size.

The co-operatives have become national monopolies. The co-operative creamery Valio, for example, was in possession of 97 per cent of the milk markets by the end of the 1970s. Correspondingly, the co-operative's market share in the meat industry was 53 per cent and its share in the egg industry was about one-third (MTK 1976: 55–9). This 'monopolar' structure in the Finnish agro-food industry, which prevented hard competition, has not been a supportive environment for any kind of innovative activities. Also, the fact that the industry was heavily subsidised became a hindrance for technological progress.

Before the Finnish EU membership and the opening of the markets in the 1990s, the structure of the Finnish agro-food industry can be described by the term 'agro-food industrial complex' (Granberg 1979: 139–55). This 'agro-food industrial complex' is an economic system consisting of the industries providing agriculture with material and technical equipment, the industries taking care of the agro-food raw material production, and to the industries taking care of the processing and delivery of the products. In this tightly coupled structure, the state and its financing, research and educational organisations are entwined with the farmers' organisations and co-operatives. Also, privately owned companies had to adapt themselves to the structure and strategies of the agro-food industrial complex. The fact that the whole education system for the agricultural sector was subordinated to the Ministry of Agriculture until the end of the 1960s is a further indicator of the closeness of the sector.

The co-operative Valio founded at the beginning of the twentieth century by co-operative dairies to export butter plays an important role in the Finnish agro-food industry. Today, Valio is engaged in processing and marketing milk, dairy products and other food products over a total product range of 800 items. During the 1980s and 1990s Valio invested heavily in the research and development of functional food products. The company has been marketing products with Lactobacillus GG (LGG) in Finland under the Gefilus brand since 1990. Gefilus products include yoghurts, cultured buttermilks, pasteurised milk, a fermented whey drink, fruit drinks, as well as capsules. Today, products containing LGG are on the market in more than twenty countries around the world, under licence agreements from Valio. The company is also the world leader in applying ultra-high temperature (UHT) technology to infant foods. The company has developed (UHT) technology in close co-operation with paediatricians. Several clinical studies have been carried out in order to improve the composition of its products. For nearly 20 years, Valio has also studied, experimented with and put into practice lactose hydrolysis in a highly sophisticated and intensive manner. The company has developed tailor-made and patented solutions for the removal of lactose in different milk products. These solutions include the use of many soluble enzymes: the Valio Hydrolysis Process, using immobilised enzyme technology, and the Valio Chromatographic Process, in which lactose is physically separated from milk.

Valio Ltd is owned by eleven co-operative dairies and 17,000 dairy farms produce milk for the company. The Valio Group comprises the parent company Valio Ltd and its subsidiaries in Finland and abroad. The Group employs 4,300 people. The whole Valio Group net sales in 1998 amounted to FIM 7.6 billion (€1.3 billion), of which exports and foreign subsidiaries made up one-third. Noteworthy subsidiaries are Valio Sverige AB in Sweden and Finlandia Cheese Inc. in the USA, for example.

Besides Valio's products, there are also other examples of successful R&D activities in the Finnish agro-food industry. Beer is a product with a long tradition in Finland. Lately malt-houses have focused on developing malting barley and new malting technologies. The most recent addition to barley breeding techniques uses genetic engineering. The first genetic barley in the world was made in 1993 by the research group of the Technical Research Centre of Finland (VTT) and was used in trials.

The best-known case is the development of the Benecol plant stanol ester, an ingredient that lowers serum cholesterol levels. The problem that triggered the innovation was to find an application for the surplus sitosterol of the chemical pulp industry of Kaukas Ltd. Raisio Ltd developed the idea of using the surplus sitosterol in margarine and vegetable oil. In the so-called North Karelia project, researchers discovered the cholesterol-lowering character of Benecol (Miettinen 1999: 166). Nevertheless, Benecol, an innovation with great economic potential, demonstrates many of the problems related to the long-term economic isolation of Finnish agro-food industries. Raisio Ltd had great problems in getting access to the US market, as it lacked the knowledge of the rules and procedures regulating the functional food market in the USA. Due to the lack of expertise, competitors were able to bypass the R&D work conducted on Benecol and develop their own products of a similar kind.

The Raisio Group was established by Finnish farmers in 1939. The first production unit was a flour mill, but the company has over the years expanded into many other areas of arable product processing, and it can claim to be ahead in this field of knowledge. The Raisio Group headquarters are in Raisio, a small town in the south-west of Finland. The Group employs nearly 2,900 people, of which about 40 per cent are based outside Finland. Today Raisio has production units at over forty locations in seventeen countries. The Group's turnover was FIM 4,950 million (€833 million) in 1998. The parent company, Raisio Group plc, has been listed on Helsinki Stock Exchange since 1989, and over 50 per cent of its shares are owned by international institutional investors and funds.

The Raisio Group exports margarine products, malt products, wheat flour, pastas, cereal flakes, potato products, cat and dog food, feeds for fur animals and farm feeds. The Chemical Division is Raisio's most international division, with production plants in fifteen countries. It is a specialist supplier to the pulp and paper industry throughout the world. Its exceptionally wide product range includes chemicals and equipment extending from pulp-making to the manufacture, coating, conversion and recycling of paper.

After the opening of markets and Finland's EU membership, the Finnish agro-food industry has approached the situation of escalating change. One example of the fundamental nature of the changes is the course of events around Cultor Ltd. The corporation employs 7,000 people in Finland. Cultor is the world's largest producer of functional ingredients for the international food industry and the world's leading supplier of feed ingredients. The company is also the leading producer of emulsifiers, functional systems, locust bean gum, fat replacers and butter flavourings, and is the world's second largest producer of pectin. The product range also includes other textural ingredients, flavourings, enzymes, sweeteners, antioxidants, and other protectants, in which Cultor is among the world's leading suppliers. Cultor has invested a lot in biotechnology-oriented R&D activities.

The development of the sweetener xylitol is one success story in applying biotechnology in the Finnish agro-food industry and Cultor. The research done in the Faculty of Dental Surgery in the University of Turku addressed the beneficial effects of xylitol for human teeth. Cultor Ltd placed xylitol in many of its products, which led to economic successes. In 1992, the R&D and the production of xylitol received the innovation reward of the Finnish National Fund for Research and Development (SITRA 1992). In March 1999, the company accepted the bid of the Danish corporation Danisco. In November 1999, Danisco was listed as the first non-Finnish company on the HEX Helsinki Stock Exchanges' Main List of blue-chip companies. Cultor continues to operate as Danisco Cultor in the ingredients sector of the Danisco concern. Most of its products are produced using natural raw materials, such as vegetable oil, seaweed, citrus fruits and seed from leguminous plants. The Danisco strategy is to establish production plants close to key raw materials. Danisco is also developing and testing the GMO sugar beet in collaboration with DLF-Trifolium A/S and Monsanto Company. The case of Cultor illustrates that even bigger Finnish companies in the biotechnology sector have difficulties in holding their own in a globalising market. This may be due to the fact that, in biotechnology, huge investments in R&D have to be made to be able to compete globally. Nonetheless, Danisco has cut the R&D

activities in Cultor, and at least 15–20 per cent of the researchers have been made redundant.

Recently, the entire agro-food sector in Finland has been undergoing major changes, turning it into a research-based modern biotechnology industry. The Agricultural Research Centre of Finland is planning the experimental production of genetically modified cheese and it has started research on GMO animals. According to the OECD's database of biotechnological field trials, two projects researching the streptococcus bacterium are being conducted in the Valio laboratories. Kemira Agro Ltd is studying the virus resistance of potatoes and Hilleshog AB is studying the glyphosate tolerance of sugar beet. In total there were six biotechnological field trials conducted in Finland before 1997.

Other key actors in the agro-food biotechnological R&D field, besides the laboratories of the agro-food industry and the Research Centre for Finnish Agriculture, are the new Helsinki Science Park in Viikki, which employs about 1,000 researchers, and the Kuopio Technology Centre TEKNIA Ltd. These new agro-food biotechnology centres of expertise represent the new technology policy of Finland. The new centres of expertise establish broader and closer linkages between universities and industries. Education, university research, knowledge-based agro-food industrial small firms, and departments of larger companies all are operating in close connection with each other in these centres.

The only Faculty of Agriculture and Forestry in Finland is now established in Helsinki Science Park. In this park, other research institutes are also operating: the Institute of Biochemistry, the Institute of Microbiology, the Institute for Animal Physiology, the Institute for Environmental Research and the Institute for Pharmacy, for example. The Helsinki Science Park is planned to become the most extensive concentration of biosciences in Europe.

In 1995, the Development Company Foodwest in Seinäjoki was launched. It is owned by twenty-four agro-food companies and thirty-two communes and communities, among them the Central Union of Agricultural Producers and Forest Owners (MTK). A few years ago, Foodwest was elected a Centre of Expertise, and today it employs about fifteen people. There is also a Development Company for agriculture production called Agropolis Ltd in Jokioinen. It is owned by local communities and other public authorities.

The wood-processing industries

In Finland, the production and export of chemical pulp – ultimately a semi-manufactured product and raw material to the paper industry – has been comparatively high. The manufacturing of chemical pulp is a representative example of mass production. For a long time, one problem in the Finnish wood-processing industry was the low degree of horizontal process integration. This is a result of the Finnish so-called smallholding policy; two-thirds of Finnish forests are nowadays privately owned by farmers or testamentary heirs of ex-farmers, one-quarter belongs to the state, and only 8 per cent to corporations.

Due to this situation, a kind of dichotomy in the production chain of the wood-processing industry emerged, which has drawn a clear dividing line between corporations on one side and farmers on the other. Both interest groups formed their own economic and commercial organisations. In the 1960s, the situation had already developed into a kind of 'double-closure' (Murphy 1998) and opposing national cartels. Not surprisingly, the research and development interests of the two key actors also diverged into two different directions. The wood-processing industry was mainly interested in research and development of end products and processes inside the factories. Correspondingly, the farmers' (or 'wood growers', as they are called) interest focused on productivity improvement of forests. In general, biotechnologically oriented research made a larger impact on the wood growers' side, and less so on the corporations' side. However, the wood growers were not greatly interested in intensifying forestry yield through biotechnological applications. Because of the fact that Finland is rich in forests, the wood growers were mainly interested in the improvement of forestry work.

The productivity of Finnish forests was defined very early as an issue of national survival (Kuisma 1993; see also Michelsen 1999, Tulkki 1996). The state has – beside the Finnish wood grower organisations – been active in forestry research and development. The great interest of the state in the wood-processing industry is self-evident, as some 40 years ago 70 per cent of Finnish exports came from this industry. Due to the polarised situation in the Finnish wood-processing industry, the state took on a kind of umbrella role. It established a broader vision in which both the interests of the corporations and of the farmers can be taken into account.

Today, there are three globally acting corporations in the Finnish forest industry. The UPM-Kymmene Group is, measured by turnover, the biggest; Stora Enso is one of the world's leading forest industry companies; and Metsä-Serla Oyj is the sixth largest forest industry and paper-producing company in Europe. The large forest industry companies, however, seem to be less active in promoting biotechnology innovations, while companies in the chemical pulp industries, being part of the forest cluster, seem to be much more engaged in research in modern biotechnology.

The most famous biotechnological innovation in the chemical pulp industry, developed by the Technical Research Centre of Finland VTT's biotechnological laboratory, is an enzyme-aided process for bleaching cellulose pulp (Miettinen *et al.* 1999: 61–88). In this process, hemicellulases are used in order to avoid using chlorine chemicals. The first pulp mill designed for complete chlorine-free bleaching was built at OY Metsä-

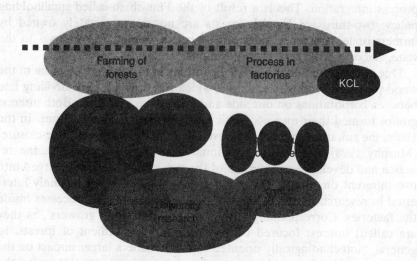

Figure 10.3 The biotechnology network in Finnish forest industries
Source: Pasi Tulkki.

Rauma Ab and started in 1996. Ahlstrom is the leading company in Finland in developing new processes and machinery for pulp and paper manufacture in which the environmental aspect is considered.

The structure of the biotechnology innovation network in forest industries differs significantly from the one in the pharmaceutical industries (see Figure 10.3). There are different research organisations functioning in the beginning and end of the production chain. The chemical pulp and paper companies and the Central Laboratory KCL co-operate in research and development of enzymes with companies like Raisio Chemicals, Primalko and Genencor International. The latter co-operate with VTT Biotechnology, which has close links to university research. In the beginning of the production chain, there are actors working on improvements in the productivity of forests, such as Forest Centres and The Finnish Forest Research Institute (METLA).

The Finnish Forest Research Institute, established in 1917, is an independent research organisation subordinated to the Ministry of Agriculture and Forestry. This central forest research organisation has a staff of 700 people, 200 of whom are research officers in the research centres located in Helsinki and Vantaa. METLA also has eight research units in different parts of the country. METLA has a strong tradition in research and development activities based on traditional biotechnology. Applications of modern biotechnology have often been delayed, mainly because of the problematic proprietorship of Finnish forests. Wood production based on applications of modern biotechnology would be easier to realise in a large and market-oriented forest industry than under the conditions of dispersed forest smallholding. Despite these difficulties, six modern biotechnological, forest genetic research projects are currently conducted at METLA.

Concerning corporations, the most interesting institutional actor has been the previously mentioned Central Laboratory KCL, which concentrates on quality control of the end products of chemical pulp and paper industry mills. But lately the interest of the laboratory has broadened from mere quality control to larger R&D activities, including also research in biotechnology. The state research organisation, the Technical Research Centre of Finland (VTT) with its biotechnological laboratory is another important actor that has close links to corporations. Although most of the biotechnology projects of METLA, VTT and other institutional actors are financed by the WoodWisdom programme, modern biotechnology has a marginal role in the whole programme entity.

The radical changes at the beginning of the 1990s broke with the customary notion of the juxtaposition of wood-processing corporations and wood grower organisations. In the new atmosphere, the wood-processing industries began to be considered as an uninterrupted production chain from forestry to consumption. According to the Technology Development Centre of Finland, the greatest future challenge for the wood-processing industry is 'to integrate forest economy and forest research to a constant part of the research of products of wood-processing industries. This means comprehension and governance of the linkages between the wood raw material quality and the end product quality' (TEKES 1998: 115–16). Research in the Bio and Food Technology Unit of the Technical Research Centre of Finland is in this direction; it applies biotechnology in the wood-processing industry in several research and development projects. The research on wood material, for example, aims at increasing biological stability and hindering the dyeing of the raw material.

Biotechnology supporting policies

The Finnish Ministry of Education established the first national research programme on biotechnology in 1987. The aim of the programme was to develop four powerful Centres of Biotechnological Expertise by 1992. These new centres were planned to affiliate with the Finnish universities that were assessed as having the capacity and resources to develop the new field of scientific research. The Centres of Biotechnological Expertise were set up in Helsinki, Turku, Kuopio and Oulu. By the end of the 5-year period, the Ministry of Education made an evaluation aiming at identifying needs to further develop biotechnology and molecular biology. The Ministry decided to continue the programme until the end of 1996. The programme period was later extended to 2000 (Jäppinen and Pulkkinen 1999: 10–13).

Besides the Ministry of Education, the Ministries of Trade and Industry, Agriculture and Forestry, and Social Affairs and Health took part in the financing of the biotechnological research programme. The four Centres of Biotechnological Expertise became part of the Finnish network of 'Centres of Expertise'. Nowadays this network consists of seventeen Centres of Expertise, of which seven are large and have an established status. Four centres have been working for some time and six are new and rather small ones (Saarinen 1999). The new Centres of Expertise in Seinäjoki, Lahti and Pori are located in regions without a local university but they are linked to large regional polytechnics or local annexes of universities.

Basic and applied research

As can be seen from Table 10.4, research and development in biotechnology is now conducted in the centres of Tampere and Seinäjoki in addition to the traditional centres. In Finland, the Centres of Expertise Programme is intended to become the core of a newly developing regional policy. The strong relationship between the state's regional financing and the Centres of Expertise Programme has led to 'excess demand' for new centres. Therefore the policy was criticised for the excessive decentralisation of

Table 10.4 The centres of expertise in Finland

	Large and established	*Medium size and stable*	*Small and new*
Centres of expertise	ESPOO: Otaniemi Science Park Ltd TURKU: Technology Centre, DataCity Centre Ltd TAMPERE: Technology Centre Ltd OULU: Technopolis Ltd	KUOPIO: Technology Centre Teknia Ltd JYVÄSKYLÄ: Science Park Ltd LAPPEENRANTA: Technology Centre Kareltek Inc.	HELSINKI: Science Park Ltd VAASA: Innovation Centre Merinova Ltd JOENSUU: Carelian Science Park Ltd SEINÄJOKI: Foodwest Ltd LAHTI: Neopoli Ltd PORI: PrizzTech Ltd
With focus on biotechnology	TURKU: BioCity Ltd OULU: Biocenter Oulu Ltd TAMPERE: Finn-Medi Research Ltd	KUOPIO: A.I. Virtanen Institute	HELSINKI: Science Park Ltd SEINÄJOKI: Foodwest Ltd

Source: Pasi Tulkki.

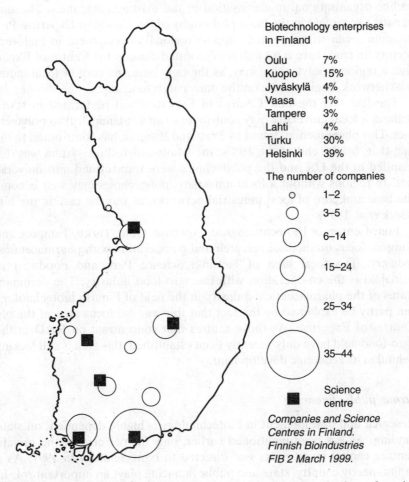

Biotechnology enterprises
in Finland

Oulu	7%
Kuopio	15%
Jyväskylä	4%
Vaasa	1%
Tampere	3%
Lahti	4%
Turku	30%
Helsinki	39%

The number of companies

○ 1–2

○ 3–5

○ 6–14

○ 15–24

○ 25–34

○ 35–44

■ Science centre

*Companies and Science Centres in Finland.
Finnish Bioindustries
FIB 2 March 1999.*

Figure 10.4 Centres of Expertise and location of biotechnology business firms in 1998

limited R&D resources. The result is that, in the field of biotechnology, no new Centre of Expertise will be set up in the near future (Kekkonen and Nybergh 1999).

Centres of Expertise (see Figure 10.4) offer local companies business services, and forge links between regional enterprises and local universities or – in some cases – local polytechnics. They are presumed to be sources of knowledge for regional economies. They also have an important role to play in the transfer of technology from high-tech centres in Finland and abroad to their own region. In addition, they are expected to generate new forms of business and to support the foundation of new enterprises, as well as to create a stimulating environment for the techno-organisational modernisation of the existing companies. The university – according to the basic philosophy of the Centre of Expertise Programme – can stimulate and support regional development in high-tech sectors. In case there is no university located close to the Centre of Expertise, a regional polytechnic may, as the only base and core of local industrial network, begin to take on the university's function.

The fact that the new Centres of Expertise will be located in towns without a local university may contribute to an academic drift to polytechnics. This phenomenon, found by Pratt and Burgess, has contributed to the fact that, by the end of the 1980s, the whole polytechnic system was dismantled in the UK and the polytechnics were transformed into universities. In regions without a local university, polytechnics may well become the base and core of local industrial networks, as was the case in the UK (Beck *et al.* 1994).

Four Centres of Biotechnological Expertise, Oulu, Turku, Tampere and Kuopio, focus on medical research and co-operation with pharmaceutical industry. The focal area of Helsinki Science Park and Foodwest in Seinäjoki is the co-operation with the agro-food industry. The dominant status of the pharmaceutical industry in the field of Finnish biotechnology can partly be explained by the fact that this was the focus area of the old Centres of Expertise. As those centres that concentrate on R&D in the agro-food field have only recently been established, this area is still lacking behind in its economic development.

Strong public financing

Research and development in biotechnology is highly dependent on state funding. As has been mentioned earlier, only 0.4 per cent of the private venture capital investments was directed to biotechnology in 1997. As a capital-needy country, state and public financing plays an important role in Finnish venture capital markets. Different parts of the idea–innovation chain are financed by different institutions. The Academy of Finland is supporting basic scientific research in universities and research centres. The Technology Development Centre (Tekes) aims at applied research and product development by supporting the co-operative activities between university research and companies. The role of the Finnish National Fund for Research and Development (Sitra) is to support promising start-up enterprises. Later on, the new knowledge-intensive companies are expected to get their financing from the capital markets.

Tekes invested FIM 535 million (€90 million) in the field of chemistry and biotechnology, which is 27 per cent of its total investments. The Academy of Finland and Tekes invest about FIM 20 million (€3.4 million) a year in research in biosciences and biotechnology as part of the Centres of Excellence Programme. In addition, Biocentrum Helsinki, Biocenter Turku and BioCity Turku are supported with FIM 4 million (€0.7 million). This means that 40 per cent of the aggregated financial support of the Academy of Finland and Tekes is directed to biotechnology. The national programme for the research on biotechnology, started in 1988, invests about FIM 80 million (€13.5 million) a year (Vihko and Pauli 1999). As state financing of Finnish biotechnology has been quite large in the 1990s, some criticism has been made about the results of this massive investment.

Presently, there are two research programmes going on within the common foundation of Tekes and the Academy of Finland. The Genome Research Programme includes gene regulation. It studies interactions between several genes and gene products, gene transfers, and knock-outs as well as gene therapy. The budget of the programme amounts to FIM 89 million (€15 million) in 6 years. The Academy of Finland financed twenty projects with FIM 37 million (€6.1 million) from 1995 to 1997. From 1998 to 2000, the Academy of Finland is financing fifteen projects with FIM 24 million (€4 million). Tekes financed five projects with FIM 5 million (€0.8 million) in 1998.

The Cell Biology Research Programme studies mechanisms of cell division and differentiation, the biogenesis of cell organelles and intracellular trafficking as well as signal transduction. The programme started in 1998 and will continue until 2001. The budget of the programme amounts to FIM 32 million (€5.4 million). The Academy of Finland is financing nineteen projects with FIM 22 million (€3.6 million). Tekes financed four projects with FIM 5 million (€0.8 million) from 1998 to 1999.

In 1993, the Ministry of Education established a new centres of excellence policy by ordering the Finnish Higher Education Evaluation Council to choose ten units and institutes as 'top units' (Ketonen and Nyyssölä 1996: 68–73). This policy of establishing Centres of Excellence has become the core of the Academy of Finland's policy (Vihko and Pauli 1999: 15). It expects that the new policy can lead to a strong concentration of research and innovative power. Currently, 6 per cent of the Academy's funding is directed to the Centres of Excellence Programme. In 2000, a total of twenty-six new Centres of Excellence will be established. Nine of them are operating in the field of modern biotechnology and biosciences (Vihko and Pauli 1999: 14). The Academy of Finland also financed research in modern biotechnology within the framework of its basic research programme. There is, for example, an ongoing programme for gene research and cell biology. In 1999, the Academy of Finland started the Research Programme for the Biology of Structures and, in the following year, the Research Programme for Biological Functions.

The Academy of Finland is financing the Research Programme in Molecular Epidemiology and Evolution. The primary areas of this programme are population genetics, concerned particularly with the evolution of genes, the adaptation of organisms to extreme conditions, genetic epidemiology and the Finnish genetic heritage, and environmental molecular genetics, including genetic factors predisposing to disease.

Tekes started a 5-year Biotechnology Development Programme in 1988. It consisted of five subjects important to Finnish industry: biotechnology for the pulp and paper industries, bio-process engineering, plant biotechnology, animal cell technology and biologically active molecules. Tekes also has an agro-food biotech programme named 'The Innovation in Foods Programme'. It aims at supporting the production of more competitive foods through research. The goal of the programme is to ensure the production of increasingly high-quality products by improving the standards of food technology and related research in Finland. The programme started in 1997 and continued until 2000. The budget of the programme will be over FIM 200 million (€33.7 million) during 4 years. All the significant Finnish agro-food companies are participating in the programme.

In 1991, the Finnish National Fund for Research and Development (Sitra), aimed at financially supporting new start-ups, invested FIM 400,000 (€67,000) in biotechnology, which was only 1.2 per cent of its total investments. Eight years later, the investments in biotechnology amounted to FIM 35.7 million (€6 million) (see Figure 10.5). Altogether Sitra has invested in eleven biotech companies; today, the share of biotech investments is already 9.5 per cent of all investments. In 1997, two special funds, Sitra Bioventures Ky and Sitra Bio Fund Management Ltd, were started with a capital of FIM 150 million (€25.2 million).

Conclusions

Biotechnology industries have only played a minor role in the Finnish industry up to now. However, the state and state-owned institutes have

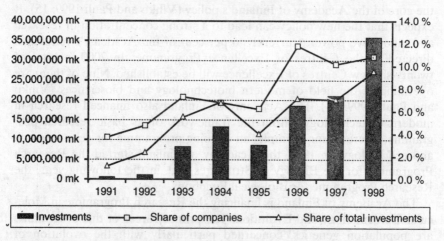

Figure 10.5 Investments of Finnish National Fund for Research and Development (Sitra) in biotechnology, 1991–8

Source: Pasi Tulkki.

started to invest heavily in biotechnological research projects, as well as in education and research infrastructure, as part of an extension policy of Finnish export's industrial basis. We are entitled to use the word 'massive' because only little R&D so far comes from the private sector, and only few business firms have started production of biotechnology-based products.

The structure of the Finnish biotechnology sector is similar to that of European biotechnology. The pharmaceutical industry represents the leading sector, while the agro-food sector and the forest industry are lacking behind partly due to the specific 'lock-ins' described in this chapter. But there are signs that the industries will be able to overcome the problems caused by the lock-ins.

The further development of the biotechnology sector in Finland depends on whether the emerging research infrastructure will soon lead to the building up of a significant number of manufacturing plants. In overall terms, the business environment in Finland seems to be less supportive for investment in and use of biotechnology than in the USA and some other parts of Europe. However, there are also some supportive factors. There seems to be widespread agreement that biotechnology could become the fourth pillar of the Finnish export sector, indicated by the massive public investment in research. Furthermore, the Finns in general are very open to technological development and their attitudes to biotechnology seem to be less negative than in other European countries. And last but not least, Finnish technical universities are known for their openness to close co-operation with industry. The Centres of Expertise seem to create a supportive environment for close university–industry co-operation.

There are also important factors that can hinder the further development of the biotechnology sector in Finland. First, there seems to be a serious shortage of highly qualified scientific staff in the sector, which the government is aiming to overcome by heavy investments in the education infrastructure. There is, however, huge demand for qualified engineers in the IT sector as well. Whether in the competition over human resources the biotechnology sector will be able to hold its own remains to be seen. Anyhow, there is a lack of students oriented in mathematics and natural sciences in their matriculation examination.

A major disadvantage is the small size of the Finnish market. Therefore, companies in Finland have to be globally oriented from the very beginning. However, as some examples demonstrate, the small Finnish biotechnology firms, particularly in the agro-food and pharmaceutical sector, often lack the management capacity to establish themselves in foreign and particularly in the most important US market. Companies operating on the national or even on the European level may soon face serious problems because they lack sufficient awareness of and access to new biotechnological knowledge.

Concerning regulatory aspects, Finnish firms suffer the same fate as other European firms. The European regulatory framework seems to have a negative effect on the competitiveness of European firms. The greatest losers in the biotechnology age are likely to be the farmers who, for regulatory reasons, have been denied access to some products. As European farmers in general, the Finnish farmers are likely to lose global market shares to farmers from other parts of the world, who are already adopting products using biotechnology.

Still another problem is the small size of Finnish firms, particularly in the agro-food and pharmaceutical industry. Small companies face serious problems as product innovation and improvement in operating efficiency come to depend increasingly on the use of biotechnology. In order to be able to develop the absorptive capacity necessary for applying biotechnological knowledge, companies have to set up respective research capacity. This is a major problem for small companies, as can also be demonstrated by the small amount of private R&D investment of Finnish firms in biotechnology. However, Finnish firms are starting to co-operate and merge not only with European but also with US companies to overcome the disadvantage of being small. As the pulp and paper industry includes some global players, the sector is not affected by this problem. As some huge mergers have already taken place in this sector, Finnish pulp and paper companies may well be able to retain their place in the biotechnology era.

Note

1 Yearly almost 5,000 Finns gain an engineering degree in universities or in polytechnics. This is 8 per cent of each age group. The number of post-graduate
   degrees in technical sciences was 350 in 1999.

References

Ahola, E. and Kuisma, M. (1998) *The biotechnological Sector in Finland: From Laboratory to an Expropriator of Premises* [*Biotekniikkasektori Suomessa: Laboratoriosta lupausten lunastajaksi*]. TEKES: Technology Development Centre Finland. *Technology review* 61/98.

Beck, U., Giddens, A. and Lash, S. (1994) *Reflexive Modernization. Politics, Tradition and Aesthetics in the Modern Social Order*, Cambridge: Polity Press.

EU (1997) *The Europeans and modern biotechnology*. EUROBAROMETER 46.1. European Commission: Science, Research, Development. Brussels–Luxembourg.

Finnish Bioindustries (2000) *Index of Biotechnology Companies*, Organisations and Science Centres in Finland.

Granberg, L. (1979) 'The Location of Agriculture [Maatalouden asema].' In: Kosonen *et al.*, *Finnish Capitalism* [*Suomalainen kapitalismi*], Helsinki: Love Kirjat.

Halme, K. (1996) *Biotechnology as a Branch of New Enterprises* [*Biotekniikka uusien yritysten toimialana*]. Helsinki: VTT: Reports 24/96.

Jalkanen, M. (1998) 'From academic networking to new bioindustries', in *High Technology Finland 1999*. Finnish Academies of Technology and The Finnish Foreign Trade Association: Helsinki-Forssa: 20–1.

Jäppinen, A. and Pulkkinen, M. (1999) 'Biotechnology as a Focus Domain in Research' [*Biotekniikka tutkimuksen painopistealana*]. Ministry of Education: Yliopistotieto 3/99: 10–13.

Jauho, M. and Niva, M. (1999) *A Risk or a Future's Commitment* [*Riski vai tulevaisuuden lupaus. Geenitekniikkaa elintarviketuotannossa koskevat käsitykset ja julkinen keskustelu*]. Kuluttajatutkimuskeskus. Julkaisuja 5/1999.

Kekkonen, T. and Nybergh, P. (1999) 'Biotechnology as a breeding ground of new technology' [*Biotekniikka uuden teknologian kasvualaustana*]. Ministry of Education: Yliopistotieto 3/99: 18–20.

Ketonen, K. and Nyyssölä, K. (1996) *Policy of Award* [*Palkitsemisen politiikka*]. University of Turku: Research Unit for the Sociology of Education. Reports 39. Turku.

Kreiner, K. and Schoultz, M. (1993) 'Informal Collaboration in R&D. The Formation of Networks Across Organisations.' Organisation Studies 1993: 14/2: 189–209.

Kuisma, M. (1993) *The Land of Wood Processing Industries. Finland, forests and the international system 1620–1920* [*Metsäteollisuuden maa. Suomi, metsät ja kansainvälinen järjestelmä 1620–1920*]. The Historical Association of Finland and The Association of Finnish Wood Processing Industries, Helsinki: Gummerus Ltd.

Lievonen, J. (1999) *Technical opportunities in biotechnology*. Technical Research Centre of Finland (VTT): Group of Technology Studies. Working Papers 43/99.

Lovio, R. (1993) *Evolution of Firm Communities in New Industries, The Case of the Finnish Electronics Industry*, Helsinki: The Helsinki School of Economics and Business Administration.

Lundvall, B-Å. (1999) 'Understanding the role of education in the learning economy: The contribution of economics', in CERI/CD (99)10: Knowledge Management in the Learning Society, Paris: OECD.

Makarov, M. (1999) '*Tutkijakoulutuksella tuloksiin*.' Ministry of Education: Yliopistotieto 3/99: 21–3.

Malerba, F. (2000) *Sectoral Systems of Innovation and Production*. Sectoral systems in Europe – Innovation, Competitiveness and Growth (ESSY), under the Fourth Research and Technological Framework Programme EU/TSER, Working Paper.

Michelsen, K.E. (1999) *The Fifth Estate* [*Viides sääty*]. The Historical Association of Finland and the Association of Technical Academics, Helsinki: Gummerus Ltd.

Miettinen, R., Lehenkari, J., Hasu, M. and Hyvönen, J. (1999) *Skills, Competences and the Creation of New in an Innovation Network* [*Osaaminen ja uuden luominen innovaatioverkossa*], Helsinki: SITRA.

Miles, I., Kastrinos, N., Flanagan, K., Bilderbeek, R., den Hertog, P., Huntink, W. and Boumnan, M. (1995) '*Knowledge-intensive Business Services. Users, Carriers and Sources of Innovation*.' In European Innovation Monitoring system (EIMS): EIMS Publication nr. 15.

MTK (1976) *Price Formation of Agricultural Products and Farmers' Commercial Co-operation* [*Maataloustuotteiden hinnanmuododtus ja maanvilejelijöiden kaupallinen yhteistoiminta*]. The Central Union of Agricultural Producers in Finland (MTK). Publications nr. 10. Tapiola.

Murphy, R. (1988) *Social Closure. The Theory of Monopolisation and Exclusion*, Oxford: Clarendon Press.

National Board of Patents and Registration in Finland. 1999. <http://www.finbio.net/>

Pratt, J. and Burgess, T. (1974) *Polytechnics*, A Report. Bath: Pitman.

Rannikko, E. and Tulkki, P. (1999) *Innovations and the Field of Biotechnology. A study of BioCity*. Unpublished manuscript. Turku.

Saarinen, N.T. (1999) 'Finnish science parks benefit companies and investors', in *High Technology Finland 1999*: 32.

Salo, A., Kauppila, J. and Salminiitty, J. (1998) *The Technological Factors of Success in Food Industry [Elintarviketeollisuuden teknologiset menetystekijät]*. TEKES: Technology Development Centre Finland. Technology review 60/98.

Science and Technology Policy Council of Finland (2000) *Review 2000, The Challenge of Knowledge and Know-How*. Helsinki.

SITRA (1992) *25 Years: Bridging the Research and the Economy [Tutkimuksen ja talouden sillanrakentaja]*. The Finnish National Fund for Research and Development 1967–1992. Helsinki.

TEKES (1998) *Technology and Future [Teknologia ja tulevaisuus]*. Technology Development Centre Finland. Technology review.

Tulkki, P. (1996) *State Service or Work in Industry? Engineer education as a social phenomenon 1802–1939*. University of Turku: Research Unit for the Sociology of Education. Report 38. Turku.

Vihko, R. and Pauli, A. (1999) 'Centres of Excellence in Bio Sciences – The Role of the Academy of Finland in Financing Bio Sciences' *[Biotieteiden huippuyksiköt – Suomen Akatemian rooli biotieteiden rahoituksessa]*. Ministry of Education: Yliopistotieto 3/99: 14–17.

White, J. (1998) 'The little country that proves it can', in *High Technology Finland 1999*. Finnish Academies of Technology and The Finnish Foreign Trade Association: Helsinki-Forssa: 10–11.

Index